Russian and Soviet Film Adaptations of Literature, 1900–2001

This book examines the importance of film adaptations of literature in Russian cinema, especially during the Soviet period when the cinema was accorded a vital role in imposing the authority of the communist regime on the consciousness of the Soviet people. The book provides many interesting case studies and brings together many leading authorities on the subject.

Stephen Hutchings is Professor of Cultural Studies and Russian at the University of Surrey. Recipient of two large AHRB grants and author of monographs on Leonid Andreev, Russian Modernism, and Russian literature's relationship with the camera. He is currently researching post-Soviet television culture.

Anat Vernitski is Lecturer in Russian at the School of Slavonic and East European Studies, University College London. She has published on twentieth-century Russian literature and on cultural representations of Orthodox Christianity. She is currently researching Russian émigré literature.

BASEES/Routledge Series on Russian and East European Studies

Series editor: Richard Sakwa, *Department of Politics and International Relations, University of Kent*

This series is published on behalf of BASEES (the British Association for Slavonic and East European Studies). The series comprises original, high-quality, research-level work by both new and established scholars on all aspects of Russian, Soviet, post-Soviet and East European Studies in humanities and social science subjects.

1. Ukraine's Foreign and Security Policy, 1991–2000
Roman Wolczuk

2. Political Parties in the Russian Regions
Derek S. Hutcheson

3. Local Communities and Post-Communist Transformation
Edited by Simon Smith

4. Repression and Resistance in Communist Europe
J.C. Sharman

5. Political Elites and the New Russia
Anton Steen

6. Dostoevsky and the Idea of Russianness
Sarah Hudspith

7. Performing Russia: Folk Revival and Russian Identity
Laura J. Olson

8. Russian Transformations
Edited by Leo McCann

9. Soviet Music and Society under Lenin and Stalin
The Baton and Sickle
Edited by Neil Edmunds

10. State Building in Ukraine
The Ukranian Parliament, 1990–2003
Sarah Whitmore

11. Defending Human Rights in Russia
Sergei Kovalyov, Dissident and Human Rights Commissioner, 1969–2003
Emma Gilligan

12. Small-Town Russia
Postcommunist Livelihoods and Identities: A Portrait of the Intelligentsia in Achit, Bednodemyanovsk and Zubtsov, 1999–2000
Anne White

13. Russian Society and the Orthodox Church
Religion in Russia after Communism
Zoe Knox

14. Russian Literary Culture in the Camera Age
The Word as Image
Stephen Hutchings

15. Between Stalin and Hitler
Class War and Race War on the Dvina, 1940–46
Geoffrey Swain

16. Literature in Post-Communist Russia and Eastern Europe
The Russian, Czech and Slovak Fiction of the Changes 1988–98
Rajendra A. Chitnis

17. Soviet Dissent and Russia's Transition to Democracy
Dissident Legacies
Robert Horvath

18. Russian and Soviet Film Adaptations of Literature, 1900–2001
Screening the Word
Edited by Stephen Hutchings and Anat Vernitski

Russian and Soviet Film Adaptations of Literature, 1900–2001

Screening the word

Edited by Stephen Hutchings and Anat Vernitski

LONDON AND NEW YORK

First published 2005
by Routledge
2 Park Square, Milton Park, Abingdon, Oxon OX14 4RN

Simultaneously published in the USA and Canada
by Routledge
270 Madison Ave, New York NY 10016

Routledge is an imprint of the Taylor & Francis Group

Transferred to Digital Printing 2009

Typeset in Times by Taylor & Francis Books Ltd

British Library Cataloguing in Publication Data
A catalogue record for this book is available from the British Library

Library of Congress Cataloging in Publication Data
A catalog record for this book has been requested

ISBN10: 0–415–30667–1 (hbk)
ISBN10: 0–415–54612–5 (pbk)

ISBN13: 978–0–415–30667–6 (hbk)
ISBN13: 978–0–415–54612–6 (pbk)

Publisher's Note
The publisher has gone to great lengths to ensure the quality of this reprint but points out that some imperfections in the original may be apparent.

Contents

List of plates

List of contributors

Joe Andrew is Professor of Russian Literature at Keele University. His main research interests are nineteenth-century Russian literature, feminist approaches to literature, and women writers. He has published numerous articles in these fields, as well as several monographs.

Birgit Beumers is a Senior Lecturer in the Russian Department at Bristol University. She specialises in contemporary Russian culture, especially cinema and theatre. Her publications include *Yury Lyubimov at the Taganka Theatre* (1997) and, as editor, *Russia on Reels* (1999).

David Gillespie is Professor of Russian at the University of Bath and teaches Russian language and culture. He has published widely on modern Russian literature and film. His book, *Russian Cinema*, London, Longman (x + 201 pp.), appeared in 2002.

John Givens is Associate Professor of Russian at the University of Rochester. He is the author of *Prodigal Son: Vasilii Shukshin in Soviet Russian Culture* (2000), co-translator of *Vasily Shukshin, Stories from a Siberian Village* (1996) and editor of the journal *Russian Studies in Literature*.

Julian Graffy is Professor of Russian Literature and Cinema at the School of Slavonic and East European Studies. His recent work includes *Bed and Sofa: The Film Companion* (2001) and *Gogol's 'The Overcoat'* (2000). He is writing a study of the classic Soviet film *Chapaev*.

Jeremy Hicks teaches Russian and Film at Queen Mary, University of London. He is the author of *Mikhail Zoshchenko and the Poetics of Skaz* (Nottingham, 2000) and has translated Zoshchenko's stories. Currently he is researching early Soviet non-fiction film.

Stephen Hutchings is Professor of Cultural Studies and Russian at the University of Surrey. Recipient of two large AHRB grants and author of monographs on Leonid Andreev, Russian Modernism and Russian literature's relationship with the camera, he is currently researching post-Soviet television culture.

Rachel Morley is completing a PhD at SSEES on the representation of women in pre-Revolutionary Russian culture. She has published on gender relations in Evgenii Bauer's films and is writing on Bauer for a critical guide to Russian cinema.

Catharine Theimer Nepomnyashchy is Ann Whitney Olin Professor of Russian Literature and Chair of the Slavic Department of Barnard College and Director of the Harriman Institute at Columbia University. Her publications include *Abram Tertz and the Poetics of Crime* (1995).

Graham H. Roberts teaches at the Lille Graduate School of Management. He has published widely on topics relating to Russian visual and literary culture. His current teaching and research interests concern the emergence of a consumer culture in post-Soviet Russia.

Russell Scott Valentino is Associate Professor of Russian and Comparative Literature at the University of Iowa. His books include *Materada* (Northwestern University Press 2000), *Vicissitudes of Genre in the Russian Novel* (Peter Lang 2001), and *Persuasion and Rhetoric* (Yale University Press 2004)

Anat Vernitski is Lecturer in Russian at the School of Slavonic and East European Studies, University College London. She has published on twentieth-century Russian literature and on cultural representations of Orthodox Christianity. She is currently researching Russian émigré literature.

Acknowledgements

In putting the volume together we have benefited from the assistance of a number of individuals and institutions and it is appropriate that we acknowledge their contributions. First, we must thank the Arts and Humanities Research Board for funding the research grant under whose auspices both the original conference and the edited volume were planned. We also owe a debt of gratitude to Professor Tony Anemone and Dr Emma Widdis for their incisive comments on individual chapters and on the volume as a whole. David Gillespie and Julian Graffy (who feature in the volume) provided invaluable advice and information for our introductory essay. Professor Richard Sakwa (University of Kent) and Peter Sowden (RoutledgeCurzon) were instrumental in encouraging us to publish with RoutledgeCurzon, and in seeing us over the various bureaucratic hurdles. The University of Surrey hosted the original 'Screening the Word' international conference and also provided Stephen Hutchings with a sabbatical in which to work on the edited volume. We much appreciated the wise counsel of Professor Peter Barta on the running of international conferences and on the pitfalls (and rewards!) of editing a volume of this kind. Vladimir Bosenko at Gosfilmofond was extremely helpful in matters relating to the whereabouts of various Russian film adaptations, as was the British Film Institute, which provided the Evgenii Bauer film shown at our conference. We should finally thank Professor Helena Goscilo and Igor Maslennikov (director of the legendary Russian Sherlock Holmes adaptations) for their sparkling keynote conference addresses which generated much discussion and which, though not included in this volume, are implicit subtexts to the discussions we engage in throughout. For the translation of Russian words and names, we use the Library of Congress system without diacritics throughout.

Acknowledgements

Introduction: The *ekranizatsiia* in Russian culture

The cultural significance of the film adaptation: theoretical approaches

This volume originated in an international conference held in 2002 at the University of Surrey under the auspices of an AHRB-funded project dedicated to the broader relationship between Russian literature and the camera. The conference included over 70 papers read by scholars from all over Europe (including Scandinavia, Poland and Russia), Israel, the USA, Australia, and from every corner of the UK. We selected 12 papers which, as well as meeting the required standards of quality, covered the most important periods/aspects of our theme. Each paper has been substantially expanded from its original version.

On the face of it, a volume dedicated to Russian film adaptations might seem self-indulgent. Surely, some will object, there is more to find in a tradition responsible for some of the great innovations of world cinema than a dozen examples of a peripheral genre which is ultimately subservient to another medium entirely? Similar arguments have led, until recently, to a lack of attention to the film adaptation amongst cinema scholars generally. A discipline that struggled for decades to establish its object of study as a bona fide art form was understandably loath to focus on a category of film liable to reinforce prejudices about cinema's status as a mass cultural form able only to aspire vainly, through imitation, to the heights of literary quality. The situation is inverted, but with similar effects, in Russia, where, for most of its history, commercialized mass culture has been non-existent. Soviet contempt for artistic essentialism meant that film, like literature, was subordinate to the political needs of the state. Film's importance, both for proponents and opponents of the regime, lay in its ability to reinforce/undermine that regime's foundations. A genre whose primary motivation is the copying of another art form appears as marginal to those concerns as it is to the articulation of cinematic purity. In this introduction we challenge such assumptions, first, via a survey of theoretical approaches to the issue, making the case for the adaptation's centrality to modern culture, then exploring its importance for Russian cinema, and finally accounting in this context for the structure of the present volume.

The perceived inferiority of film adaptations with respect both to the literary sources upon which they parasite themselves, and cinema in its essential form, is reflected in the early history of adaptation studies and indeed in much current writing on the theme.[1] Typically, adaptations are compared to their literary sources, and/or to examples of 'non-parasitic' original cinema, only to be found wanting on both counts. Adaptations are condemned to fail perpetually either to live up to their textual originals, or to realize the inherent potential of the cinematic medium in its authentic, non-literary form. However, inspired by the pioneering work of André Bazin, one of the few early commentators to take the adaptation seriously, and by the still earlier interest in the genre expressed by the Russian Formalists, film and literary scholars have slowly begun to reassess its significance. In what, then, might consist the rationale for such a reappraisal?

It was Bazin who suggested that, rather than remain imprisoned within a rhetoric of fidelity (either to literary originals, or to cinematic essences), we should examine adaptations in terms of a dialogue in which, in the best examples, we are dealing with 'the refraction of one work in another creator's consciousness' (Bazin 2000: 20). Rejecting the simplistic notion of film's inability to convey the subtleties of authorial tone, style and linguistic register, Bazin suggests that the successful adaptation utilizes the full array of cinematic technique (soft-focus and 'dissolve' shots, montage, flashback, etc.) to create an 'equivalence in meaning of the forms' (ibid.: 20). Taken to its extreme, for Bazin, who uses Renoir's film of a Maupassant story as his example, this approach leads to the conclusion that the screen version 'is a different work from the novel and is equal … to its model because Jean Renoir is … an artist of the same rank as Maupassant' (ibid.: 21). Bazin's pioneering essay was written in 1948. It was not until 1957 that G. Bluestone took up his baton, arguing that 'the end products of novel and film represent different aesthetic genera, as different from each other as ballet is from architecture' (Bluestone 1957: 5).

Bluestone viewed the adaptation as a tool of translation between film and literature conceived as possessing fixed, essential qualities. This model influenced Seymore Chatman whose seminal 1981 essay implies, however, that the essential qualities of the novel are superior to those of film. The word order and parentheses in the essay's title are revealing: 'What novels can do that films can't (and vice versa)'. The zenith of such adaptation studies was reached in 1996 with Brian McFarlane's *Novel to Film*, still the most systematic analysis of the genre. Having exposed the fallacy of the fidelity notion as a measure of value when judging film versions of books, McFarlane devotes much of his attention to demonstrating how film, through the use of techniques specific to it, generates its own versions of literary qualities like semantic ambiguity, point of view, focalization, narrative irony, intertextuality, figure of speech, etc.

Robert Stam takes us beyond the 'translation' approach by conceiving of the text–film relationship in terms of the cinematic medium's *response* to its sources articulated through 'a complex series of operations: selection, amplification, concretization … critique … analogization, popularization, and reculturalization' (Stam 2000: 68). But even Stam gives implicit precedence to the literary source as the site of these various transformations, which is why his concluding remarks welcoming the differences between literature and cinema in the interests of intermedia dialogism employ a verbal rhetoric of 'readings, critiques, interpretations, and rewritings of prior material' (ibid.: 76).

The volume in which Stam's essay appears also contains a contribution from Dudley Andrew recognizing the adaptation's cultural hybridity. Andrew makes the often ignored point that, since 50 per cent of all films are based on literary texts, definitions of what constitutes an adaptation are problematic. He proposes that for the purposes of genre analysis 'we confine ourselves to those cases where the adaptation process is foregrounded … where the original is held up as a worthy source or goal' (Andrew 2000: 29). Such constraints exclude several adaptation-related issues: (i) the economic relations between cinema and popular fiction (how fiction is sustained through the selling of film rights); (ii) the question of prestige (whilst not always openly 'revering' literary sources, cinema has, from its inception, often enhanced its status by grounding itself in them); (iii) the logic of mass production (the adaptation as an illustration of film's status as a medium belonging to Benjamin's era of mechanical copies). Nonetheless, Andrew's definition is useful, as is his typology dividing adaptations into three basic modes: borrowing, intersection and fidelity of transformation (ibid.: 29). Of these, the last is of least interest, both to Andrew and to ourselves. The first, in which 'the artist employs … the material, idea or form of an earlier … successful text', covers films in which 'the audience is expected to enjoy basking in a certain pre-established presence and to call up new or especially powerful aspects of this cherished work' (ibid.: 30). Andrew Davies's recent BBC adaptations of Austen and Eliot conceived with a contemporary audience in mind are one example. The second category – intersection – describes films where 'the uniqueness of the text is preserved to such an extent that it is intentionally left unassimilated', enabling cinema to 'initiate a dialectical interplay between the aesthetic forms of one period and the cinematic forms of our own period' (ibid.: 30–1).[2]

Commenting on the 'borrowing' mode, Andrew notes the two-way movement between the adapted text, which gains new audiences thanks to its cinematic popularization, and the adapting film, which gains prestige from its association with the literary canon (ibid.: 30). He thus returns us to the state of affairs which originally led to formalist-inspired attempts to rehabilitate the adaptation as a serious form: its perceived (and often self-acknowledged) inferiority before its literary sources. In so doing, he opens up a fruitful avenue by encouraging us to take this perception at face value and examine the adaptation as a site of mediation between different cultural registers. Later, Imelda Whelehan reframed the debate in terms of the adaptation's centrality to an understanding of the relationship between 'high' and 'low' culture and of the acquisition of what Bourdieu calls 'cultural capital'. However, when concluding that 'such a study ... inserts the reading of literary texts into the same critical sphere as the consumption of more explicitly commercial texts' (Whelehan 1999: 19), she herself feels it necessary to assign the adaptation to one of the categories that it straddles (literature/popular culture). Some might accuse Whelehan of avoiding formalist essentialism at the cost of skirting content-led reductionism (assimilating both adaptations and their sources to a diffuse, Marxist-inspired concept of cultures of consumption). Nonetheless, her approach is highly productive, as is the related 'heritage model' that treats the genre in terms of its role in the construction of national identity in the global era (Giddings and Sheen: 2000).[3] The same cautionary note applies, however: it is all too easy to reduce the film adaptation to a function of a particular ideology of national identity and thus to ignore its specificity as a cultural form.

The opposite extreme is to elevate the genre into a meta-level cultural model. James Naremore takes this approach, locating the adaptation at the centre of modern, mass-produced culture, claiming that:

> [t]he study of adaptation needs to be joined with the study of recycling, remaking and every other form of retelling in an age of mechanical reproduction and electronic communication. By this means, adaptation will become part of a general theory of repetition, and adaptation study will move from the margins to the center of contemporary media studies.
>
> (Naremore 2000: 15)

He does so, however, by sidelining the mechanisms by which the *transmutation* of literary word into cinematic image is accomplished. To present the adaptation as the *paradigm* of modern culture is an elegant way of avoiding pinpointing the genre's specific modes of operation *within* modern culture.

Naremore is correct, however, to link film versions of literature with the very principle of representation which, as Andrew clarifies, invariably involves the adaptation of a 'prior concept' (Andrew 2000: 29). Therein lies a means of both retaining the adaptation's cultural centrality, yet ensuring that its specific features are not ignored. When W.J.T. Mitchell claims that 'the interaction of pictures and texts is constitutive of representation as such' and that 'all media are mixed media, and all representations are heterogeneous' (Mitchell 1994: 5), he implicitly exhorts us to address the particular kind of picture–text interaction embodied in the film adaptation (which, as part of the heterogeneous mix, differs from such interaction in theatrical productions, for example, and touches upon fundamental ideological issues).[4]

Mitchell insists that conflicts at the 'word-image threshold' drive the development of human culture (Mitchell 1987: 44). For this reason, 'the tensions between visual and verbal representations are inseparable from struggles in cultural politics and political culture' (Mitchell 1994: 3), a point well illustrated by Stalinist film adaptations of nineteenth-century Russian classics. Mitchell's theory is grounded in examples from painting. Its modes of operation must be adjusted to account for the fact that, in the case of the filmed adaptation, we are dealing with mass-produced, moving images, not with static scenes. As Walter Benjamin observes, film subverts the link between the camera and the eye by tilting perceptions towards artifice (ibid.: 78). Moreover, photography embraces a radically different ontology from painting. For Walter Benjamin, the capacity for infinite reproduction defines the camera, since it destroys the painterly image's 'aura of authenticity', severing its ties with tradition and ritual. Benjamin links this process with a diminution in reality's uniqueness and permanence (ibid.: 74–5). Photography thus undermines the image's association with natural vision, aligning it with the disembodied word. But this is to ignore photography's 'indexical' ties to its object. As Susan Sontag argues: 'The force of photographic images comes from their being … richly informative deposits left in the wake of whatever emitted them, potent means for turning the tables on reality' (Sontag 1999: 93). Photography replicates within itself the original dichotomy of (abstract) word and (concrete) image, freeing the image from its context, enabling it to partake in projects driven by ideological or commercial agenda, and balancing its links to objectivity with a capacity for the subjectivism normally associated with the word.

Far from diminishing the usefulness of Mitchell's model for adaptation theory, Benjamin's and Sontag's insights lend it greater historicism. Sontag's perception of the camera's paradoxical embrace of both subjectivism and objectivity, for example, provides a tool for analysing Stalinist screenings of socialist realist texts which, through the use of aerial panoramas superimpose an anonymous, objectifying perspective over idiosyncratic authorial voices, yet also subjectivize their representations of reality via shot/reverse-shot techniques.

However, the word-image paradigm's very flexibility means that it demands to be applied beyond the generic boundaries of adaptations themselves. Verbal discourse is not restricted to literature, nor images to film, nor is literature's encounter with film defined by screenings of particular works. Acknowledging this, some have called for adaptation studies to be subsumed into a more general study of the relationship between literature and film, expanding 'heritage cinema' to encompass films which, whilst not adaptations *sensu strictu*, employ the latter's rhetoric of venerating national tradition and attention to period detail. Bellen Vidal Villasur proposes that we consider the broader category of the 'literary film', of which adaptations are one example. She invokes Jakobson's definition of 'literariness' as 'language calling attention to itself', associating such literariness with intertextuality understood as the 'reflexive quality of [a film's] images'. She argues that the 'literary' considered as an intertext can 'open paths to the work of memory in … certain narrative of the past … but also to the … operations of intertextuality that rewrite those received narratives'. Villasur concludes that the term 'literary film' may 'encompass better than "adaptation" a wide range of films that present different levels of play between the central intertext and the modes of subjectivity inscribed in the films' mise-en-scene of the past' (Villasur 2002: 8). Villasur's approach is likely to prove of particular value in the context of Russian cinema culture in which the shadow of the literary word looms across films that one would not conventionally classify as adaptations.

Villasur is not alone in questioning the narrow focus on relations between two single texts which has characterized adaptation studies. Apart from ideologically motivated commentators prone to discuss the genre in terms of cultural capital and/or national identity, a new model has emerged in the form of Sarah Cardwell's call for us to 'view adaptation as the gradual development of a "meta-text" … a valuable story or myth that is growing and developing, being retold, reinterpreted and reassessed' (Cardwell 2002: 25). For Cardwell, the question of subordinating cinema to literature (or vice versa) does not arise, since both film and text are adaptations which represent 'points on a continuum as part of the extended development of a singular, infinite metatext' (ibid.: 25). Thus, each new *Macbeth* is 'an adaptation of a sort of "myth", an "ur-text" which stands outside and before each retelling of the story, and which contains the most fundamental parts of the tale without which an adaptation would lose its identity as that tale' (ibid.: 26).

However, a work's narrative core is not always its most important aspect. For Shakespeare scholars, *Macbeth*'s greatness has to do less with its plot than with its attention to psychological detail and its treatment of universal human themes – aspects which any serious adaptation would address. Although it replaces one fetishized hierarchy (that of the literary source) with another (that of the dominant *ur*-text), and despite ignoring the dynamics of the dialogue between literature and cinema central to many effective adaptations, Cardwell's theory offers distinct advantages over others in that it usefully questions precisely what it is that is being responded to in film adaptations. Rather than simply transpose text into film, it can be argued that an adaptation mediates the literary original through a secondary text or set of texts. Thus, Western adaptations of nineteenth-century horror novels such as *Frankenstein* and *Dracula*, and Soviet adaptations of socialist realist texts like *Chapaev*, filter the literary original through the stock of myths surrounding the central figures. Many of these myths arise not from the literary originals but from the installation by earlier screen adaptations of the narratives in the popular consciousness.[5]

Rather than Cardwell's infinite variations on an essential *ur*-text, we might be said to be dealing with a three-way struggle for representational pre-eminence between film, legend and text (a struggle to assert a claim to be the authentic representation of Dracula, or of Chapaev) inseparable from the material context in which the struggle unfolds. This comes close to Mitchell's notion of a battle for 'proprietary rights on nature' and of the word-image threshold as the site of a culture's 'fundamental conflicts and tensions' (Mitchell 1987: 44). Mitchell's word-image border can be re-expressed as the threshold of embodiment: the point at which abstract concepts (or ideologies) are incarnated in tangible form. The point at which word becomes image is thus also the point at which ideas become flesh and, as controversies over the original incarnation indicate, it is a point of immense cultural significance. Such controversies are, as Terry Eagleton recognizes, capable of taking political form, as suggested in his remarks on the reason why modern states rely on imagery to consolidate their power:

> [M]en and women do not easily fall in love with abstractions and love … lies at the root of social order … Only by coming to feel affection for the law will we obey it, which means that we need tangible images. If power does not infiltrate our hearts … it is likely to prove alarmingly fragile.
>
> (Eagleton 2001: 26)

Eagleton notes, however, that 'sensual mediation … places a limit on the universality of reason. Reason, to preserve its august authority, must give the slip to all fleshly representation, and so can be brought to bear upon our sensibilities only with difficulty' (ibid.). Thus, to retain its force, an ideology must at once ensure that it transcends each individual instantiation of itself, yet convince us that such instantiations are complete expressions of its meaning. The film adaptation is crucial to an understanding of this dilemma since it (a) constitutes a prime example of sensual mediation at work (it can popularize difficult, yet ideologically important, texts) (b) offers a microcosm of its workings (the mediation of ideological abstractions is replicated in the translation of verbal texts into cinematic images).

Eagleton's insight into the conflict between the universality of reason and the limit placed on that universality when rendered in 'tangible images' has particular relevance for the role of the screen adaptation (*ekranizatsiia*) in Russian culture. Issues to be interpreted in this light include: (i) the use of the *ekranizatsiia* to shape (and subvert) the Soviet literary canon; (ii) changing attitudes to popular cultural forms from within the Soviet 'high art' establishment; (iii) cinema's difficulties in using the Russian literary tradition to unify the multi-ethnic Soviet state; (iv) approaches to the embodiment of the authority invested in omniscient literary narration; (v) the clash of the subjective identification mechanisms characteristic of cinema with the 'objective' authorial voice of Party doctrine; (vi) post-Soviet attempts to reconcile within the screen adaptation Russian logocentrism with Western image-based commercial culture. The present volume tackles a number of these issues, incorporating aspects of several theoretical approaches detailed above.

The film adaptation in Russian and Soviet culture I: Previous scholarship

Russian screen adaptations have been under-researched. In the West, where study of Russian cinema as a whole is in its infancy, the only treatments of the *ekranizatsiia* as a genre are Evgenii Dobrenko's essay dealing with its function in enabling Stalinist culture to appropriate the Russian classics for ideological purposes (Dobrenko 2001), and our own article which builds on Dobrenko's insights, attempting to subdivide the genre into subcategories according to how the demands of socialist realism are met (Hutchings and Vernitski 2002). Other, substantive treatments of the *ekranizatsiia* are rare, although the issue receives cursory treatment in Baudouin and Heller's work on the dominance of verbal culture over the image in Stalinist Russia (Baudouin and Heller 1991). Iurii Tsiv'ian's book on the emergence of early film audiences frequently refers to the prevalence of the film adaptation at the dawn of Russian cinema (Tsiv'ian 1994). Chapters 4 to 7 of the companion to the present volume (Hutchings 2004) focus on the *ekranizatsiia*'s role in (de)constructing a Soviet official sphere.

A number of Western analyses treat individual Russian film adaptations. In the only Western book on Russian film adaptations, Nikita Lary berates Soviet screenings of Dostoevskii for their lack of fidelity (Lary 1986). Ian Christie accounts for the relationship of Protozanov's 1924 film *Aelita* with A. Tolstoy's original science fiction novel (Christie 1991). Stephen Crofts (1997) and Mark Ferro (1976) examine the ideological structures and discourse status of the classic socialist realist adaptation, *Chapaev* (issues developed by Jeremy Hicks in this volume). Milena Michalski's reading of Avraam Room's ill-fated screen realization of Olesha's film scenario, *A Strict Youth* (*Strogii iunosha*, 1934) spotlights the politics of censorship as applied to literary films in the early Stalin period (Michalski 2000). Kevin Moss reads *That Same Miunkhauzen* (*Tot samyi Miunkhauzen*, 1980), the Soviet television version of Rudolf Erich Raspe's classic, as a subversive political allegory (Moss 1993). Anat Vernitski analyses the complex political and aesthetic implications of differences between a Stalin-era narrative by Vera Panova and its 1964 screen version (Vernitski 2003). Adaptations receive passing mention in two authoritative general histories of Soviet cinema (Leyda 1960; Woll 2000). The most notable work on post-1991 *ekranizatsii* is David Gillespie's study of the fate of three nineteenth-century Russian classics on the post-Soviet screen (Gillespie 1999), which he expands upon in a chapter in his recent book (Gillespie 2002).

When we consider Russian scholarship on the *ekranizatsiia*, we must recall that cinema was bound up with the revolutionary avant-garde whose aim was, in the words of the Futurist manifesto, to 'throw Pushkin overboard the ship of modernity'. Central to the project of at least one branch of the avant-garde movement was a move to reconcile Marxist materialism with an emphasis on the material specificity of each artistic medium; thus, cinema was to free itself from subordination to literature, just as literature was to cease being the 'handmaiden' to philosophy and psychology. Literary adaptations might appear to offer little to this project, particularly in light of fiction's associations with the very bourgeois culture that the likes of Dziga Vertov, the great experimental film director, set out to crush with his new aesthetic of proletarian documentary fact (Vertov 1984: 71). But, paradoxically, literature's influence on cinema was greater in the avant-garde period than at any time. The Formalist movement, which was so important to avant-garde culture as a whole, retained a strong literary bias. The danger that cinema might overpower literature was noted by Shklovskii, who warned in 1926 that the growing emphasis on non-fictional cinema represented by Dziga Vertov's Cine-Eye was leading to a crisis in literature (Shklovskii 1988a: 151). More extreme reactions against Vertov's dogmatism included Viktor Pertsov's defiant claim in 1927 that 'literature will serve in the next few years as the principle source of raw material for Soviet cinema' (Pertsov 1988: 166). To be sure, Eisenstein affirmed montage as the aspect of film that confirms its uniqueness as a form of art, regarding it as the only way to liberate cinema from the 'reverence of literary tradition' which could stifle cinema's natural development (Eisenstein 1998a: 31). Yet he resorted to a literary comparison to explain montage, claiming that it resembled poetry in that 'its rhythm emerges as a conflict between the metric measure adapted and the distribution of sounds that ambushes that measure' (Eisenstein 1998b: 95).[6]

Shklovskii, Eikhenbaum, Jakobson and Tynianov nonetheless consistently applied the 'specificity' theory to cinema. This resulted in some of the most sophisticated analyses of early Russian cinema. Indeed, the scholars made a lasting contribution to film semiotics by being the first to exploit Saussurean formulations of film as a system of conventions rather than the recording of natural phenomena. In a 1927 anthology edited by Eikhenbaum and called *Poetika Kino* (*The Poetics of Cinema*), with contributions by Eikhenbaum, Shklovskii, Tynianov and others, the Formalists identified a 'poetic' use of film similar to the 'literary' use of language posited for verbal texts (Eikhenbaum 1982). Another aspect of Formalist literary theory imported into cinema theory was the concept of 'inner speech', explained by Eikhenbaum as a discursive glue which holds the meaning of a film together in the spectator's mind. Eikhenbaum also discusses film images which translate linguistic colloquialisms, where figures of speech anchor meaning. Film adaptations provided Eikhenbaum with the perfect illustrative tool for these notions.

It is not surprising that Formalists drew attention to the *ekranizatsiia*, since, as the point at which cinema and literature intersect, it highlights the implications of the formalist approach. Their findings were, however, ambiguous. Tynianov categorized visual devices capable of translating literary texts into a self-sufficient cinematic language (Tynianov 1977). On the other hand, Shklovskii found film adaptations of the classics lacking in artistic essence since they duplicate ideas and images no longer relevant in post-Revolutionary culture (Shklovskii 1988b: 163).

By comparison, official decrees adopted a deeply unimaginative approach to the literature-cinema relationship which later became the norm under Stalin. Lenin, who famously declared cinema the most important art, nevertheless required that propaganda films be tried out on 'old Marxists and literary men' so as not to repeat the sad mistakes that have occurred several times in the past, when propaganda achieves the opposite effect to that intended' (quoted in Taylor and Christie 1988: 56). By the late 1930s and early 1940s the official literary approach dominated. At the First Soviet Writers Congress in 1934, when the official dogma of socialist realism was enunciated, Natan Zarkhi, the scriptwriter of the experimental film-maker, Pudovkin, declared: 'Comrades, you know very well that the successes of Soviet cinema are determined by what lies at the basis of the film: a literary work, a script?' (quoted in Taylor and Christie 1988: 331). In 1940, even Eisenstein wrote: 'If we take the majority of successful films, we see that the most successful images … occur when there are literary prototypes available' (Eisenstein 1998c: 151). Reviews of adaptations insisted that the use of literary sources was desirable as long as both 'fidelity' to the original and socialist realist principles were observed. Grigorii Roshal, a prominent adapter of the 1930s, claimed 'All creative potential should be mobilized … to interpret the original from the standpoint of socialist realism … to reveal its deep-seated progressive tendencies' (quoted in Dobrenko 2001: 62). These two principles often clashed. Thus a review of an adaptation of Polevoi's World War II classic, *Tale of A Real Man* (*Povest' o nastoiashchem cheloveke*) which, on the one hand, praises the film for its accurate rendition of the far from unambiguously socialist realist original, on the other hand, begins with Molotov's insistence that art should express the ideological meaning of the work of the Soviet people (Chakovskii 1948). Often, adaptations were seen as a way to correct ideological flaws in their literary originals. A review of the film of Fadeev's war epic *Young Guard* (*Molodaia gvardiia*) claims that it 'improved upon many weaknesses of the novel' expressing the political struggle of the Soviet people and the Communist Party's leading role (Anonymous 1948: 5).[7]

Because of the precedence given to literary sources, Soviet writing on *ekranizatsii* distinguished consistently between the literary scenario (*avtorskii stsenarii*) and the director's scenario (*rezhisserskii stsenarii*). Adaptations in which the original author was involved (of which there are many in Soviet cinema) worked with three texts: 1) the literary original; 2) an intermediate text (the literary scenario) written by the author in literary style, but with the cinematic version in mind; and 3) the director's translation of the latter into 'film language'. Even non-literary film-makers often began with a past-tense literary scenario. O. Bulgakova notes that the literary scenarios were censored especially rigorously (a reflection of Stalinist logocentrism), although there are numerous examples of films falling victim to the censor at the final stage (Bulgakova 2000: 150).

Soviet criticism continued to pay lip-service to the 'fidelity approach' beyond the Stalin years. As late as 1973, U.A. Gural'nik identified the *ekranizatsiia*'s main task as that of 'conveying the spirit of the literary original', quoting with approval Sergei Bondarchuk's comments on his epic adaptation of *War and Peace* to the effect that he aimed to 'convey by cinematic means what Tolstoy wrote on paper' (Gural'nik 1973: 20, 2).[8] This set film critics (who were close to the ideological centre of gravity) at odds with the directors of adaptations (who began to establish artistic independence following Stalin's death). Iulii Raizman instantly attacked the 'excessive' subjectivism of *Pavel Korchagin* (1958), a reinterpretation of Ostrovskii's canonic socialist realist text, *How The Steel Was Tempered* (*Kak zakalialas' stal'*), complaining that Korchagin 'stops being an expression of the ideals of the Komsomol, and becomes simply an individual personality' (quoted in Alov and Naumov 1989: 43). The 'fidelity' concept was invoked to attack Mikhalkov-Konchalovskii's dangerously nostalgic adaptation of Turgenev's *Nest of Gentlefolk* (1968).[9]

Nonetheless, the post-Stalin period saw the gradual emergence of alternative ideological currents. Birgit Menzel argues that as early as the mid-1930s a subjective-lyrical trend began to infiltrate Stalinist culture (Menzel 2000: 954). These trends eventually made themselves felt in approaches to the *ekranizatsiia*. By 1973, in *The Book Argues with Film* (*Kniga sporit s fil'mom*), whose title reflects the fact that the literature–film relationship was more problematic than had traditionally been thought, A. Macheret claimed of adaptations that 'there is no objective Pushkin, Tolstoi or Chekhov, but only 'my Tolstoi', 'my Pushkin', 'my Chekhov'' (Beliaev, Macheret and Dmitrieva 1973: 239). And Maia Turovskaia supported the aesthetic independence of makers of adaptations, recognizing the futility of the fidelity principle and arguing that adaptation critics should not look for copies of literary originals, but rather see the films as individual artistic statements (Turovskaia 1973: 226, 233). During the 1960s and 1970s, Soviet film adaptations bifurcated into adaptations proper and those freer adaptations defined as films according to the motifs of a literary source (*po motivam* ...). Pre-empting Villasur's notion of the 'literary film', V. Kozhinov explains that the dividing line between the two is fluid, yet cites the distinction as evidence, on the one hand, of the strong heritage of the written word in Russian culture (the two categories cover a vast range of Soviet films), and, on the other hand, of the tradition's elasticity (Kozhinov 1973: 12).

The glasnost period took Turovskaia's argument to its conclusion, returning the debate on the *ekranizatsiia* to Formalist notions of cinema and literature as independent, albeit mutually influential, art forms. Andrei Tarkovskii, himself responsible for several original adaptations, even declared that when literature is adapted it is transformed into an entirely new art form (Tarkovskii 1990: 23).

Post-Soviet studies of *ekranizatsii* are, unlike their Soviet predecessors, numerous and varied. A multi-volume collection of work on the cinema–literature relationship published throughout the 1990s included volumes on literature and silent cinema (Vartanov and Zor'kaia 1989), literature and sound cinema (Bogomolov 1994), the modern period (Vartanov *et al.* 1994) and literature and television (Vartanov *et al.* 2000). Much of the scholarship, like other post-Soviet humanities scholarship, aims to reassess conventional wisdoms, rather than strike out on radical new paths. Thus, early Russian cinema is now seen not only from parochial Soviet viewpoints, but in the context of other European cinema movements (Zor'kaia 1989: 107). Regarding the 1920s, emphasis is now switching from the analysis of revolutionary cinema to adaptations of popular literature which are seen as providing the framework for official socialist realist heroic cinema (Khrenov 1991: 229–30). Stalinist *ekranizatsii*, meanwhile, are being reassessed within contemporary adaptation poetics. E. Levin, for example, examines 1930s adaptations in terms of the dialogue between historical times and cultures that they institute, and as a reflection of attempts by the official guardians of Soviet culture to construct a new mythography based on nineteenth-century radical critic Dobroliubov's reinterpretations of Russian literary classics (Levin 1994: 73, 91). Levin's work is representative of a new-found interest in a cultural form whose importance to the mechanisms driving Soviet culture is becoming ever clearer.

The screen adaptation in Russian and Soviet culture II: Overview

The history of Russian cinema is inseparable from that of the film adaptation. From its inception, Russian film engaged in a dialogue with literature, first modelling itself upon theatre and classical fiction in order to consolidate its own cultural status, then attempting to establish itself as 'high art' in its own right. Many early Russian films were adaptations of nineteenth-century Russian fiction. The birth of cinema coincided with a surge of national feeling and adaptations of the quintessentially Russian works of Lermontov and Dostoevskii exploited the new medium to promote a revitalized Russian self. Whilst most of these films paid homage to their originals, as Rachel Morley's chapter on Evgenii Bauer shows, Russian cinema was always capable of challenging its sources. Morley demonstrates how, in transforming nineteenth-century Russian literary types within his film *A Child of the Big City*, Bauer undermines old morality codes, relocating his re-reading of nineteenth-century classics within the concerns of modern twentieth-century culture.[10]

Literature's influence on cinema continued, as we know, to reverberate within revolutionary avant-garde cinema through Formalist involvement in *ekranizatsii*. Shklovskii contributed the scenario for an adaptation of Dostoevskii's *House of the Dead* (1932). Tynianov wrote the scenario for the 1926 version of Gogol's 'The Overcoat' ('*Shinel'*') which differentiates itself from its source by incorporating elements of another Gogol story, and by substituting for Gogol's cumbersome *skaz* narrative expressionistically lit scenes shot from the angle of a detached viewer. Its indulgence in visual puns, for example, a literalization of the Russian idiom 'Delo v shliape!' ('It's in the bag!', literally 'The thing is in the hat!'), marks its awareness of its intermediary verbal–visual status.

One reason for Formalism's prominent role in cinema was the ability of many of its protagonists (Tynianov, Shklovskii, Brik, and others) to compensate for the lack of good scenario writers who would also be ideologically sound (a recurrent problem in Soviet cinema history up to the 1950s). For this reason, following Stalin's clampdown on avant-garde culture (including Formalism), film occasionally provided both writers and critics with a refuge from the ravages of the repressions. Since cinema's nationalization in 1919, it remained close to the levers of Soviet power and a reliable tool of propaganda. The switch to cinema, however, occasionally backfired, as evidenced by Avram Room's screening of Iurii Olesha's scenario *A Severe Youth* (*Strogii iunosha*, 1934). Room adjusted Olesha's scenario to bring it into line with political orthodoxies, omitting Olesha's negative references to an emerging 'Soviet aristocracy' and replacing invocations of 'equality for all' with references to 'the masses' and their 'leaders'. Nonetheless, the film was assailed for its formalist indulgences. This indicates the complex balance of power between word and image under Stalin: literature's position at the summit of Stalin's cultural hierarchy explains Room's need to manipulate Olesha's scenario, yet the lingering importance of visual rhetoric meant that ideological corrections to the script were outweighed by deviations from emergent cinematic orthodoxies.

For a while, Formalist notions of the essential differences between film and literature coincided with Bolshevik sensibilities. Formalist technique and radical Marxism merged in one of the most important early Soviet films: Pudovkin's adaptation of Gor'kii's novel, *Mother* (1926). Pudovkin's striking use of montage and cinematic synecdoche, and his presentation of the characters as expressionist archetypes (they are introduced with intertitles identifying them as 'mother', 'son' and 'father') mark the film as a conscious visual reinterpretation of a source whose revolutionary message it distils into stark blocks of cinematic meaning. Another early Soviet film, Protozanov's adaptation of Aleksei Tolstoi's science fiction novel *Aelita* (1924), a melodramatic potboiler with political subtext, turns Tolstoi's original on its head by transferring most of the action from the planet Mars to NEP-era Russia. Sequences juxtaposing the old aristocracy's opulent lifestyles are juxtaposed with crowd scenes depicting the hardships of ordinary Russians. Corrupt NEP-regime officials are also targeted and, unlike the novel, the film ends with the hero abandoning his love for the Martian princess Aelita and committing himself to the rebuilding of orphanages ravaged by the Civil War.

Another example of a cinematic 'Bolshevization' of a literary classic is the 1934 film *The Great Citizen* (*Velikii grazhdanin*), based very loosely on

Dostoevskii's *Devils*. Here the nineteenth-century author's mordant satire on Lenin's murderous precursors is transformed into an equally sardonic assault on the counter-revolutionaries purportedly responsible for the assassination of Kirov, the Leningrad Communist Party leader, proving the screen adaptation as capable of 'decanonization' as of canon-formation.

As the utopian experimentation of the early 1920s waned, the purpose of the *ekranizatsiia* changed as it became ever more subordinate to the demands of a repressive state apparatus desperate to consolidate its still precarious hold on power. For example, screen versions of the Caucasian tales of Pushkin, Tolstoi and Lermontov produced by Georgian State Cinema between 1926 and 1928 provided a potent means of cementing ties between the disparate republics of the newly formed Soviet Union.[11]

Cinema's ability to make arcane concepts accessible to the masses gave the screen adaptation a vital pedagogical function. The Soiuzdetfilm (children's films) and Soiuzmultfilm (cartoons) studios set up in the early 1930s generated suitably uplifting texts tied to rigid school literature curricula which contributed to the formation of a Soviet literary canon, and to the overall propaganda mission (many such adaptations reinforced points of Stalinist orthodoxy absent from the literary originals, using their parasitic dependence on the status of the latter to legitimate those points). In 1935, an animated version of *Gulliver's Travels* was made under the title *New Gulliver* (*Novyi Gulliver*) in which Swift's text provides a platform for an entertaining satire on the rising tide of Fascism in Europe. In 1933, Saltykov-Shchedryn's satirical novel, the *Golovlev Family* (*Gospoda Golovlevy*), was screened under the title *Iudushka Golovlev*. Saltykov's semi-surreal plot is fragmented into a series of episodic scenes in which aspects of country estate life under the tsar (attitudes towards the peasants, corruption, estate mismanagement) are highlighted.

The same contradiction emerged in what became the chief rationale for the Stalinist screen adaptation: its ability to reinforce the dogmas of socialist realism whose official inauguration in 1934 confirmed the word's reinstallation at the summit of Soviet discourse after the demise of the visually oriented avant-garde. With a remit to furnish a middlebrow culture capable of appealing to the masses, cultural policy makers placed a premium on accessibility. Bridging the divide between highbrow literature and popular film, the *ekranizatsiia* was ideally suited to this purpose. It facilitated the rapid canonization of key texts. Fadeev's *The Rout* (*Razgrom*) and Sholokhov's *Quiet Don* (*Tikhii Don*) were adapted as early as 1931, *Chapaev* in 1934, with Ostrovskii's *How the Steel was Tempered* (*Kak zakalialas' stal'*) following later in 1942. As Jeremy Hicks's chapter on *Chapaev* indicates, adaptations of socialist realist texts frequently reinterpreted their sources to ensure their conformity with ideological principles. Hicks shows how the Vasil'ev brothers played down the problematic, semi-documentary status of Furmanov's original in favour of a convenient folklorization of the figure of Chapaev.

The *ekranizatsiia* also legitimated socialist realism by demonstrating the movement's links with pre-revolutionary literature and with progressive world culture as a whole. Nineteenth-century classics featuring criticism of the old tsarist order were milked for all they were worth. Eisenstein's *Bezhin Meadow* (*Bezhin lug*) (1935), however, reconfirms the precarious nature of the 'contract' between literature and cinema. Despite subjecting Turgenev's original to a contemporary rewriting in which the rural idyll is replaced by a brutal, collectivist logic, the film was banned for its purportedly modernist aesthetics.

Early twentieth-century works which openly embraced the coming revolution (such as Gor'kii's autobiographical trilogy), and Soviet fiction set in the pre-revolutionary period, were prominent amongst 1930s and 1940s adaptations. In the 1937 version of Valentin Kataev's semi-autobiographical novella, *A Lone White Sail Gleams* (*Beleet parus odinokii*), set in the aftermath of the abortive mutiny on the battleship Potemkin in 1905, Kataev's vestigial modernistic quirks are expunged. References to tsarist pogroms are replaced with socialist realist motifs and the young hero's friendship with a sailor on the run from the tsarist authorities is expanded to fit the framework of the 'Party Mentor'–'Young Initiate' model axiomatic within socialist realist aesthetics. Inter-titles address the viewer in the omniscient voice of revolutionary history and the film's ending is replete with rousing speeches to righteously angry crowds. As well as grounding socialist realism in pre-revolutionary culture, such adaptations offer a convenient solution to the representational paradox of how to demonstrate the immanence of the socialist utopia within an everyday reality stubbornly resistant to the optimistic paradigm imposed upon it.

The 1930s and '40s also saw a steady stream of *ekranizatsii* of judiciously selected world classics (predominantly those dealing with social themes or popular uprisings), providing socialist realism with organic roots in world history, just as *White Sail* rooted the movement in domestic tradition. However, the *ekranizatsiia* was compelled to engage with some of the tensions entailed in managing the relationship between the verbal and the visual, the official and the popular. Film's visual regime entails a subjectivization of experience at odds with the pseudo-objective rhetoric of the narrative voice it translates into cinematic language. In classic socialist realist adaptations like *The Quiet Don* and *The Rout*, the camera, through shot-reverse shot techniques, frequently adopted the viewpoint of the leading character, subjectivizing viewer experience in a manner subversive of the official rhetoric of the transcendence of 'spontaneity' by Party consciousness.

In the later Stalin period, the *ekranizatsiia*'s allegiances with the new rhetoric of the outstanding individual accorded more readily with official discourse which was, by now, fully engaged with fostering the Stalin personality cult. One of the most important films of the late 1930s was Vladimir Petrov's 1937 adaptation of Aleksei Tolstoi's historical novel *Peter the Great*

(*Petr Pervyi*). Whilst the novel evoked favourable comparisons between Stalin and Russia's first iron-willed reformer, Petrov ensured that the parallels conformed to contemporary ideological orthodoxies. The bulk of the first part of the novel dealing with Peter as a precocious child and his obsession with the Germans is omitted, as is Aleksandr Menshikov's positive influence on the young tsar. The tsar is presented as a ready-made myth (the distinctive image he cuts became part of the iconography of the Stalin period), rather than the product of a complex biographical line of development. Peter's affinity with ordinary people and hands-on involvement in military affairs are underscored and the frequent scenes depicting the tsar at the centre of crowds reconcile images of heroic leadership with collectivist politics.

The dual tendencies observed in the *ekranizatsiia* of the 1930s intensified during and after World War II. On one hand, they continued to serve as a means of popularizing, canonizing and 'correcting' key texts, as with Gerasimov's 1948 version of Fadeev's *Molodaia gvardiia* in which scenes depicting the planned, disciplined nature of the young heroes' struggle with Nazism proliferate (see Figure 0.1). Stephen Hutchings's chapter shows how adaptations of 1940s' children's literature reconceived their sources in order to naturalize the moral ideology of the mythologized Soviet war hero, and, by fostering oscillations of viewer identifications between child hero and paternalistic state, to ameliorate the contradictions of Stalinist society.

Figure 0.1 A scene from Gerasimov's *Young Guard* (*Molodaia gvardiia*, 1948)

Source: Courtesy of British Film Institute, London

On the other hand, it was during the war that the rigid dogmas of socialist realism began to splinter under pressure from twin imperatives: the need to unite the Soviet people under the banner of a revived Russian national spirit, and the need to celebrate individual acts of heroism. Here, too, with its grounding in native literary tradition, the screen adaptation was a useful tool. An interesting, if contradictory, example is A. Stolper's 1948 adaptation of Boris Polevoi's socialist realist paradigm, 'Tale of a Real Man' (1946). Polevoi's text centres on the true story of Aleksei Mares'ev (renamed Meres'ev by Polevoi), a double amputee who, overcoming bureaucratic hurdles to his desire to fly again for his squadron, finally takes to the air in battle again. The tale's singularity and its theme of resistance to impersonal, institutional obstacles, are, in themselves, at odds with socialist realist convention and are omitted in the film. However, by expanding on a brief scene in the novella in which Meres'ev dances to a folk song in his new prostheses, the film underscores the Russian nationalist theme.

In the early 1950s, film adaptations returned to more conventional Stalinist themes. Films were made of some of the most trenchantly socialist realist novels. Thus, V. Kochetov's production novel, *The Zhurbins* (*Zhurbiny*), was adapted by Iosif Kheifits in 1954 as *The Big Family* (*Bol'shaia semia*). Set in a shipbuilding yard and featuring the working lives of several generations of the Zhurbin family, the novel is dominated by conversations about welding techniques and the sacrosanct value of labour, and authorial interventions celebrating the idyllic socialist future. Kheifits's title assimilates Kochetov's novel to the Stalinist cult of the Soviet Union as a family headed by a stern, loving father. He eradicated most of the production novel excesses and established an extra-marital affair involving Viktor Zhurbin and a woman called Zina at the centre of the narrative, replacing Kochetov's tract-like, plotless text with something resembling a socialist realist soap opera (see Figure 0.2).

Kheifits's reworking of Kochetov is unsurprising in the context of the infiltration into post-Stalinist cinema of the concerns of the individual and private. Two of the main characteristics of early Thaw film adaptations were (a) a reshaping of the literary canon to include some previously ignored or suppressed works and (b) a reinterpretation of canonic texts to reflect the shifting of values away from the tenets of Stalinist collectivism. Thus, Ivan Pyr'ev used his position at the summit of the Soviet film hierarchy to rehabilitate the works of Dostoevskii (directing versions of *The Idiot* (1958), *White Nights* (1959) and *The Brothers Karamazov* (1968)), and 1958 saw a new version of Fadeev's *The Rout* (*Razgrom*) retitled as *The Youth of our Fathers* (*Iunost' nashikh ottsov*) in a manner indicative of the wave of early Thaw-era nostalgia for the purity of Leninist principles.

As Julian Graffy's contribution indicates, the Thaw also saw the screening of the audacious writing of the Young Prose movement (Graffy analyses two very different adaptations of stories by Vasilii Aksenov). Later, the literature of the anti-urban Village Prose movement enjoyed success in screen

Figure 0.2 A poster advertising Kheifit's *The Big Family* (*Bol'shaia sem'ia,* 1954)
Source: Courtesy of British Film Institute, London

form, as John Givens indicates in his chapter on Vasilii Shukshin. At the same time, cinema itself was advancing in new directions and, rather than fade into insignificance, screen adaptations often spearheaded these innovations. For example, the career of Andrei Tarkovskii, who achieved world recognition for articulating a pure cinematic vision inspired by his veneration of his father's poetry, began with a highly impressionistic interpretation of the tale of a war orphan, *Ivan's Childhood* (*Ivanovo detstvo*). David Gillespie's chapter reminds us that Grigorii Kozintsev, who had prospered in the Stalin years with a series of conventional socialist realist films, was originally part of the 1920s cinematic avant-garde; in his visually stunning 1964 adaptation of *Hamlet*, Kozintsev rediscovers his former creative talent.

Experimentation ground to a halt with Khrushchev's demise. The new repressive atmosphere accounted for the banning or shelving of several groundbreaking *ekranizatsii*, including Askol'dov's iconoclastic *Commissar* (*Kommissar*), a reinterpretation of Vasilii Grossman's 1942 tale, *In The Town of Berdichev* (*V Gorode Berdichev*), set during the hallowed Civil War period. As

Graham Roberts's chapter suggests, Askol'dov 'sins' on three counts: his formalism, his sympathetic portrayal of Jews, and his hostility to the inhumane consequences of dogmatic collectivism. Nonetheless, the role of the *ekranizatsiia* in expanding the Soviet literary canon did not cease with Brezhnev's accession to power. The increasing premium placed on 'culturedness' (*'kulturnost'*), a reflection of late Soviet class politics, and anxiety over the deleterious influences of Western mass culture, meant that there remained a place for tasteful adaptations of the Russian classics, a large number of which appeared in the Brezhnev period. The latter concern also produced the opposite result: the rapid adaptation of works of popular literature able to satisfy the growing demand for cultural products that entertained as well as edified.

Another approach to the issue was to cast popular media stars in serious literary adaptations. Vladimir Vysotskii, who had attained popularity of mythical proportions through his guitar poetry and appearances in war films, is one example. Vasilii Shukshin, who, as Givens shows, managed successfully to combine the roles of serious writer, film director of his own literary scenarios and popular screen star, is another. An unanticipated consequence of this phenomenon was that it contributed towards the growing trend towards interpretations of *ekranizatsii* which stressed parallels between the represented literary past and the Soviet present, making it difficult to avoid the sense that these films were replete with hidden allegorical meaning. Loyal renditions of Turgenev were open to perceptions of discrepancies between freedom to travel across Europe in novellas like *Asia* (adapted by Iosif Kheifits in 1977) and the lack of such freedoms in the Soviet present. Even faithful renditions of classics could barely avoid the taint of ideological oppositionism through their pointed contrast with Stalinist adaptations which subjected nineteenth-century literature to all manner of political distortions.

The *ekranizatsiia* also became the locus for a revitalized Russian nationalism which could now be grounded in nostalgia for the lost splendour of the pre-revolutionary years. Birgit Beumers and Russell Valentino treat Nikita Mikhalkov's revalorization of a Russian landscape idealized through adaptations of nineteenth-century country estate classics. Valentino's analysis of Mikhalkov's version of Goncharov's *Oblomov* focuses on a single cinematic device, the freeze-frame tableau, which Valentino reads as a symbol of the false aestheticization practised by Stolz, the Eurocentric foil of Goncharov's indolent hero who, in turn, is associated with lyrical scenes of a childhood spent amidst the authentic beauty of the Russian countryside. Beumers contrasts Mikhalkov's *ekranizatsii* with his brother's version of *Uncle Vanya* showing how Mikhalkov 'elevates nature to an artistic image containing the national past within its value system'.

Under Brezhnev, television adaptations assumed greater importance. The televisual appearance of stock characters from the international literary canon like Sherlock Holmes, Tom Sawyer and the heroes of J.K. Jerome helped sate the mounting curiosity of ordinary Soviet people about all things Western. Such adaptations also complemented international policies of détente, promulgating cosy stereotypes of the eccentric English gentleman which enabled official culture to claim that it was 'fostering international understanding', but, at the same time, to ensure that progressive views of the iniquities of capitalism prevailed. A 1979 production of *Three Men in a Boat* uses J.K. Jerome's original as a platform from which to indulge in stereotypical images of 'Misty Albion' and Big Ben. By contrast, a 1981 television production of *Tom Sawyer* exploits Twain's original to expose American racism, and simultaneously celebrate negro culture, whilst aiming for realist authenticity in its sets and scenery. The series is framed with anachronous shots of a negro jazz-band, juxtaposed with images of a sweating black stoker on a steamboat. Sawyer's misdemeanours are portrayed as a sublimated form of protest against social injustice, whilst Huck Finn is represented as an outsider, exasperated at bourgeois hypocrisies. Cathy Nepomnyashchy's chapter on parallels between the Soviet and nineteenth-century British imperial missions as reflected in the Sherlock Holmes stories provides another angle on the function of late Soviet television adaptations of foreign classics as vehicles by which contemporary political tensions are articulated.

With the coming of glasnost, coded allegorizations were replaced by open polemic, as film began to reflect the ideological challenges posed to communist orthodoxy mounted across the breadth of Soviet culture. In one sense, the *ekranizatsiia* resembled other films of the period. A major cinematic innovation in the late 1980s was the introduction of taboo subjects: crime, explicit sex and anti-social behaviour. Balaian's 1989 adaptation of Leskov's 'Lady Macbeth of the Mtsensk District' ('Ledi Makbet Mtsenskogo uezda') places the controversial topic of serial murder at its core. Moreover, like better-known films of the period such as Pichul's *Little Vera* (*Malen'kaia Vera*) and Piotr Todorovsky's *Intergirl* (*Interdevochka*), both released in 1989, the film is abundant in sex scenes. Adaptations of the late 1980s were also a key forum for the re-evaluation of Soviet history. Thus, Tsymbal's 1988 adaptation of Il'ia Zverev's short story 'Defence Attorney Sedov' ('Zashchitnik Sedov'), deals with the manipulation of an honest attorney by the Stalinist regime during the 1930s purges.

But the *ekranizatsiia* did not merely duplicate tendencies common to all 1980s Soviet cinema. It had a crucial role to play in reshaping the literary canon in line with new political realities. The satirical fantasies of Mikhail Bulgakov, whose novel the *Master and Margarita* had served as a banner of opposition during the Stagnation, finally arrived on the Soviet screen. In 1988, V. Bortko's adaptation of Bulgakov's 'A Dog's Heart' ('Sobach'e serdtse') was released. 1990 saw the screening of the same writer's 'The Red Crown' ('Krasnaia korona'). Mikhail Iakzhen's version of Bulgakov's *Notes of a Young Doctor* (*Zapiski iunogo vracha*) followed in 1991. In 1989 Odessa Studios issued a film based on Babel's stories under the title *The Art of Living in Odessa* (*Iskusstvo zhit' v Odesse*) which, apart from rehabilitating a previously repressed writer, indicated that *ekranizatsii* set in the non-Russian republics earlier used to cement Russia's control over the Soviet Union were now functioning as a site at which local concerns might be asserted against Russian centralism. The glasnost-era *ekranizatsiia* fostered new, post-communist identities, complementing the political dismantling of Soviet ideologies with which glasnost is habitually associated.

The introduction under Gorbachev of market forces inspired an awareness of cinema's commercial potential, resulting in adaptations of contemporary crime thrillers, both Russian and Western: *The Big Game* (*Bol'shaia igra*, 1988), a television detective series based on Iulian Semenov's novel, *Press-Centre* (*Press-tsentr*), and *The Bay of Death* (*Bukhta smerti*, 1991), based on James Chase's detective novel *Stone Jungles*, to name two.

However, few non-commercial Russian writers of the glasnost period were adapted for screen in the 1980s or the 1990s. Tatiana Tolstaia's short story 'Sonia', released in 1991 under the title *House on the Sand* (*Dom na peske*), is one exception. The early post-communist period was marked by a prolonged financial crisis throughout the arts and resource-hungry cinema was particularly harshly affected; the likes of Tolstaia (whose 'Sonia' relied on German co-funding for its film version), Erofeev, Pelevin and Petrushevskaia were generally deprived of the opportunity to see their works on screen.[12]

In the post-Soviet period, the removal of state subsidies for cinema and television entailed a significant reduction in the number of film adaptations.[13] Literary films hardly offer the money-spinning potential provided by the likes of Aleksei Balabanov's post-Soviet gangster films, *Brother* (*Brat*, 1997) and *Brother 2* (*Brat 2*, 2000), although adaptations of Russian mass literature have enjoyed significant commercial success. (A recent example is Pavel Lungin's 2002 version of Iulii Dubov's novel *The Big Ration* (*Bol'shaia paika*), tracing the career of the rich entrepreneur, Boris Berezovskii, and entitled *Oligarkh* (*The Oligarch*.) Market-led post-Soviet television has tended to abandon literary programming owing to its lack of commercial viability, though the introduction in 1997 of a Culture Channel (Kul'tura) has proved a durable exception). *Ekranizatsii* are still widely shown, but these are mostly old films screened repeatedly for economy's sake.

Nonetheless, large-scale literary adaptations are not extinct. The early 1990s witnessed a number of provocative post-Soviet reinterpretations of nineteenth-century classics. Several are treated in this volume. Joe Andrew explores the cinematic transposition of Tolstoi's *Prisoner of the Caucasus*, set in the tsarist Caucasus, onto latter-day Chechnya, highlighting the film's critique of both gender and ethnic stereotypes. Anat Vernitski discusses adaptations of Leskov's 'Lady Macbeth of the Mtsensk District', Pushkin's *Captain's Daughter*, and Dostoevskii's *The Idiot*, illustrating the way post-Soviet culture defines itself in a three-way relationship with the pre-Revolutionary and the Soviet periods.

In a reprise of Stalinist policy, but to reverse ideological effect, established literary classics are now screened to bolster an officially sanctioned Russian national identity. Whereas Pushkin's portrayal of Pugachev's eighteenth-century peasant revolt was once appropriated into revolutionary mythology, it now emblematizes the stain on authentic Russian-ness that is Bolshevism's current symbolic status. Thus, the new Pushkin adaptation polemicizes with a 1958 Soviet *ekranizatsiia* of the tale, underscoring, as does *Prisoner of the Caucasus*, the fact that adaptations are interpretations (rather than translations) which establish intertextual relations with their predecessors, as well as with literary sources.

With (albeit unofficially, and partially) state-controlled television now spearheading the Russian national identity project, the *ekranizatsiia* has once again emerged as a key cultural form. Money is now abundantly available, provided it is spent on the (re)canonization of approved texts. Ambitious television serials based on Dostoevsky's *Idiot* and Bulgakov's *A Theatrical Romance* (*Teatral'nyi roman*) have recently been shown. In 2002, Channel 1 (now a Putin mouthpiece) adapted Boris Akunin's detective thriller, *Azazel'*, set in an idealized nineteenth-century Russia in which once demonized tsarist secret policemen are portrayed as intrepid heroes fighting against a world domination plot implicitly reminiscent of the Jewish–Masonic conspiracy central to Russian nationalist mythology.

In short, reports of the death of Russian literary culture are premature. This is thanks in no small part to the vitality of the *ekranizatsiia*, whose dialogue with its verbal sources, with the cinematic art whose fraught relationship with literature it mediates, and with the official culture to which it so often lends support will continue long into the twenty-first century.

The volume: structure and scope

The twelve chapters making up this volume are divided into four chronologically sequenced sections each of which is relatively unified in the broad issue around which it is centred. The theme running throughout our overview has been the *ekranizatsiia*'s contribution to the rise, decline and eventual supplanting of the political mythology that has animated Russian society through the twentieth-century. Each section treats an aspect of this process relevant to the period in question. Part I examines how the twentieth-century Russian *ekranizatsiia* emerged from its early subservience to its sources to become a primary tool by which the Stalinist mythology at the heart of Soviet culture authenticated itself. Whilst she refers to the pre-Soviet period, Morley demonstrates that the *ekranizatsiia*'s ability to desacralize its source, and exploit it to influence contemporary mores was not an invention of cynical Soviet ideologues but rather inherent within the logic of the genre itself. The remaining two chapters in this section examine how Stalinist adaptations 'corrected' their sources in order to generate texts free from the demands of historical accuracy (Hicks), and to turn the 'innocent' settings of children's wartime literature into metaphoric models of Stalinist society as a whole (Hutchings).

Part II focuses on the challenges posed to axiomatic socialist realist principles by Thaw-period adaptations. Gillespie's chapter on Kozintsev provides the transition from Part I by showing how a director steeped in socialist realist aesthetics produced Shakespeare adaptations which, whilst embracing conventional, socially grounded interpretations of the playwright, nonetheless draw parallels between contemporary Soviet society and negative aspects of the historical situations Shakespeare depicts. Roberts's chapter addresses the *ekranizatsiia*'s contribution to the replacement of Civil War mythology by existential concerns of freedom and identity. Graffy reveals the contradictory process by which Thaw cinema edged towards the alternative mythologies emerging within the Soviet youth generation. Givens's chapter on Shukshin touches on the emergence of 1960s *auteur* cinema in which Stalinist collectivist myths are replaced by those of the individual genius.

In Part III, Beumers's and Valentino's chapters move us chronologically to the Brezhnev and early Gorbachev period, and thematically to the adaptation's role in articulating the Russian nationalist ideologies which emerged as alternatives to worn-out Marxist platitudes. Nepomnyashchy discerns in the legendary Sherlock Holmes series of the 1970s and '80s, not only a site for the playing out of the tensions of imperialism, but also an example of late Soviet stereotypes of the English detective.

Part IV addresses the *ekranizatsiia*'s role in the contradictory process of identity-building which has characterized contemporary Russian culture. Andrew's analysis indicates that the *ekranizatsiia*'s subversive, de-mythologizing function continued into the post-Soviet period. Vernitski confirms this trend and return us to Morley's account of the deliberately quirky adaptation of the canonic classic as a means of commenting upon contemporary societal problems. However, as Vernitski suggests, by polemicizing with readings of nineteenth-century classics canonized during the Soviet period, the *ekranizatsiia* lays the ground for the re-recruitment of those same texts to the services of new ideological trends.

Every decade of the twentieth-century is represented in the volume, but with the important exceptions of the 1920s and the 1950s. Moreover, that the balance of the films analysed is tilted heavily towards the 1960s and 70s is only in part a reflection of the virtually unmatched volume of films made during these decades. We have attempted to correct these imbalances and omissions in our extended overview. We should also refer readers to the companion to this volume which discusses *ekranizatsii* of the under-represented periods in detail.[14] Overall, we hope that readers will come away from the book with a feeling for the range of complex issues that the Russian *ekranizatsiia* raises, for the theoretical approaches to which it responds, and for the path of development that it has followed.

Notes

1 Louis Giannetti's claim in 1975 that '[t]he overwhelming majority of what's been written about the relationship of film and literature is open to serious question' is, sadly, still relevant (Giannetti 1975: 89).
2 Baz Luhrman's cinematic transpositions of Shakespearean text to modern America offer a good illustration.
3 The function of Merchant-Ivory productions of the English classics as carriers of post-imperial values is one much-discussed example of this phenomenon.
4 For instance, screen representations of the autobiographical 'I', a common dilemma for the film adaptor, is not merely a formal problem, but the function of a set of tensions centring on viewing as voyeurism, and reification of the other.
5 This is why recent 'faithful' adaptations, such as Kenneth Branagh's version of *Frankenstein* announce themselves with titles like 'Mary Shelley's Frankenstein'.
6 Moreover, if we are to insist on determining cinema's unique features, then amongst those features are its natural syncretism, its tendency towards synaesthetic combinations of linear narrative, visual image, music, sound: its refusal, precisely, of material specificity.
7 Other *Pravda* reviews, devoting inordinate attention to the Party role, praise Gerasimov for 'correcting the novel's weak parts in response to criticism' (Tass 1948: 3) and for making the Bolshevik Protsenko 'the point at which all the strands of underground activity converge' (Anonymous 1948: 2).
8 For this view, see also Dzigan (1973).
9 See the debate between Ol'gin (1969) and Anninskii (1969) in *Iskusstvo kino*.
10 Even faithful adaptations of the silent period achieved considerable sophistication. The 1917 version of Tolstoy's *Father Sergii* is one of the best pre-revolutionary Russian films.
11 See Chapter 4 of Hutchings (2004) for more detail on this process.
12 Pelevin's story 'The Blue Lantern' ('inii fonar') was, however, adapted in 1997 in a non-commercial student production at the Russian film school (VGIK) under the title *Nothing Terrible* (*Nichego strashnogo*)
13 Film production in the former Soviet Union declined from 300 per annum in 1990 to 46 in 1995, although it has recovered a little since.
14 See Chapters 4–6 in Hutchings (2004).

Part I

Film adaptations from the start to Stalin

Manufacturing the myth

1 'Crime without punishment'

Reworkings of nineteenth-century Russian literary sources in Evgenii Bauer's *Child of the Big City*

Rachel Morley[1]

As many commentators on early Russian cinema have noted, the use of nineteenth-century Russian literary classics as sources for film scenarios was a common strategy of pre-Revolutionary Russian directors, who often sought thereby to increase the cultural and social 'respectability' of their new art form (Zorkaia 1976: 99–111; Tsiv'ian 1991: 8; Youngblood 1999: 15, 61–71, 115; McReynolds 2003: 260–4).[2] In this respect, Evgenii Bauer (1867–1917) is an anomaly. While he adapted several works of Russian and European literature for the screen, Bauer chose none of the classic nineteenth-century Russian texts, preferring works by lesser-known writers or those not generally considered literary classics.[3] The only extant Bauer film based on a work by one of the nineteenth-century Russian greats is *After Death* (*Posle smerti*, 1915), a modernized version of Ivan Turgenev's 1882 story 'Klara Milich', not one of the author's best-known works.[4]

Bauer's relatively late entry into cinema, in 1912, may explain this peculiarity of his oeuvre.[5] As Denise Youngblood notes: 'By 1912, it had become apparent to studio heads that the works of "sensational" living writers … could attract even larger audiences than those for the classics' (Youngblood 1999: 9). Despite this shift towards popular literature, however, adaptations of the classics continued to be made. Moreover, Bauer did not entirely ignore the nineteenth-century Russian classics. In fact, in his many films that have original scenarios, he exploited a wide range of nineteenth-century literary sources, most notably works by Pushkin, Gogol', Dostoevskii and Tolstoi, drawing on their stock protagonists, themes and images. Bauer did not merely replicate the commonplaces of this literary tradition, however. Instead, he frequently subverted, reversed and developed them in surprising ways. This makes the films Bauer based on original scenarios more complex and challenging intertextual works than those that are straightforward adaptations of single texts.

Bauer's subversion of the staple protagonists, motifs and themes of this literary tradition is a recurrent characteristic of his directorial style and thus seems to be an intentional strategy. The aims of this chapter are therefore twofold: to give examples of Bauer's appropriation of nineteenth-century Russian literary sources, and to consider why he preferred such intertextual play to direct adaptation of the Russian classics. In so doing, I shall focus on Bauer's 1914 melodrama *Child of the Big City* (*Ditia bol'shogo goroda*), subtitled *A Girl from the Street* (*Devushka s ulitsy*), for its density and range of literary and cultural allusion are such that only a detailed reading can do it justice.[6]

Set in contemporary Moscow, *Child of the Big City* tells the story of a beautiful seamstress, who improves her lot by captivating a rich young man whom she ruins and then abandons. The film's sententious title and subtitle both situate the viewer in the context of the realist literature of nineteenth-century Russia, and lead us to expect that Bauer, too, will focus on moral and social concerns. The opening sequence further encourages this assumption, for we witness the orphaning of Man'ka, the eponymous child: her mother, a laundress, dies of consumption in a dirty basement, surrounded by tearful, God-fearing women and watched by her distraught daughter. Having, during her lifetime, performed the prototypical work of nineteenth-century lower-class women – and not only of those in Russia –, Man'ka's mother dies in one of the two conventional locations for such a scene, the other being a miserable garret. Furthermore, she dies what Susan Sontag has shown to be the quintessential death of nineteenth-century female protagonists. In *Illness as Metaphor*, Sontag demonstrates that in nineteenth-century works tuberculosis is repeatedly represented as 'the prototypical passive death' and 'the disease of born victims' (Sontag 1991: 25–6); it was also seen as 'a redemptive death for the fallen' (ibid.: 42). Bauer's use of this general nineteenth-century trope is not intended to continue this tradition, however, but rather to disrupt it. It is not his central female protagonist who suffers from consumption, but the peripheral character of her mother, and, moreover, Bauer ultimately dismisses the type of the passive and victimized consumptive heroine altogether; after the opening sequence, the action leaves the dirty basement and the nineteenth century and instead moves out and up into the high society of the modern city, focusing on the story of a twentieth-century woman's self-creation. Although Man'ka's story may begin like that of so many nineteenth-century heroines, we shall see that it does not progress in the same way.[7]

While the opening sequence of *Child of the Big City* draws on these commonplaces of nineteenth-century art, it is also Bauer's first direct reference to a specific nineteenth-century Russian text, Fedor Dostoevskii's 1867 novel *Crime and Punishment* (*Prestuplenie i nakazanie*). In many of its details this sequence recalls the scene from Part 5, Chapter 5 when Katerina Ivanovna Marmeladova – Sonia's stepmother – dies from consumption in Sonia's garret room, surrounded by her weeping children and other onlookers (Dostoevskii 1973b: 332–4). Although Katerina Ivanovna is not a laundress by trade, her obsessive concern with remaining awake to wash her family's clothes at night, detailed especially in Part 2, Chapter 7 (ibid.: 140), further links Man'ka's mother to her. Bauer thus encourages the viewer to identify his young heroine not only with Sonia's stepsister Polen'ka, but also with the twice-orphaned Sonia herself, for, throughout his novel, Dostoevskii presents Polen'ka less as a character in her own right and more as a young version of Sonia, for whom Raskol'nikov repeatedly predicts the same fate of prostitution.

The film's action then jumps forward nine years, however, and immediately weakens the connection between Man'ka and Sonia. Bauer's heroine, who has blossomed into the beautiful Mania, has not fallen into prostitution, but instead works in a sewing workshop as a seamstress, another prototypical profession of nineteenth-century Russian literary heroines, and a type, moreover, whom, according to Nikolai Gogol', one may often see as she 'runs across Nevskii Prospect with a hatbox in her hands' (*'perebezhit chrez Nevskii prospekt s korobkoi v rukakh'*) (Gogol' 1994: 11).[8]

At this point in the narrative, Bauer introduces his central male protagonist, Viktor Kravtsov, a wealthy, idealistic but unhappy young man. An intertitle informs us of his romantic disillusionment, revealing that he is searching for 'an unspoilt young creature, unlike the "cultured" women who surrounded him' (*'naivnoe molodoe sushchestvo, nepokhozhee na okruzhavshikh ego <kul'turnykh> zhenshchin'*). Viktor is thus immediately cast as a twentieth-century Moscow version of the nineteenth-century literary type of the naive and intense 'Petersburg dreamer'. In this, Bauer's filmic hero joins a long line of nineteenth-century literary heroes, including Piskarev, the timid Petersburg artist of Gogol''s 1835 story 'Nevskii Prospect' ('Nevskii prospekt'), the Underground Man of Dostoevskii's *Notes from Underground* (*Zapiski iz podpol'ia*, 1864), his Raskol'nikov in *Crime and Punishment*, and others. Viktor's fantasies of finding the love of an 'unspoilt' woman perhaps also link him, albeit less directly, to Pushkin's Byronic hero Aleko in *The Gypsies* (*Tsygany*, 1824).

These allusions to general nineteenth-century literary types again narrow into a direct reference to a specific nineteenth-century text, this time Gogol''s 'Nevskii Prospect'. In both text and film the central male protagonist is further characterized by his relationship with a friend whose personality is diametrically opposed to his own. In the same way that Gogol' contrasts the idealism of the naive Piskarev with the pragmatism of his worldly promenading companion, Lieutenant Pirogov, so Bauer creates a down-to-earth foil for the romantic Viktor in his friend Kramskoi. Moreover, this surname cannot have been chosen by chance: through it Bauer alludes to the nineteenth-century Russian realist artist, Ivan Kramskoi, whose most famous work is his 1883 portrait of a knowing and challenging 'Unknown Woman' (*'Neizvestnaia'*). By thus linking Viktor's friend with this realist artist, Bauer highlights Kramskoi's matter-of-fact approach to women. He also subtly underlines Viktor's naive idealism, both by contrasting him with Kramskoi and by identifying him with Gogol''s Piskarev, for Viktor is thus associated with an art and an outlook of a very different kind from Kramskoi's worldly realism, one that is rooted in a sentimental romanticism that has little to do with everyday reality. Gogol' describes his artist hero as belonging to a class of people that 'has as little in common with the citizens of Saint Petersburg as a person who appears before us in a dream has with the real world' *('stol'ko zhe prinadlezhit k grazhdanam Peterburga, skol'ko litso, iavliaiushcheesia nam v snovidenii, prinadlezhit k sushchestvennomu miru'*) (Gogol' 1994: 13).

As Piskarev and Pirogov did before them in Saint Petersburg, Viktor and Kramskoi go out into the Moscow streets to continue their 'search' for a suitable woman. There they encounter Mania, hatbox in hand, and, as in 'Nevskii Prospect', the chase is on. Viktor and Kramskoi first notice Bauer's heroine as she stands, transfixed, before a flower shop; for them, she is as much an object to be bought or possessed as the luxury goods she admires (see Figure 1.1). With Kramskoi leading the way, the two men follow her and watch as she gazes into a jewellery shop and bursts into tears of frustrated longing. Viktor hangs back as Kramskoi invites Mania to dine, then the three of them repair to the private room of a restaurant, where Kramskoi plies Mania with wine, laughs indulgently at her lack of *savoir-faire* and makes an attempt to seduce her that is as clumsy and aggressive as Pirogov's attempted seduction of Schiller's blonde wife in Gogol''s story. It is also as ineffective; Viktor, ostensibly more gallant than his businesslike

Figure 1.1 Viktor (Mikhail Salarov, on the left) and Kramskoi (Arsenii Bibikov, on the right) encounter Mania (Elena Smirnova) in the Moscow streets.

Source: Courtesy of Gosfil'mofond Rossii, Moscow

friend, 'protects' Mania, but, when Kramskoi leaves, he seduces her himself. Encountering no resistance, yet believing he has at last found his 'unspoilt young creature', Viktor sets Mania up as his mistress.

The unsophisticated Mania is thus presented by Bauer as Viktor's equivalent of Aleko's nineteenth-century feminine ideal, embodied by the uncivilized Zemfira. However, as with both Pushkin's Aleko and Gogol''s Piskarev, Viktor's assessment of Mania's character proves to be misguided, for she is neither as 'unspoilt' nor as 'naive' as he believes. From the outset Bauer stresses that Mania, like Zemfira, who is entranced by Aleko's account of his life in the civilized world (Pushkin 1978a: 155), is attracted by the trappings of the high society to which Viktor belongs. The street scene, described above, unequivocally links Mania with the innately materialistic *habituée* of Nevskii Prospect who, Gogol' notes ironically, turns 'her little head to the sparkling shop windows, as a sunflower turns to the sun' (*'svoiu golovku k blestiashchim oknam magazina, kak podsolnechnik k solntsu'*) (Gogol' 1994: 8). Bauer also draws attention to Mania's longing for luxury in the earlier workshop sequence. Here Mania is framed in medium close-up, sitting pensively by the window. The window seat was the favoured position of the dreaming heroines of sentimental literature, and also of Pushkin's Tat'iana in *Evgenii Onegin* (1823–31, published in full in 1833). Mania is transfixed not by dreams of love, however, but 'was carried away by dreams of a make-believe life, full of luxury and wealth' (*'unosilas' mechtami k nesbytochnoi zhizni, polnoi roskoshi i bogatstva'*). Moreover, as she looks out at the Moscow cityscape, far from being horrified by the ugliness of the view and scared by its unfamiliarity, as Tat'iana is when she visits Moscow in Chapter 7, Stanza 43 of *Evgenii Onegin* (Pushkin 1978b: 136–7), Mania longs to be part of that exciting world. Mania's more pragmatic aspirations link her with Pushkin's Lizaveta in *The Queen of Spades* (*Pikovaia dama*, 1833), who also sits by the window dreaming of finding a man to help her improve her social standing (Pushkin 1978c: 218).

Mania's desire for a 'better' life thus explains Viktor's appeal for her. Through him she goes up in the world, a fact Bauer conveys visually in a lengthy shot of the huge flight of stairs leading to the glamorous *café-concert* to which Viktor introduces her. Mania quickly settles into her new way of life. She abandons her Russian name in favour of its Western equivalent, Mary (*Meri*), and enjoys the soirées, the life of leisure, the glamorous clothes and the tasteless knick-knacks that Viktor's money buys her. Like Zemfira again, however, Mary values her 'freedom' and is not prepared to commit herself to one man. She flirts with Viktor's valet and basks in the attention of male guests at the *café-concert*. It therefore comes as no surprise when Mary, like Zemfira, eventually transfers her attention and her affection to another man.

Like Gogol', who dismisses Piskarev as 'completely ridiculous' (*'chrezvychaino smeshon'*) (Gogol' 1994: 17), Bauer does not sympathize with his suffering hero; instead he mocks Viktor's delusions and romantic aspirations by linking him increasingly closely with the hapless Piskarev. Indeed, the two men share so many traits that Viktor at times appears to be Piskarev's double. Both Piskarev and Viktor are shown to aestheticize women. Piskarev describes his beloved as 'the very image of Perugino's Bianca' (*'sovershenno Perudzhinova Bianka'*) (ibid.: 12) and fantasizes that, had she not existed in reality, but instead been 'the creation of an inspired artist' (*'sozdanie vdokhnovennogo khudozhnika'*), he would have been able to worship her as he chose (ibid.: 24). Typically, Bauer uses details of *mise-en-scène* to reveal Viktor's similar tendency towards the aestheticization of his beloved. This would-be Pygmalion is surrounded with artistic representations of his feminine ideal: in his study neo-classical statuettes of women abound and even the base of his desk lamp has the form of a scantily-clad woman (see Figure 1.2). Moreover, after Mary has left him, Viktor seeks refuge from the truth about her by venerating her photograph.[9]

Both men also idealize the objects of their infatuation. Piskarev considers the prostitute a divine being, with 'divine features' (*'bozhestvennye cherty'*), who 'has flown down from heaven directly on to Nevskii Prospect' (*'sletelo s neba priamo na Nevskii prospekt'*) (ibid.: 13–14). As Piskarev loses himself in dreams and opium-induced visions, so Viktor sits daydreaming at his desk. They both construct fantasy images of the women they love that have little to

Figure 1.2 Surrounded by statuettes, Viktor and Kramskoi peruse Viktor's album of society belles.

Source: Courtesy of bfi Video Publishing, London

do with reality, and again coincide to a remarkable degree. In his favourite dream, Piskarev casts the prostitute as his faithful wife and pictures her devotedly watching him at work before 'she leant her delightful little head on his chest...' (*'ona sklonila k nemu na grud' prelestnuiu svoiu golovku...'*) (ibid.: 24). Viktor similarly constructs a passive, compliant and faithful lover, who is content to adore and be adored, as she rests her head on his shoulder. Gogol' states outright that these images are false, noting that in Piskarev's dreams the prostitute always appears 'in a guise completely contrary to reality' (*'v polozhenii protivopolozhnom deistvitel'nosti'*) (ibid.: 24); Bauer underlines the divergence cinematically. In a skilfully constructed sequence, he shows Mary reclining on her chaise-longue, indulging herself in erotic daydreams. As an image of Viktor's valet fades in, superimposed in the centre of the frame, Mary arches her back and reaches out to him ecstatically. Throughout this sequence, one of Viktor's statuettes can be seen on a shelf behind Mary, a constant reminder of the gap between Viktor's ideal image of his lover and the self-image of the real woman with whom he is involved (see Figure 1.3).

Later, when Viktor surprises Mary and his valet in an embrace, he raises his gun and shoots at her. The bullet, however, misses, and instead shatters Viktor's reflection in the mirror. This telling misaim is symbolic of something the viewer already knows: the ideal female whom Viktor loves has no existence except as a projection of his own psyche.

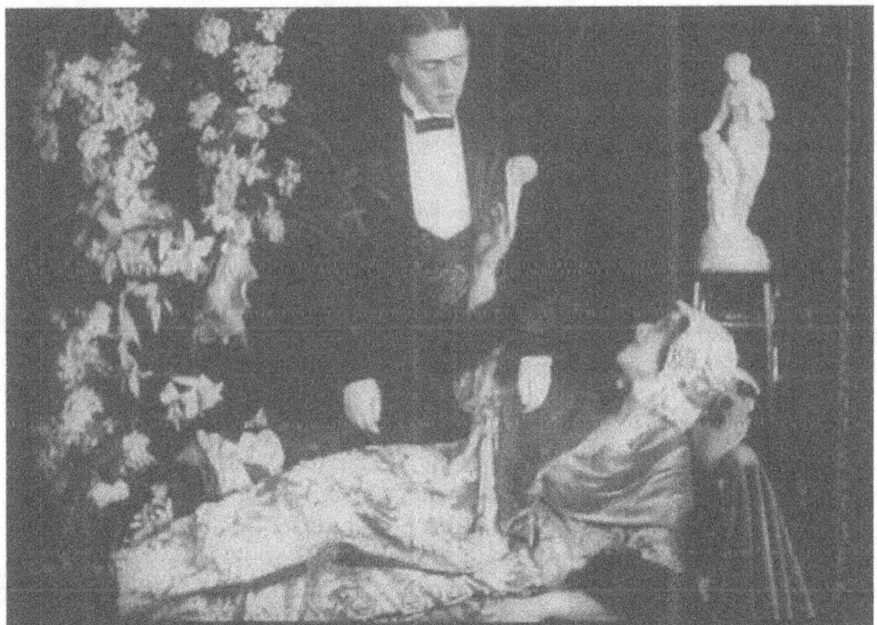

Figure 1.3 The juxtaposition of idealized aesthetic image and real self-image: the faithless Mary indulges herself in erotic daydreams of Viktor's valet (Leonid Iost)

Source: Courtesy of bfi Video Publishing, London

Furthermore, neither Gogol' nor Bauer presents his hero as a 'good' man, nor accepts his unworldliness as an excuse for his attitudes and behaviour. Instead, both writer and director emphasize the unpleasant sides of his hero's personality. While Piskarev is repeatedly described as pure and chaste (Gogol' 1994: 15, 17, 24), other details of Gogol''s narrative reveal something different about him. Piskarev's dreams show him to be self-aggrandizing, exploitative and vain, for they focus to a large extent on his hopes for worldly success and suggest that the prostitute is in fact more valuable to him as a 'muse', or an artist's appendage, than as a real person. Piskarev's repeated use of the dehumanizing noun 'creature' (*'sushchestvo'*) to refer to his beloved suggests the same: as he pursues her, Piskarev describes her as a 'delightful creature' (*'prelestnoe sushchestvo'*) (ibid.: 13), the 'unknown creature' ('[*n*]*eznakomoe sushchestvo'*) (ibid.: 14), a 'weak, beautiful creature' (*'slaboe prekrasnoe sushchestvo'*) (ibid.: 15), while, when he arrives at the brothel, he describes it as a place in which woman turns into 'a sort of strange, ambivalent creature … and ceases to be that weak, beautiful creature so different from [man]' (*'kakoe-to strannoe, dvusmyslennoe sushchestvo … i uzhe perestala byt' tem slabym, tem prekrasnym i tak otlichnym ot nas sushchestvom'*) (ibid.: 16). Moreover, while Piskarev sees himself as a chaste and chivalrous knight (*'rytsar''*) who, through marrying the prostitute, would accomplish a 'deed' (*'podvig'*) that would be 'disinterested and may even be great' (*'beskorysten i mozhet byt' dazhe velikim'*) (ibid.: 25), the details of his favourite dream are far from innocent and disinterested. As the prostitute – now imagined as Piskarev's wife – sits watching him at his work, Piskarev notes with rapture that 'the burden of bliss was manifest in her languorous, weary eyes' (*'[v] ee glazakh tomnykh, ustalykh, napisano bylo bremia blazhenstva'*) (ibid.: 24), and the discreet ellipses with which his description tails off at that point in the dream when she leans her head on his chest (cited earlier, ibid.: 24) leave the reader in no doubt as to how this dream continues, especially when Gogol' notes that Piskarev awaits his dreams 'with the passion of a lover' (*'so strastiiu liubovnika'*) (ibid.: 24). Moreover, despite his professed disapproval of the prostitute's life style, Piskarev is willing to paint a suggestive portrait of a seductive woman for the lascivious Persian who supplies him with opium (ibid.: 23).

In these respects again, Bauer creates a parallel between his hero and Gogol''s. He uses the same dehumanizing noun 'creature' (*'sushchestvo'*) in the intertitle that describes Viktor's ideal woman, and the half-naked statuettes that decorate Viktor's study suggest an erotic interest in worldly, sexual women that his stated preference for an 'unspoilt' woman attempts to deny. So, too, does his photograph album that contains portraits of the knowing society belles he affects to dislike (Hansen 1992: 14) (see Figure 1.2). Indeed, Viktor's aim of finding a woman of a lower social class to love is itself unattractive; it recalls the abusive attitude of Petr Luzhin in *Crime and Punishment*, who selects Dunia as his bride because she satisfies similar criteria (Dostoevskii 1973b: 32). The erotic satisfaction Luzhin derives from the thought of this unequal match is clear: he fantasizes 'with delight' ('*so slastiiu*') and 'with ecstasy' ('*s upoeniem*') about the time when 'such a creature would be slavishly grateful to him all her life for his deed, and would reverentially humble herself before him, while he would have absolute, unbounded power over her!' ('*takoe-to sushchestvo budet rabski blagodarno emu vsiu zhizn' za ego podvig i blagogoveino unichtozhitsia pered nim, a on-to budet bezgranichno i vsetselo vladychestvovat'!*') (ibid.: 235). Finally, although Viktor is not physically aggressive towards Mary, like Kramskoi, he is nevertheless shown by Bauer to prey on her, taking advantage of her fear and inexperience to seduce her in the restaurant.

The resemblances between Piskarev and Viktor do not end here, however. When Viktor realizes that Mary is ruining him and herself, he writes to her in an attempt to show her the error of her ways. Bauer thus draws directly on the general theme common in nineteenth-century Russian literature of the 'innocent' young man attempting to save the 'fallen woman'.[10] He also again engages very specifically with 'Nevskii Prospect', for Viktor's letter mirrors the speech Piskarev makes to his beloved when he finally accepts that she is, after all, 'one of those [women] who walk Nevskii Prospect at night' ('*iz tekh, kotorye khodiat vvecheru po Nevskomu prospektu*') (Gogol' 1994: 12). Gogol''s hero waxes lyrical, lecturing the object of his infatuation thus: 'It's true that I am poor ... but we will begin to work .... I will sit at my painting, you, seated next to me, will inspire my work and embroider or do other needlework – and we will want for nothing' ('*Pravda, ia beden ... no my stanem trudit'sia .... Ia budu sidet' za kartinami, ty budesh', sidia vozle menia, odushevliat' moi trudy, vyshivat' ili zanimat'sia drugim rukodeliem, – i my ni v chem ne budem imet' nedostatka*') (ibid.: 26). Viktor pleads with Mary in the same vein: 'Mary, I beg you, let us go away, let us rent a cheap flat. We will live modestly, for each other' ('*Meri, moliu tebia, uedem, snimem nedoroguiu kvartiru. My budem zhit' skromno, drug dlia druga*').

As Piskarev's attempt to redeem his fallen woman is dismissed by Gogol' as an 'ill-conceived plan' ('*legkomyslennyi plan*') (ibid.: 25), so Viktor's efforts are shown by Bauer to be misguided, for the responses of the two women are also very similar. Like Piskarev's dark-haired beauty, Mary has no desire to be 'saved'. Neither woman is ashamed of her way of life or in the least inclined to repent of it. Driven not by abstract moral concerns, but by worldly practicalities, neither of these pragmatic heroines is prepared even to consider relinquishing the material advantages of her 'immoral' lifestyle for the privations and hardships of a more 'respectable' way of life, and they both give their would-be saviours short shrift. Piskarev's lady interrupts him 'with an expression of contempt' ('*s vyrazheniem prezreniia*'): 'I am no laundress or seamstress, to be setting myself to work' ('*Ia ne prachka i ne shveia, chtoby stala zanimat'sia rabotoiu*') (ibid.: 26), while Mary is even more dismissive: 'For a modest flat, get yourself a modest girlfriend. I grew sick of your love a long time ago' ('*Dlia skromnoi kvartiry podberi sebe podrugu po sredstvam. Ty davno opostylel mne s svoei liubov'iu*').

Just as Gogol"s fallen woman spurns Piskarev's suggestion of sewing as an alternative to prostitution, so, tacitly, does Bauer's heroine. During the course of the film Mary discards her 'respectable' job as a seamstress in favour of a morally dubious life as a courtesan/kept woman, and this choice is shown by Bauer to result in Mary exchanging a 'poor' life for a 'better' life, with both these adjectives being seen in social and material, not moral, terms. Bauer therefore echoes Gogol"s rejection of a pervasive and powerfully suggestive trope in nineteenth-century Russian literature: that of sewing and sewing machines as the means and symbol of the fallen woman's spiritual redemption.[11] Bauer does not, therefore, use Mary's rejection of sewing only to link his heroine to one specific nineteenth-century fallen woman. He also exploits it to distance her from the many fallen heroines of this literary tradition who do wish to be redeemed, and in whose redemption sewing and sewing machines often play a part. Significantly, Dostoevskii's Sonia is one of these heroines. In Chapter 1 of the Epilogue of *Crime and Punishment*, Dostoevskii signals her redemption by having her take up dressmaking. Dunia and Razumikhin learn from one of her letters that: 'she does sewing and, as there are practically no dressmakers in the town, she has even become indispensable in many houses' (*'ona zanimaetsia shit'em, i tak kak v gorode pochti net modistki, to stala vo mnogikh domakh dazhe neobkhodimoiu'*) (Dostoevskii 1973b: 16).

Thus, while the opening sequence of *Child of the Big City* encouraged the viewer to identify Bauer's heroine with Dostoevskii's Sonia, the film's development progressively negates this connection. Unlike Sonia, who falls into prostitution but is ultimately redeemed, Mary falls, but rejects redemption. Furthermore, while Sonia adopts this way of life in order to help others, Mary does so to help nobody but herself. The relationship between Viktor and Mary thus turns that between Raskol'nikov and Sonia on its head. Raskol'nikov and Viktor both hope to rescue their female counterparts from their demeaning way of life. However, while Raskol'nikov succeeds, Viktor, like Piskarev, fails. Moreover, while Sonia also determines to save Raskol'nikov, Mary sets out to do the exact opposite for Viktor and instead ruins him, a Gogolian intertitle informs us, 'with a rare, perhaps innate, skill' (*'s redkim, mozhet byt', vrozhdennym umeniem'*). That Mary's rise on the property ladder is paralleled by Viktor's fall from it – he ends up as the tenant of a gloomy garret room – is perhaps an ironic reference to Nikolai Nekrasov's famously earnest poem about the rescue of a fallen woman by an upright young man, 'When from out of error's darkness...' (*'Kogda iz mraka zabluzhden'ia...*, 1845). This poem, which is also pilloried by Dostoevskii in the second part of *Notes From Underground*, concludes with the poetic persona's exhortation to his redeemed fallen woman:

> And boldly and freely enter my house,
> As its full mistress!
> (*I v dom moi smelo i svobodno*
> *Khoziaikoi polnoiu voidi!*)
>
> (Dostoevskii 1973a: 171)

Bauer thus also adapts that commonplace of nineteenth-century Russian literature according to which the female protagonist is stronger than her male counterpart; the relationships between Pushkin's Zemfira and Aleko, his Tat'iana and Onegin, Dostoevskii's Sonia and Raskol'nikov, Turgenev's Natal'ia and the eponymous Rudin (1856), his Odintsova and Bazarov in *Fathers and Sons (Ottsy i deti*, 1862), and Goncharov's Ol'ga and the eponymous Oblomov (1859) are but a few examples of this tendency. On one level, Bauer continues this tradition, and thus, like his nineteenth-century predecessors, Viktor is weaker and less attractive than the woman he loves. Mary does not use her strength positively to revive Viktor, however, as Sonia revives Raskol'nikov. Instead, vampire-like, she gradually drains from him the little strength he had. Moreover, the way in which Mary is strong bears no resemblance at all to the way in which Sonia and many other nineteenth-century Russian heroines are strong. While they gain their strength from their deeply held moral, spiritual – and what are often termed 'Russian' – values, Mary's strength has nothing to do with either morality, spirituality or Russia, a fact underlined by her adoption of the Western version of her Russian name; she is driven by purely selfish, pragmatic and material goals.

Viktor's reaction to Mary's rejection is, unsurprisingly, the same as Piskarev's before him: he commits suicide. But, while Piskarev used a razor blade in his garret room, Viktor chooses a more modern method – shooting himself in the head on the steps of Mary's house. Bauer's ending thus reverses that of Pushkin's *The Gypsies* where Zemfira is murdered by the jealous Aleko. Here, the victim who lies dead is the cuckolded man, while the unfaithful woman not only survives, but is implicated as the cause of his death, as Maia Turovskaia acknowledges by including Mary in her discussion of the murderess in the Russian cinematic tradition (Turovskaia 1997: 111).

Bauer suggests Mary's responsibility for Viktor's death cinematically in a skilfully constructed sequence, which begins when the impoverished, lovesick Viktor arrives at her house to deliver a desperate letter. As Viktor hands the letter to Mary's doorman, Bauer cuts inside to the drunken dinner party where Mary and her new lover are entertaining their guests with an elaborate tango routine. Described by film historian Iurii Tsiv'ian as 'disturbingly libidinous', the tango arrived in Russia from Paris in late November 1913 and was an immediate *succès de scandale*, inspiring intense debates, with most commentators agreeing that its defining characteristic was its tragic and vaguely sinister sexual nature (Tsiv'ian 1996: 317–18). The sensual atmosphere of their performance is highlighted by Bauer's *mise-en-scène*: a thick black velvet curtain is drawn three-quarters of the way across the set, putting the viewer in the position of frustrated voyeur, by allowing only brief glimpses of Mary as she dances. The arrival of Viktor's letter interrupts the performance, but elicits only a sneer from Mary. In a gesture that enables Bauer neatly to illustrate the complete shift in the balance of power in their relationship, Mary reverses society's traditional gender roles and gives her maid three roubles to pass to Viktor. This action both mirrors and overturns the scene in Part 2, Chapter 9 of Dostoevskii's *Notes From Underground*, when the Underground Man, having sobbed before Liza 'for a quarter of an hour in real hysterics' (*'chetvert' chasa … v nastoiashchei isterike'*), suddenly realizes 'that the roles were now definitively reversed, that she was now the heroine, and I was precisely the same crushed and humiliated creature as she had been before me on that night four days ago' (*'chto roli ved' teper' okonchatel'no peremenilis', chto geroinia teper' ona, a ia tochno takoe zhe unizhennoe i razdavlennoe sozdanie, kakim ona byla peredo mnoi v tu noch', – chetyre dnia nazad'*) (Dostoevskii 1973a: 175). Although Dostoevskii discreetly passes over what happens between them next, the reader understands, especially when, in Chapter 10, the Underground Man thrusts a crumpled five-rouble note into Liza's hand. This act is, the Underground Man acknowledges, maliciously and cruelly intended to offend, and Mary's action seems to have the same motivation. Without giving another thought to Viktor, she dismisses the maid and resumes her tango performance. Bauer cuts briefly to his hero, however, and, just as Dostoevskii's Liza flings the money on to the table before rushing from the room, so Viktor throws Mary's insulting 'gift' to the ground.

This scene also recalls the conclusion of Pushkin's prose story 'The Postmaster' ('Stantsionnyi smotritel''), from his *The Tales of the Late Ivan Petrovich Belkin* (*Povesti pokoinogo Ivana Petrovicha Belkina*, 1830). Like Viktor, the Postmaster calls uninvited at a grand town house in order to save a 'fallen woman', who, like Mary, does not wish to be saved. Her lover gives the Postmaster ten roubles before seeing him off the premises, and the Postmaster throws the money to the ground in a noble gesture, although he later returns to attempt, without success, to retrieve it. Ultimately the Postmaster drinks himself to death. While the relationship between the would-be saviour and the presumed fallen woman in Pushkin's text is that of father and daughter, there is an erotic ambiguity about their relations. The Postmaster is a widower and as aware of his daughter's beauty as are the young men who travel past their house. Moreover, Viktor and the Postmaster have much in common, both being idealistic, yet exploitative, and mistaken about what the women they love want from life. Finally, in the same way that Viktor relies on literary prototypes in constructing his attitude to Mary, so the Postmaster's understanding of Dunia is conditioned by a literary source, the biblical parable of the 'lost sheep', retold in the pictures on his wall (Pushkin 1978c: 88–98).

Having thrown Mary's money to the ground, Viktor raises his pistol to his head. At this dramatic point in the narrative Bauer unexpectedly cuts away from his hero, however, and returns his attention to Mary. For almost two minutes the camera looks on as she and her lover tango, and it is only when the revellers leave for Maksim's, a fashionable Moscow tango club, that we discover that Viktor has shot himself. The cultural associations of the tango as a dance of tragic sexuality thus combine with Bauer's evocative *mise-en-scène* and his euphemistic cross-cutting between Mary and Viktor to suggest that Mary's sexuality is the cause of Viktor's death.

The discovery of Viktor's body is not the climax of the film, however. Rather, Bauer focuses on Mary's reaction to her former lover's death. In a macabre inversion of the expected, Mary's initial shock turns, not to grief or horror, but first to annoyance and then to absolute indifference. Even the cynical narrator of 'Nevskii Prospect' confesses, after Piskarev's suicide, that: 'I do not like corpses and dead bodies' (*'Ia ne liubliu trupov i pokoinikov'*) (Gogol' 1994: 22). Mary, however, is not so squeamish. Announcing that discovering a dead body is said to be a sign of good luck to come, Mary urges her companions to hurry lest they arrive late at the tango club. Then she lifts her gown and, revealing a dainty foot clad in a modish tango slipper (Tsiv'ian 1996: 318), steps over Viktor's inert body (see Figure 1.4).

Bauer thus also indicates Mary's guilt in another, more subtle way. By homing in for a close-up of her foot as she steps over Viktor's body and by making this close-up extra-diegetically lengthy, Bauer very deliberately stresses Mary's action of stepping over the corpse both spatially and temporally. In this way he contrives to link his heroine to the most famous murderer of nineteenth-century Russian literature, Dostoevskii's Rodion Raskol'nikov, who repeatedly – twenty-four times, in fact (Ando, Yasuo and Mochizuki 1994: 760–1) – uses the two verbs 'to step over' (*'pereshagivat'/*

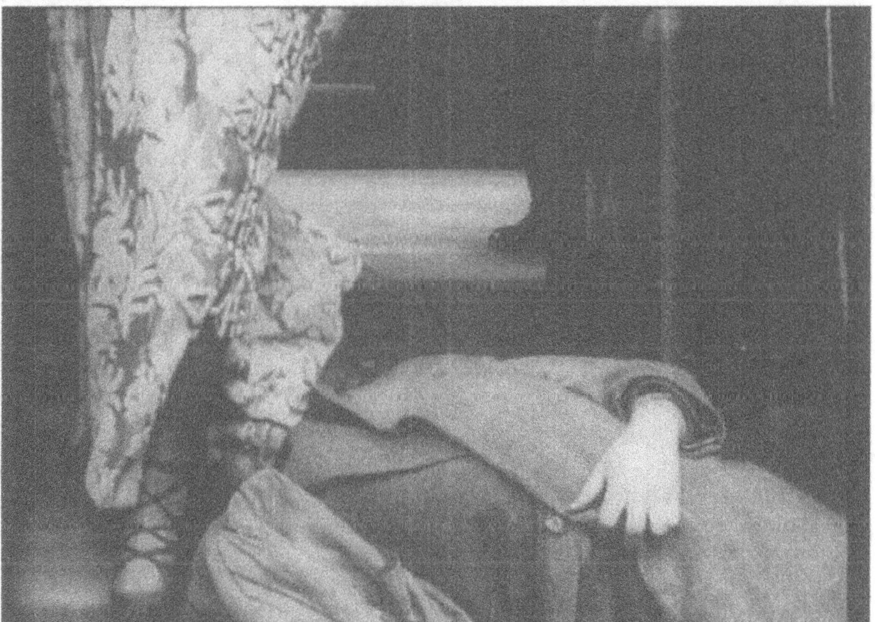

Figure 1.4 Mary steps over Viktor's corpse

Source: Courtesy of bfi Video Publishing, London

pereshagnut" and *'perestupat'/perestupit"*) as a metaphor for committing a crime against morality. In Part 3, Chapter 5, when Raskol'nikov meets the chief detective for the first time, Porfirii questions him about the theories behind his article 'On Crime' (*'O prestuplenii'*), whereupon Raskol'nikov declares: 'the "extraordinary" person has the right – not an officially sanctioned right, that is – to permit his conscience *to step over* ... certain obstacles, but only if it is absolutely necessary for the fulfilment of his idea on which, quite possibly, the welfare of all mankind may depend' (*'<neobyknovennyi> chelovek imeet pravo... to est' ne ofitsial'noe pravo, a sam imeet pravo razreshit' svoei sovesti pereshagnut'... cherez inye prepiatstviia, i edinstvenno v tom tol'ko sluchae, esli ispolnenie ego idei (inogda spasitel'noi, mozhet byt', dlia vsego chelovechestva) togo potrebuet'*) (Dostoevskii 1973b: 199; emphasis added).

Using it figuratively here, Raskol'nikov later uses this verb more literally: 'if, for the sake of his idea, such a person has *to step over a corpse* or through blood, he is, in my opinion, absolutely entitled, in accordance with the dictates of his conscience, to permit himself to wade through blood, all depending, of course, on the nature and scale of his idea – note that, please' (*'esli emu nado, dlia svoei idei, pereshagnut' khotia by i cherez trup, cherez krov', to on vnutri sebia, po sovesti, mozhet, po-moemu, dat' sebe razreshenie pereshagnut' cherez krov', – smotria, vprochem, po idee i po razmeram ee, – eto zamet'te'*) (ibid.: 200; emphasis added).

By thus linking Mary with Raskol'nikov, Bauer underlines once and for all the huge gulf between his heroine and Dostoevskii's. Mary is emphatically not Sonia. However, Bauer also shows her to be very different from Dostoevskii's gloomy intellectual, Raskol'nikov, who murders to test out a serious – albeit naive – moral theory. After the murder, Raskol'nikov is tormented first by his belief that he did not succeed in 'stepping over' and therefore failed to prove himself a great man, and, ultimately, by his recognition of the awfulness of his crime.

Mary, however, does not ruin Viktor in pursuit of any Dostoevskiian moral agenda. Despite the fact that the 'nature and scale of her idea' are frivolous and selfish – she does not want Viktor's suicide to ruin her night out – Mary steps over the obstacle that lies in her way (Viktor's corpse) without the slightest twinge of conscience. Unlike Raskol'nikov, Mary is not in the least tormented by the part she has played in a person's death. Indeed, she does not even reflect on her responsibility. The moral concerns central to Dostoevskii's novel and his protagonists are therefore ignored. Bauer's female character behaves badly – commits 'moral suicide' and 'moral murder', the core of Sonia's and Raskol'nikov's dilemmas – without any sense of guilt, without any punishment or retribution, either from without or from within, and without any repentance.[12] For, while Dostoevskii's novel begins with the crime and goes on to chart the process of Raskol'nikov's repentance, Bauer's film ends abruptly with the crime itself. Bauer therefore deliberately rejects the conventional nineteenth-century 'moral' ending, by showing that Mary is not shocked into guilt and repentance at the sight of Viktor's lifeless body, and especially by declining to explore her reaction to her crime over time.

Even at the end of the film, however, Bauer withholds sympathy from his male protagonist, and ultimately he achieves this through his sustained appropriation of nineteenth-century prototypes. For, by linking Viktor very closely to one 'ridiculous' and long out-dated nineteenth-century hero, Bauer contrives to sideline his male protagonist; he becomes one-dimensional, a cardboard cut-out, and is therefore incapable of engaging the viewer's interest. Floundering in nineteenth-century clichés, Viktor does not stand still, but actually regresses. Although a man of the twentieth century, he has yet to learn the lessons Gogol' drew from the fate of Piskarev nearly eighty years previously.

By contrast, Mary is based on a number of different nineteenth-century protagonists, both female and male. As she is both like and radically unlike these characters, she moves beyond her nineteenth-century literary prototypes and transcends the clichés of this tradition. Bauer emphasizes this by adding to his portrayal of Mary contemporary literary and cultural resonances. In the *café-concert* sequence, for example, as she enjoys the compliments of admirers and accepts flowers from one of them, Mary recalls, in attitude and appearance, the ambiguous female personae of many of Aleksandr Blok's urban poems, particularly those of 'The Unknown Woman' ('Neznakomka', 1906) (Blok 1997a: 122–3) and 'At the Restaurant' ('V restorane', 1910) (Blok 1997b: 16). She is also cast as a 'tango-woman' (*'zhenshchina-tango'*), a twentieth-century Lilith defined in the following archetypical terms in a 1914 article entitled 'The New Eve' ('Novaia Eva'): 'as lithe as a serpent, pale to the point of transparency, with almost holy eyes and dissolute lips' (*'gibkii do zmeinosti i blednyi do prozrachnosti, s pochti sviatymi glazami i razvratnymi ustami'*) (Nikol'skaia 1990: 33). In this way Mary is shown to be dynamic; she changes, moves forward and adapts to the challenges of modernity. This makes her an ambivalent, complex and interesting figure, a disturbing 'new woman', who engages the viewer's full attention. In this way Bauer also overturns the tendency of nineteenth-century literature to be centred on the male protagonists. In the works of most nineteenth-century Russian writers it is invariably the hero who holds the reader's attention while, as Barbara Heldt has argued, the female protagonists remain underwritten and are not the equal of their male counterparts in 'fictive fullness' (Heldt 1987: 13–14). In this and other films by Bauer the opposite is true.

We have seen, then, that in *Child of the Big City* Bauer's intertextuality takes two forms: he draws widely on the common topoi of the nineteenth-century Russian literary tradition that recur from text to text and from author to author, and he also makes extremely precise and sustained reference to several key texts of this tradition, specifically Gogol''s 'Nevskii Prospect' and Dostoevskii's *Crime and Punishment*. Bauer's treatment of his sources is often subversive, but when he alludes to Gogol', whose work is itself more ironic and worldly-wise than that of his nineteenth-century realist contemporaries, Bauer's references are more faithful in both content and tone.

Bauer's use and subversion of the prototypical male and female protagonists, their conventional relationships and other staple motifs and themes of the nineteenth-century Russian literary tradition, is a deliberate, recurrent directorial strategy, and is of fundamental importance to the thematics of Bauer's film, to the presentation of his protagonists and to his expression of his worldview.[13] Rejecting straightforward adaptations of individual nineteenth-century classics in favour of creating original scenarios that subvert nineteenth-century Russian literary sources enables Bauer, a twentieth-century filmmaker, to suggest that the old codes of morality are being undermined and dismissed as invalid in the new century. In the twentieth-century city that appears on his screen, we witness crime without reason, crime without punishment, and, most shockingly, crime without remorse. The moral certainties of the old century and its classic literature have collapsed, but nothing has taken their place; what remains is an amoral vacuum, where self-interest is the only criterion for action. Bauer also suggests a similarly disruptive shift in gender relations, a theme of central importance to him throughout his cinematic career. Here, too, the old male certainties about women have lost all validity. Bauer's twentieth-century cinematic heroine is shown to be very different from the conventional nineteenth-century literary heroine, and his rejection of the various clichés that surrounded her makes it clear that such mythologies have no relevance, either for him or for the twentieth-century woman he seeks to portray in this film. By contrast, Bauer's central male protagonist appears to be stuck in the past; unwilling or unable to change, he attempts to relate to his female counterpart as the heroes of nineteenth-century literature once did. As Bauer warns, such anachronistic behaviour threatens to render him 'superfluous' to the requirements of the dynamic, exacting and disturbing twentieth-century woman we watch on the screen.

Notes

1 I thank Professor Julian Graffy, both for reading drafts of this article with characteristic patience and enthusiasm, and for making many invaluable suggestions. I am also grateful to Dr Philip Cavendish and Professor Peter Kenez for supplying me with visual material.

2 A selective list of pre-Revolutionary Russian films based on literary sources appears in Vishnevskii 1945: 157–60. A fuller catalogue of Russian and Soviet adaptations of literary texts (1907–1944), compiled by the Literature and Visual Media Research Group of the Russian Section of the Department of Linguistic, Cultural and International Studies, University of Surrey, can be viewed at http://www.surrey.ac.uk/LIS/LVMG/catalogue.html.

3 Extant adaptations of literary works directed by Bauer include: *Her Heroic Feat* (*Ee geroiskii podvig*, 1914), based on a foreign farce; *Cold Showers* (*Kholodnye*

dushi, 1914), based on a French vaudeville; *The Thousand and Second Ruse* (*Tysiacha vtoraia khitrost'*, 1915), based on Vladimir Azov's play *The Thousand and First Ruse* (*1001aia khitrost'*); *Leon Drei* [*Lady-Killer*] (*Leon Drei* [*Pokoritel' zhenskikh serdets*], 1915), based on S. S. Iushkevich's short story; Daydreams [Deceived Dreams] (*Grezy* [*Obmanutye mechty*], 1915), based on Georges Rodenbach's novel *Bruges la Morte*; *After Death* [*Motifs from Turgenev*] (*Posle smerti* [*Turgenevskie motivy*], 1915), based on I. S. Turgenev's story 'Klara Milich'; *A Life for a Life* [*For Every Tear a Drop of Blood*] [*The Rival Sisters*] (*Zhizn' za zhizn'* [*Za kazhduiu slezu po kaple krovi*][*Sestry-sopernitsy*], 1916) based on Georges Ohnet's novel *Serge Panine*; *The Tocsin* (*Nabat*, 1917), based on Elizaveta Werner's novel *On the Open Road* (*Vol'noi dorogoi*); *The King of Paris* (*Korol' Parizha*, 1917) based on Georges Ohnet's novel of the same title.

4 Available on DVD and video, *Mad Love: Three Films by Evgenii Bauer*, *bfi* Video Publishing. In 1914 Bauer based a film (not preserved) on another late Turgenev story, *Song of Triumphant Love* (*Pesn' torzhestvuiushchei liubvi*, 1881); as in *After Death*, Bauer set the film in the twentieth-century present.

5 For biographical information about Bauer, see Tsiv'ian (2002) and Tsiv'ian (1989).

6 Available on video, *Early Russian Cinema*, vol. 7, *Evgenii Bauer*, *bfi* Video Publishing.

7 It is telling that none of Bauer's later female protagonists suffers from consumption. Indeed, Bauer had been similarly dismissive of this nineteenth-century trope in the early *Twilight of a Woman's Soul* (*Sumerki zhenskoi dushi*, 1913), available on DVD and video, *Mad Love: Three Films by Evgenii Bauer*, *bfi* Video Publishing. For a discussion of this, see Morley (2003: 53–4).

8 Translations from Russian are mine, unless otherwise indicated.

9 Photographs and portraits, statuettes and other artefacts provide many of Bauer's weak male protagonists with a 'safe' and manageable version of the women they find so threatening. For a discussion of this, see Morley (2003: 55–8).

10 For a discussion of this theme, see Siegel (1970).

11 Laurie Bernstein suggests that the source of this trope is Nikolai Chernyshevskii's 1863 novel *What Is To Be Done?* (*Chto delat'?*), in which two prostitutes abandon their trade when given the opportunity to join a sewing cooperative (Bernstein 1995: 212–13). For a survey of this theme, see McMillin and McMillin (1999).

12 In Part 4, Chapter 4, Raskol'nikov tells Sonia that when she became a prostitute she committed moral suicide: 'You, too, have stepped over … were capable of stepping over. You've laid hands on yourself, you've destroyed a life – your own life (it's all the same!)' (*'Ty tozhe perestupila … smogla perestupit'. Ty na sebia ruki nalozhila, ty zagubila zhizn' … svoiu (eto vse ravno!)'*) (Dostoevskii 1973b: 252).

13 Another Bauer film with an original scenario that can be read as a reworking of a specific classic nineteenth-century Russian literary text is *Children of the Age* (*Deti veka*, 1915, not available on video or DVD; copies held at the Library of Congress, Washington DC and Gosfil'mofond Rossii, Moscow), which 'modernizes' and subverts Lev Tolstoi's novel *Anna Karenina* (1873–77) in similar ways, and to similar ends, as those described here. In *Children of the Age*, as in *Child of the Big City* and many other films, Bauer also reworks many of the general stock protagonists, motifs and themes that recur in classic nineteenth-century Russian literature. For reasons of space, detailed discussion of the ubiquity of this technique in Bauer's oeuvre lies outside the scope of the present chapter.

2 Educating Chapaev

From document to myth

Jeremy Hicks

Chapaev, Dmitrii Furmanov's 1923 autobiographical account of the experiences of a commissar in Chapaev's 25th Rifle Division, is typically regarded as a canonical Socialist Realist text (Clark 2000: 84). Indeed it has even been said to fit perfectly the definition of Socialist Realism adopted at the First Congress of Soviet Writers (Vroon 1996: 220).[1] Nevertheless, despite its ultimate elevation to this status, *Chapaev* can be seen as incompatible with what later became Socialist Realism. *Chapaev*'s assimilation as a Socialist Realist text was a process of reinterpretation during which its original documentary and historical nature was underplayed as it was redefined as a novel, before finally being undermined by its transformation into legend and folklore. Its adaptation for the screen in the hugely successful film directed by Georgii and Sergei Vasil'ev, (*Chapaev*, Lenfil'm, 1934) was a turning point in this reassessment. Yet the underlying causes for this shift cannot be attributed solely to the contrasting demands of literature and film. Rather the contrast between the literary source and the adaptation of *Chapaev* reflects a wider shift in Soviet approaches to nonfictional forms. Furmanov's *Chapaev* exemplified a powerful trend in Soviet culture of the early 1920s in which the striving to record, characteristic of documentary, prevailed over more properly artistic concerns (Levin 1978: 123). Yet, as the 1920s progressed, the status of art and of fiction grew so that nonfictional material was consistently reworked according to the norms of fiction and subordinated to an official pre-existing narrative. By the time the film version was made, all narratives had to extol heroes and heroic deeds, and the dividing line between fictional and nonfictional modes had been blurred. In order meaningfully to distinguish these two approaches we need first to examine and define notions of the documentary in literature and cinema.

Chapaev and definitions of the documentary

Although Ronald Vroon has described Furmanov's *Chapaev* as a hybrid text, employing both fictive and non-fictive discourse (Vroon 1996: 221), opinion is divided as to how and even whether such a distinction can be meaningfully maintained. In particular, productive currents of contemporary thought, largely working from the perspective of structuralism's bracketing and denigration of reference, argue that it is impossible to distinguish fiction and nonfiction.[2] Robert Scholes typifies such views by arguing that all experience is mediated by textual categories usually associated with fiction: 'the conditions of our being come to us already scripted, textualized, shaped in patterns into which we must fall, almost like actors given a script that they must follow. The human condition is a condition of textuality' (Scholes 2001: 77). Nonfiction is inconceivable from such a perspective in that it suggests the possibility of accessing experience or events other than through patterns tied to fictional texts and to language in general. 'All writing, all composition is construction … There is no mimesis, only poesis. No recording. Only constructing' (Scholes 1975: 7).

Nevertheless, those critics who make a defence of the notion of nonfiction (sometimes under the title of documentary) for the most part accept that it may share textual characteristics with fiction, but argue that, whereas fiction is seen as a kind of analogy with the experiential world (Sauerberg 1991: 44), nonfiction demands that the reader see textual elements such as characters, events, letters and other documents as having referents in his or her world (Foley 1986: 26). For a nonfictional text to function as such, it must be read as nonfiction, and not as fiction. The fiction/nonfiction opposition is an either/or choice: a given textual element can be see as one or the other, but not as both (Foley 1986: 28; Sauerberg 1989: 88–9). Consequently textual elements alone cannot define a work as nonfiction, since, although certain styles or rhetorical modes may, at certain times, be seen as more properly nonfictional, they are never exclusively so, since fiction has a tendency to appropriate them, and nonfiction also uses techniques borrowed from fiction.

But given that a nonfictional text may outwardly resemble a fictional text, what enables a reader to approach it as a work of nonfiction? Broadly it is a question of context, although there is some disagreement as to what constitutes this context. Some critics stress that it is the author alone who determines whether a text is fact or fiction (Heyne 1987: 480; Foley 1986: 40). Lars Ole Sauerberg provides a more expansive sense of the context determining the indexing of a work as nonfictional, arguing that readers understand by testing texts against the competing fictional and nonfictional conventions and traditions of representation and reference (Sauerberg 1989: 83–4). Authorial aims are subsumed under a larger category of intention extended to include a large range of contextual items such as the advertising blurb on a book (Sauerberg 1989: 51, 85).[3]

In film, this debate is complicated somewhat by the fact that the photographic image, unlike that of language and literature, resembles its referent and is a recording capable of bearing a certain trace of the profilmic event as the result of a photochemical process. Despite this intrinsic difference, much of the argument follows a remarkably similar pattern to that observed in literature. On the one hand, we have influential structuralists such as

Jacques Aumont asserting that all film is fiction, since it employs the same devices regardless of the filmmakers' intentions (Aumont *et al.* 1983: 71). On the other hand, those defending the concept of nonfiction film stress these texts' relations to the extra-textual as their distinguishing feature (Carroll 2001: 155; Carroll 1996: 286). Carl Plantinga is particularly eloquent in expounding this view. He argues that nonfiction films assert that what they show was the case, whereas fiction films merely invite the spectator to consider a possible scenario. Yet Plantinga retains the notion of there being textual as well as extra-textual conventions that may index a film as nonfictional (Plantinga 1997: 19).

So how do these definitions fit *Chapaev*? In essence, they suggest that for *Chapaev* to be a nonfictional text, the readers, spectators and critics would have had to have perceived that they were dealing with a nonfictional work, either through contextual factors identifying the work as nonfictional such as Furmanov's or the Vasil'evs' stated intentions for their works, or through corroboration from other witnesses to the events and other reliable sources, or by recognizing in the text certain conventions either of representation (fiction) or of reference (nonfiction). Moreover, in the case of the film we can examine the ways in which the filmic text has been altered and seek to determine the purpose of these changes: so as better to coincide with historical record, or so as to create a more compelling or more politically acceptable narrative. To examine *Chapaev* in these broader contexts would enable us to avoid the self-acknowledged 'historical half-truth' of Vroon's anachronistic reading of *Chapaev* in the light of the *Novyi Lef* theories of factography systematically expounded from approximately 1927, some time after the publication of the first edition of *Chapaev* in 1923 and Furmanov's death in 1926 (Vroon 1996: 223).[4] In fact these attempts to define nonfictional texts seem to suggest that it is particularly important to avoid such sleight of hand since the reception context of a work plays a crucial role in determining whether or not it is read or viewed as a work of nonfiction. As we shall see, *Chapaev* underwent reissue in a different series, critical redesignation as a novel, and adaptation for cinema. Finally, after a marked blurring of the boundaries between fiction and nonfiction had expanded exponentially what was acceptable practice in nonfiction, it was ready to become a nonfictional text of a radically different kind, sharing more in common with myth than with documentary.

Furmanov's *Chapaev*: publication and critical context

The context of the initial publication of Furmanov's *Chapaev* was somewhat ambiguous in that Furmanov clearly had literary ambitions, but was playing on his authority as an eyewitness to the events depicted so as to launch his literary career. The work appeared in a series called *'Istpart'* comprising nonfictional, historical works devoted to the history of the Communist Party. This circumstance reveals Furmanov's ability to exploit his Civil War past to the benefit of a nascent literary career, a factor which coloured critical reactions, leading at least one review to treat it as a work of history (Lelevich 1923: 189–91). Moreover, Furmanov's preface to the first edition states: 'I have no pretensions as to the literary quality (*khudozhestvennost'*) of its finish' (Furmanov 1923: 3).[5] Maksim Gor'kii was the most famous of a number of prominent critics (Kogan 1926: 75; Lelevich 1923: 189) who found the work valuable solely as nonfiction, but neither this nor Furmanov's protestations prevented him reacting to the book's failings as literature:

> You write carelessly, very untidily and recount like an eyewitness, you don't represent as an artist (*khudozhnik*) does. That's why there are a mass of completely unnecessary details in the story that drag it out.
>
> (Gor'kii 1957: 308)

In responding to Gor'kii, Furmanov restates the historical and nonfictional purposes of the work insisting that these aims required the explanation and commentary Gor'kii deemed excessive: 'for a fictional (*khudozhestvennyi*) work in the strict sense of the term, my explanations are unnecessary, superfluous and detrimental' (Furmanov 1960–61, IV: 471). But Gor'kii is right. *Chapaev* lacks plot development. Even as a *Bildungsroman* it does not function well, since it is far from clear that Chapaev himself develops. Although, as we have seen, textual features alone do not define a work as nonfictional, it is nevertheless noteworthy that literary devices most frequently employed in nonfiction predominate. Rhetorical persuasion and argumentation outweigh narrative. In general, the work is circumscribed by the logic, or rather the haphazard nature, of events and the need to record what happened rather than by the logic of narrative. It also reproduces a number of letters, orders and resolutions verbatim so as to underline their value, and thereby its own value, as historical document. These elements can all be verified by reference to other sources and only make sense in that context. Moreover, there are no fictional characters chosen to typify historical or social processes, as in the historical novel. The characters all have historically verifiable counterparts, although the names of the living are changed out of consideration: 'The names of the living have been changed, those of the dead are their own' (Furmanov, 1960–61, I: 57) or, in the case of Lenin, Trotskii and Frunze, still alive at the time of the first edition, not changed, because everyone would recognize them anyway.

However, if Furmanov's *Chapaev* started out as a work of history pursuing nonfictional aims, the process of adapting and redesignating it according to the textual norms of fiction and the novel was initiated by Furmanov himself. At the same time as defending his book as history, in the same letter to Gor'kii, Furmanov also concedes that the style of *Chapaev* leaves something to be desired. He states that he intends to write a new epic work about the Civil War but that this time it would be a novel, and that his hands would not be tied by 'historicism' (*istorizm*) as they were with *Chapaev* (Furmanov 1960–61, IV: 477). Moreover, shortly after the correspondence with Gor'kii, possibly stung by this criticism, Furmanov decided to rewrite the third edition of *Chapaev*, to make the style more literary.[6] In the 82 pages reworked, the language becomes more overtly literary through its use of metaphor, but also in its incorporation of colloquial elements of speech. At times it even resembles ornamental prose, a style of writing then associated with literary sophistication. Such reworking of course does nothing to undermine the nonfictional, referential claims of the work, but, at the same time, it does suggest an increasingly significant reorientation on the part of Furmanov, whereby he tries to present himself as a writer and his work as literary rather than historical. The apologetic preface playing down the work's artistic merits was likewise discarded from subsequent editions, possibly further confirming Furmanov's growing literary pretensions.

Yet this re-emphasis is not simply due to Furmanov's career aspirations, but is also part of a change occurring in Soviet culture and the Proletarian Literature movement (of which Furmanov was part until his death in 1926). The sense that the revolution brought cultural discontinuity and the notion of a new proletarian culture radically breaking with the past were increasingly played down in favour of a greater sense of cultural continuity and a respect for the professional qualities required of the writer and of writing. So it was that the Proletarian Literature movement's leading journal, *Na postu,* started in 1923 by calling for the creation of a wholly new, proletarian, culture and rejecting the heritage of the nineteenth-century novel, but by 1926 its successor, *Na literaturnom postu*, was praising realism, and calling for writers to imitate the example of Lev Tolstoi (Sheshukov 1984: 139–45). The contrast between the documentary approach of Furmanov's *Chapaev* and the more traditional literary style of Aleksandr Fadeev's *The Rout* (*Razgrom*), published in 1927, may be seen as exemplifying this shift.[7]

An indication of the increasingly precarious discrete status of documentary discourse can be seen in the prominent Proletarian critic Averbakh's defence of Furmanov in 1931, in which he claims that Furmanov was a writer, writing literature throughout even in his diaries (Averbakh 1931: 11–12). Indeed the Russian term used by Averbakh '*khudozhestvennaia literatura*' usually means fiction and can be used as an antonym to documentary. Averbakh argues that Furmanov selects typical details not in order to represent reality, nor for the sake of actual reference to what happened (Averbakh 1931: 12). He is an artist because he selects typical details that demonstrate the wider picture, a consistent concern in Marxist literary theory (Fadeev 1959–61, IV: 25; Bisztray 1978: 56). Furmanov then, according to Averbakh, is not at all a 'factist' ('*faktovik*'), simply recording what happens, but a proletarian writer. In Averbakh's terms, for a writer to have followed what actually happened would be to risk missing the deeper meaning in events. Essentially Averbakh's argument is that there is no distinction between fiction and nonfiction because, in pursuit of coherence, which is not necessarily apparent in what actually happens, a writer has every right to employ invention (*vymysel*). Furmanov's account is true not because of its reliable, verifiable recording of events, but because Furmanov, as a proletarian writer, has the correct ideology.

Demystification or '*strakh pered legendoi*'?

While the primary purpose of Furmanov's narrative is to record what Chapaev was actually like, another of Furmanov's purposes in writing the work was polemical: to confront what he saw as widespread and pernicious myths about Chapaev. In the spirit of much Marxist historiography he attempts to strip the heroic and legendary aura from Chapaev so as to reveal him as a product of his class, and his epoch.[8] However, subsequent criticism not only redefined Furmanov's work as art, but redefined Chapaev as a hero.

A particularly telling example of Chapaev's redefinition as a hero is an article on the twentieth anniversary of the October Revolution in 1937 which argues that Furmanov is too close to the events and too close to Chapaev to see that he is truly a great hero (Makarenko 1937: 119). Supposedly, Furmanov's account is too painstakingly cautious to permit him to grasp this and suffers from 'nihilism with regard to heroes and … fear of legends' ('*strakh pered legendoi*') (ibid.: 113). In a startling paradox, the article asserts that Chapaev's legendary status is the result of a legendary reality:

> The legend of Chapaev is the memory of the real but truly titanic deeds of the men and women of the Civil War years. The normal scale and normal everyday realism cannot measure these deeds, just as they cannot measure many present day events.
>
> (Makarenko 1937: 113)

In fact the triumph of the legend ran in the face of the basic aim of Furmanov's documentary narrative, and despite the fact that his book was reprinted many times and became effectively canonized. Why was this? A clue may lie in this article's praise for the Vasil'ev Brothers' 1934 film above the book for presenting a true image of the authentically legendary Chapaev unspoilt by Furmanov's modesty and his excessively schematic approach. Without doubt, the cinematic reinterpretation of Furmanov's account marked a turning point in the rehabiliatation of Chapaev, the legendary hero (Makarenko 1937: 119).

'The country must know its heroes'

This 'reheroization' of Chapaev cannot be understood except as part of a shift in attitudes to heroes and to nonfictional forms evident in Soviet culture during the first Five Year Plan period (1928–32). Indicative of this was an article entitled 'The Country Must Know its Heroes' ('*Strana dolzhna znat' svoikh geroev*') which appeared in *Pravda*, 7 May 1931, signed by Fedor Panferov and other Proletarian writers. This argued that Furmanov's *Chapaev* showed the heroism of the Civil War. The efforts of present-day labourers are no less heroic, but very little has been written about them: 'Every day labour becomes more and more a matter of honour, glory, prowess and heroism' (Panferov *et al.* 1931). The article goes on to argue that fictional and nonfictional forms should both pursue this agenda with equal vigour:

> This Land of Soviets demands of us that we show (*pokazali*) the triumphant collectives and the heroic shockworkers of factories and of collective-farm fields, both in the broad canvases of fiction (*khudozhestvennymi polotnami*) that are raising still further the quality of artistic creation, and in the genre of the sketch (*ocherk*), the short story (*rasskaz*), the poem, and the portrait.
>
> (Panferov *et al.* 1931)

This article, and others like it, demonstrate that Furmanov's account had already become a shorthand for the heroic exploits of the Bolsheviks in the Civil War. What is more, it indicates, as we saw intimated by Averbakh, that the distinctions between fictional and nonfictional texts were increasingly being elided in this period as both were conjoined to pursue the same agenda of 'showing' heroic images of Soviet workers in particular, and the Soviet order more generally. This had distorting influences upon both modes: fiction was held to have a referent in the real world, as the word 'show' implies, and it was compelled to 'show' the contemporary world. It was no longer free to offer an analogy of the real world, or to invite the spectator to consider a state of affairs. In other words it was almost indistinguishable from nonfiction. Likewise, nonfiction was to show, but only certain things in a certain way. It was still to assert that what it showed existed, but it was freer than ever before to stage and rewrite so as to ensure the correct, pre-established, message. Crucially, neither fiction nor nonfiction, despite their assertions that the events they portray had real extra-textual referents, were subjected to critical scrutiny as to the reliability of their accounts or compared with other sources. On the contrary, critical reactions tended to bolster these tenuous nonfictional claims. This unexacting and obfuscating critical atmosphere was central to the radical shift in the image of Chapaev. Yet before examining the critical discourse surrounding the reception of the Vasil'evs' *Chapaev*, we need first to examine precisely what was different about the film version.

Chapaev, the movie (1934)

The idea of a screen adaptation of *Chapaev* occurred to one of the book's earliest reviewers (G.V. 1923). Within a few months of the book's publication, Proletkino asked Furmanov to work on a screenplay (Furmanov 1960–61, IV: 320). A year later, in June 1924, having looked at his screenplay, Goskino told him they were not impressed and Furmanov washed his hands of the project. Although Furmanov was told that shooting would begin at the end of the year, it was not until 1931, after his death, that his widow produced the second attempt at adapting the book (Dolinskii 1945: 16–21). These two previous efforts propose some of the changes introduced in the film, such as the idea of having scenes from the White camp, and one of the most obvious points of divergence between book and film – the renaming of Klychkov as Furmanov. However, Furmanov's widow edited the text of 1930s editions of the book so as to give real names where Furmanov had used pseudonyms, so that Klychkov becomes Furmanov (Kuprianovskii 1981: 174). Since it was her screenplay that initially caught the Vasil'evs' attention, this would appear to be why the film retains this change from the more authoritative editions of the book. On the whole though, the primary responsibility for the changes between book and film can be attributed to the Vasil'evs.[9]

Another change which immediately strikes a viewer of the film is the fact that it begins with the arrival of the Ivanovo-Voznesensk textile workers detachment, and of course Klychkov-Furmanov, whereas the book introduces Chapaev only in the fifth chapter. This change is highly significant, because Klychkov in the missing chapters of the book confronts the legend of Chapaev before he confronts the real Chapaev. This is a structurally important part of Furmanov's narrative since one of its major themes is the difference between the real Chapaev and the legend of Chapaev. The film does exactly the opposite. It introduces us to the character by giving us an example of Chapaev's legendary power, showing him photographed from a low angle directing Pet'ka's machine-gun fire, inspiring fleeing soldiers to return to the battle even without their rifles. The low angle shot is clearly chosen to heighten the spectator's sense of Chapaev's charisma, and it became one of the film's most famous shots, a still from which featured on contemporary posters (Figure 2.1). The scenes from the Whites' camp (not present in the book of course) likewise corroborate Chapaev's charismatic power by showing how legendary he is even for the enemy. As Colonel Borozdin says: 'He and his reputation are equally dangerous to us'. Like Borozdin, the Vasil'ev brothers are not interested in distinguishing between a real and a legendary Chapaev. Their film, made for people who had forgotten the legend, recreates it by directly showing us its power over others, and implicitly over us.

Chapaev's enhanced status in the film is also signalled by the shift of narrative focus from Furmanov to Chapaev. This is indicated at the beginning by the latter's joking response as to why the men are in the river: 'They're swimming. It's hot'. The narrative until this point has followed Chapaev, albeit briefly, but long enough for the spectator, like Chapaev, to know that they are in fact looking for their guns, ditched in the retreat. The

Figure 2.1 Chapaev directing Pet'ka's fire from *Chapaev* (1934)
Source: Courtesy of the British Film Institute, London

effect is to produce a joke at the commissar's expense, and to align us with Chapaev. Moreover, the Chapaev with whom we are aligned is a substantially different one.

In the book Chapaev has many faults, such as his habit of referring to the Red Army command (with the exception of Frunze) as 'bastards' ('*svolochi*') and of swearing (not just the relatively mild 'sons-of-bitches' ('*sukiny deti*') as in the film). This was a deliberate strategy, as is clear from Furmanov's diary for 19 August 1922:

> Question: to really give people a Chapaev with the petty details and faults, with all the innards of a human being, or as usual, to give them a larger than life figure, one that might be colourful, but would in many respects be castrated. I tend more towards the first.
>
> (Furmanov 1960–61, IV: 285)

These flaws are not eradicated. Development in the book is provided by the story of the growing friendship between Klychkov and Chapaev. Klychkov gains more influence over him, and this bears fruit in their military campaigns, but Chapaev is not easily changed.

By contrast, the Vasil'ev Brothers' film adaptation is clever in its creation of a larger than life, heroic figure, while maintaining some of Chapaev's faults; his slovenly habits of dress, his temper, his prickly attitude to the newly arrived commissar and to the army chiefs of staff are all depicted. However, in the film these faults are educated out of him by Furmanov, in a classic Socialist Realist spontaneity/consciousness (*stikhiinost'/soznatel'nost'*) dialectic (Clark 2000: 15–24) and his death is that of a completely remade, new man. Indicative of this is the fact that Klychkov makes no reference to Chapaev's 'shabby appearance' ('*zatrepeznyi vid*') in the book, whereas in the film, Furmanov's success in awakening in Chapaev a sense of discipline is demonstrated not only by Chapaev's own changed conduct, but in his own ticking off of Pet'ka for going around with a 'shabby appearance'. This use of dialogue is emblematic of the way in which the film adapts the book into neat literary structures: rather than striving to correspond with known fact, it imposes upon the material a clear *Bildungsroman* plot, the archetypal story of the Party educating the people, after the model of Gor'kii's *Mother* (*Mat'*) so as to make Chapaev's transformation explicit.

The film narrative is a radically distinct story from that presented in Furmanov. Here, the issue of Chapaev's development is left open, and his death is a tragedy precisely because he is still so far from becoming a new man. In the book, if anyone changes it is Klychkov. His inexperience and fear, shown in the scene where he runs away in the first battle, quickly turn into military maturity. The film makes Furmanov older, and, like Stalin, a pipe-smoker, suggesting greater authority. We see no evidence of fear and his lack of military experience is instead treated in a light-hearted way; the directors transfer his weaknesses onto the figure of Anna, a female member of the Ivanovo-Voznesensk detachment not present in the book. Her relationship with Chapaev's orderly, Pet'ka, parallels the relationship between Furmanov and Chapaev by reversing the didactic theme present in the latter: whereas Furmanov teaches Chapaev discipline, it is Pet'ka who teaches Anna how to use a machinegun. In both cases a strong bond (friendship, love) is formed and both Chapaev and Anna prove to be good pupils. The episodes involving Anna also serve to echo the soldiers' light-hearted suspicion of the detachment of textile-workers as Pet'ka is surprised to find a woman at the front, and does not take her desire to learn about machine guns entirely seriously. The humour and general effectiveness of the narrative here, entirely dependent on an assumption about the incompatibility of women and warfare, are more typical of prevailing 1930s attitudes to women rather than those associated with 1919 or the early 1920s.

These and other structures of parallels, called 'character couples' by Marc Ferro (Ferro 1988 [1977]: 62), lend the work a greater sense of cohesion and give it the polished air of a work of art. The film succeeds in freeing the story from the constraints of its context and its time, from the inconvenience and messiness of what actually happened, and from the limitations of history. In its place, the Vasil'ev Brothers, brothers only in name, create a film resembling its primary source likewise in little more than name.

Adaptation, myth and socialist realism

Yet how many of these changes are attributable to the contrasting natures of film and literature? Audiences of the 1930s would have less of a sense of Chapaev's legendary reputation: where Furmanov could assume prior knowledge of it, the Vasil'ev Brothers had to give audiences a direct sense of what it was by showing us his charm, his charisma and his power over his men. In doing this they end up paying more attention to the character of Chapaev and presenting him as the main figure in the piece. The cinematic medium has an often noted proclivity for the rendering of screen presence, and the power over spectators of this presence may be witnessed, for example, in the phenomenon of the star (Dyer 1979: 16–17). It is often seen as far poorer in its representation of interior worlds such as that created by the diary narrative form of Furmanov's *Chapaev*. Furmanov's first person perspective, while adding immediacy and authenticity to his account, also discusses the act of writing, referring to the commissar recording events in his diary. This thematization of the process of writing and representation raises the possibility of an alternative version of events that the sequential medium of film has great difficulty presenting, particularly in dramatic form.[10] To have retained Furmanov's narrative perspective would have required specific cinematic narrative devices such as the voice-over, reaction shots of the commissar (although we have some) and maybe even point-of-view shots. Similarly, the better narrative organization, as well as the addition of parallel scenes in the White camp and the romantic subplot of Anna may all also have been added so as to create a better story and enable it to appeal to a cinema audience.

Yet despite the distinct qualities of film and literature, the transformation effected by the Vasil'ev Brothers cannot be attributed to these factors alone. That processes at work transforming the story of Chapaev are part of a greater shift in Soviet culture can be witnessed in other literary transformations of the story. As early as 1923 there were abridged editions of Furmanov's book that emphasized the heroic and legendary character of Chapaev, including the myth that he survived (Prokhorov 1967: 47). These popular myths of course predated Furmanov's account, but they gained strength in the 1930s culminating in neo-folkloric accounts (e.g. Kriukova 1937: 45–64; Sokolov 1938: 106–10) and finally a short film sequel during World War II: *Chapaev is with Us* (*Chapaev s nami*) (V. Petrov, Lenfil'm, 1941) in which Chapaev makes it to the other side of the Ural river and returns to aid the Soviet war effort of 1941 (Babochkin, 1968: 73) (see Figure 2.2).

In reworking Furmanov's material, the Vasil'ev Brothers' film adaptation amplifies the heroic and mythical aspects of the story so that their Chapaev resembles myth more than document. This reworking of the story is less an individual reinterpretation than an updating of it in accordance with the cultural norms of 1934. As Régine Robin has argued, Socialist Realism incorporated a certain kind of folklore for its ritualizing, heroicizing and mythologizing functions while at the same time disregarding folklore's less

Figure 2.2 A scene from Petrov's *Chapaev is With Us* (*Chapaev s nami,* 1941)
Source: Courtesy of Gosfie'mofond, Moscow

exalted aspect (Robin 1992: 53–4). In fact the most famous advocate of the use of myth and folkloric hyperbole in portraying the real was Furmanov's old nemesis, Maksim Gor'kii. In his speech at the 1934 First Congress of Soviet Writers, he argued that myth is an accurate expression of the hyperbolic abilities of humanity: 'In idealizing peoples' abilities and as it were anticipating their mighty future evolution, mythmaking was basically realistic' (Gor'kii [1934] 1990: 6); 'Myth is invention. To invent is to draw from the sum of real data its fundamental meaning and embody it in an image: that's how we get realism' (ibid.: 10). This 'revolutionary romanticism' was very much tied up with the earlier mentioned notion of heroism, as Zhdanov's definition at the same Congress made clear: 'the combination of the most stern and sober practical work with a supreme spirit of heroic deeds and magnificent future prospects' (Zhdanov [1934] 1990: 4).

These statements date from August 1934, a few months before *Chapaev* was released, on 7 November. Despite not being conceived to do so, *Chapaev* fitted these formulae very well in its hyperbolic representation of Chapaev as a hero, but one who truly existed. The factual historical basis of the film is emphasized throughout contemporary reviews. Indeed, the Vasil'ev Brothers take care to assert their use of authentic documentary sources (Vasil'ev and Vasil'ev 1934). Veterans of Chapaev's Division, such as A.D. Mikhailov, are also used to confirm that that the film is an accurate record of what happened:

> It happened long ago. But now, watching the film *Chapaev*, you forget that so many years have past since the Civil War. The film is so powerfully done, that you sit in the cinema, and once more relive all those events yourself … once more it's as if you were involved in the events unfolding on the screen along with the rest of Chapaev's men.
>
> (Mikhailov 1934)

Reviews such as this stress not only authenticity, but also the fact that time has changed nothing; the film makes the spectator feel the continuity between the Civil War and Soviet Russia of 1934. This emphasis upon a sense of continuity had very definite political objectives. The film's evocation of the Civil War ethos coincided with both an atmosphere of increasing military tension provoked especially by the Japanese invasion of Manchuria. *Pravda*, in particular, ran a series of articles commemorating the fifteenth anniversary of a number of key moments in the Civil War of 1919, including the defeat of Wrangel' and Denikin's unsuccessful push on Moscow. The purpose of these commemorative articles was clear: to suggest to readers that the Soviet Union was once more under threat and that a new war was looming. Stories of the Red Army seeing and approving of the film were given particular prominence (Anonymous 1934a). A large number of reviews and audience responses to the film also drew a direct patriotic message of relevance to the present day from Chapaev's heroism: 'Chapaev's reputation, his heroism and courage call every private and commander, every labourer to courage, to infinite love and devotion to their socialist motherland' (Anonymous 1934b). This emphasis upon the continuity between the Civil War and the present day has another aspect too. As well as holding up Chapaev as an example to all, such responses also attempt to construct a vision of a timeless continuity that has more in common with myth than with history. In one viewer's reaction in the same issue of *Pravda* this is made especially clear:

> We came out of the theatre and saw on Arbat Square the mirror of tarmac, Soviet cars and buses, the skeleton of the new underground station. We saw Red Army men in strong boots and sturdy greatcoats … We were overcome with joy, we realized Chapaev hadn't drowned, shot from the precipice by White machineguns; Chapaevs live on.
>
> (Nikulin 1934)

Accounts such as these bespeak an atemporal continuity redolent of myth which, as Lévi-Strauss argues, is timeless. All is justified on the basis that 'the ancestors taught it to us'. Myth starts with a stable ready-formed structure to which all events are fitted so as to retell the same fundamental story (Lévi-Strauss 1962: 236).[11] So it is with the Vasil'evs' *Chapaev*. The film recounts a story of heroism which has little to do with historical record, and in accordance with which the events of Furmanov's narrative are manipulated (or discarded) until they fit. It is now a work which coincides with a referent or with extra-textual fact only minimally. As Thomas Lahusen has argued, the nonfictional referent of Socialist realist works was 'ever-shifting': 'what was considered to be based on fact depended on the current definition of what was considered typical and general' (Lahusen, 1997: 28). In place of Furmanov's documentary account, the Vasil'evs present us with a heroic Chapaev whose story corresponds far better to the myth-like 'master plot' (Clark 2000: 4–5) of nascent socialist realism. *Chapaev* had not discarded its pretensions to the status of nonfiction, but these pretensions were now meaningless, because they were now entwined inextricably with textual characteristics and a critical discourse of reception determined to conflate the fictional and the nonfictional so as to render accurate nonfiction impossible. The film version of *Chapaev* dispenses with the problematizing, questioning, reflexive drive of Furmanov's account and proposes in its stead a narrative that pretends to be incontestable in its elevation of Chapaev as a hero. The apparatus of Soviet criticism plays no small part in this by failing to contest the film on the grounds of historical objectivity by which nonfictional works should, as we have argued, be measured.

The Vasil'ev Brothers certainly mythologized Chapaev in line with an officially sponsored revalorization of heroes, folklore and myth, but their adaptation drew on the original legendary aura of Chapaev which Furmanov sought to explode. This reinvigoration of a popular myth, authorized from the top, did not succeed unopposed for long. Although *Chapaev* was a hugely successful film seen by millions of people, popular culture fought back so that by the 1970s Chapaev jokes had become widespread. The following example deliberately ridicules the notion of Chapaev's immortality, while at the same time making fun of his stupidity and placing him in the incongruous context of a 1970s Soviet school:

Pet'ka: Vasilii Ivanovich, why have you gone and painted a stripe across your forehead?

Chapai: The English teacher asked us to prepare for the lessons using the immersion method and I haven't forgotten my water-line from the Ural.

(Endlin 1983: 57)

These jokes served to emphasize Chapaev's stupidity, his Sovietness, and his backwardness. They often also supplied an obscene subtext to the Chapaev–Pet'ka relation, as well as the Pet'ka–Anna relation so markedly pure in the film. They are an attempt to strip from Chapaev the aura imparted to him by the film and by mainstream Soviet culture: they ridicule his legendary status and place him in an unhallowed contemporary setting. Paradoxically, in attempting to demythologize this figure and bring Chapaev down to earth, these anti-communist jokes aim for the same effect as Communist Commissar Furmanov's original account.

Notes

1 Not all critics, however, see Furmanov's *Chapaev* as a proto-Socialist Realist text. A notable example is Jürgen Rühle, a Leftist East German dissident (Rühle 1969: 44–5).

2 I shall here primarily employ the terms 'fiction' and 'nonfiction' although the critics differ in their usages. The term 'documentary literature', while more widely employed, is both narrower and less helpful for a rigorous definition of the distinction with fiction proper.

3 It should, however, be noted that Sauerberg is alive to the potential ambiguities and conflicts over the generic classification of texts and the historical relativism of such definitions (Sauerberg 1991: 14).

4 *Lef* had advocated journalistic and propagandistic forms from late 1923, but not in a consistent and systematic way, and not under the title 'factography.' Instead they had vague slogans such as 'Art Must Enter Life, and Become Part Of It!' (Tret'iakov 1924: 197).

5 All translations from Russian are mine.

6 Prokhorov rejects the notion that it was in response to Gor'kii's letter that Furmanov began rewriting Chapaev (Prokhorov 1967: 58).

7 However, this is not to suggest that the shift occurred in all media at the same time, nor that factographical tendencies were banished by the mid-twenties. Notably the First Five Year Plan period was one in which documentary literature of a kind flourished, and with photography and cinema a shift occurred somewhat later. Graham Roberts gives an account of the shift in cinema (Roberts 1999: 100–101).

8 Clark argues that this is not demythologization but remythologization. (Clark 2000: 88).

9 Dolinskii gives a detailed comparison of the various stages of the adaptation. (Dolinskii 1945).

10 There are, however, exceptions. Chris Marker explores a range of alternative accounts of events in his documentaries.

11 In the study of film the concept of myth that has gained the most widespread use is that of Claude Lévi-Strauss (Caughie 1981: 157–64), and it is his work on myth that seems most helpful in describing *Chapaev*. However, the Vasil'evs' *Chapaev* may also be said to be embracing what Roland Barthes called myth since it empties Chapaev's story of history and presents it as nature, that is to say it conceals its own textuality (Barthes 1993: 129). Evgenii Dobrenko and Jeffrey Brooks have also commented upon the myth-like, timeless quality of Socialist Realist culture (Dobrenko 1993: 64; Brooks 2000: 66–79).

3 Ada/opting the Son

War and the authentication of power in Soviet screen versions of children's literature

Stephen Hutchings

Introduction

The role played by World War II mythology in consolidating Soviet power is well established. War in general enables societies to legitimate their guiding ideologies by making the effects of hostility to those ideologies painfully palpable at the heart of everyday existence. Nowhere was this more true than in the case of the appalling sufferings unleashed upon the Soviet population by the Nazi invaders in 1940. Whilst, during the almost unremittingly repressive Stalin years, the Soviet Union had less need for legitimating mythologies than other societies, the ever-waning influence of Marxist–Leninist ideology in the post-war period meant that the iconography and narratives of the Great Patriotic War were accorded a vital role in shoring up the Soviet regime's totalizing authority. By maintaining the all-too-real pain and all-too-heroic sacrifices of the war at the forefront of the Soviet collective consciousness, the weary abstractions of Party rhetoric could be revitalized and given new expressive form. As Peter Kenez puts it, in the Soviet experience of war 'the present came alive and was no longer suspended between a richly embellished past and an imminent future' (Kenez 1995: 184). Because war throws ordinary people into extreme situations in which it is the essential human qualities of courage and self-sacrifice which are at a premium, bookish platitudes about an international proletariat triumphing over global capital can suddenly be accorded vivid meaning, established humanistic values like bravery and endurance conveniently meshed with blatantly ideological notions of class consciousness. Soviet man becomes identical with Man in his ideal form. As Rosalinde Sartori contends, the 'typically Soviet' turned out to be 'merely the embodiment of universal qualities such as perseverance, along with a strong sense of purpose' (Sartori 1995: 181). In Catriona Kelly's words, war mythology furnished 'a supremely efficient basis of national identity in the post-Stalin era. Unlike ... even revolutionary history, it invoked what was universally revered as a just cause: the righteousness of war was never questioned, even in private' (Kelly 1998: 265). The tribulations of the Great Patriotic War offered post-Stalin mythmakers the capacity to naturalize the deeply political principles on which Soviet society was organized, to ground them in timeless human spirit.

Equally familiar is cinema's function in promoting the mythology through which the authentication process operated. Suffice it to recall the popularity of Grigorii Chukrai's *Ballad of a Soldier* (*Ballada o soldate*, 1959), or the powerful resonances of the imagery in *The Cranes Are Flying* (*Letiat zhuravli*, 1958). Indeed, cinema's war mythology industry went into production with the war still in progress, and by the end of the 1940s powerful images of the titanic efforts of the Red Army, the unthinkable sufferings of the Soviet people and the unspeakable crimes of their Nazi tormentors were already etched in the consciousnesses of Russians of all ages. Bereft, as M. Gallagher notes, of the concerns of class or economic system (Gallagher 1963: 126), Stalinist war films were able to locate the source of moral authority motivating their brave heroes in the eternal Russian soul rather than in a (potentially) transient political ideology. Paradigmatic in this respect is the legendary 1944 film, *Zoia*, based on the life of a real female partisan's death at the hands of the Germans, but glorifying her martyrdom in hagiographic manner (the film ends with a shot panning across the blue 'heavenly' sky in which Zoia's immortal soul now implicitly resides).

Within the context outlined, the film adaptation genre had an important role to fulfil. Literature never lost its position at the summit of the Soviet cultural hierarchy. Socialist realism, the dogma which dominated all the Soviet arts, was itself of literary origin (it was formulated at the 1934 Writers' Union Congress and its master texts and figureheads were all literary). Indeed, the movement's optative modality (it famously claimed 'to represent the tomorrow in the today') accorded uneasily with visual media dealing in photographic indices of present reality. The word remained the ultimate arbiter of cultural value, the primary code in the representation of power, even when embodied in a non-literary form. Thus, if the war film served to authenticate the foundations of Soviet power through its mythologizing potential, then, cinema, in its turn, was able to gain in authenticity, prestige and authority by reference to the hallowed realm of literature cited in the *ekranizatsii* it generated in the 1940s. Indeed, during this period, screen versions followed their literary sources with an unparalleled rapidity and purposefulness.

Some of the most enduring war films were adaptations of literary works: Fadeev's *Young Guard* (*Molodaia gvardiia*), adapted in 1948 with a Shostakovich music score, a 1944 version of Konstantin Simonov's *Days and Nights* (*Dni i nochi*), published in the same year and treating the battle for Stalingrad, and the 1948 film of Polevoi's paradigmatic socialist realist war epic, 'The Tale of a Real Man' ('*Povest' o nastoiashchem cheloveke*'). In 1959, a version of Sholokhov's 'Fate of a Man' ('*Sud'ba cheloveka*') rapidly became one of the most frequently cited Soviet war movies, and a year later Tarkovskii's controversial film, *Ivan's Childhood* (*Ivanovo detstvo*), adapted from Vladimir Bogomolov's story, 'Ivan', was at the forefront of Thaw-era reassessments of Stalinist mythology.

We are dealing, then, with two intersecting realms of authority – the political and the literary – and the fact that the *ekranizatsiia* is located at the point of intersection is in itself reason enough to pay it attention. However, the situation is rendered still more fraught by cinema's proximity to the levers of power. Heavily reliant on central funding, film tended to be both a more reliable barometer of shifts in policy during the Soviet period than literature, and a more rigorous implementer of the values on which those policies rested. For this reason, the *ekranizatsiia* was liable to counter incipient literary centrifugalism with its own centripetal force, functioning as a vital corrective to literary waywardness and exchanging its authenticating activity for the reverse: that of guarantor of ideological rectitude. The supreme example is the fate suffered by the adaptation of *Young Guard*. The film was praised for restoring to Fadeev's tale of a young partisan unit the importance of the Party's role which the author was attacked for ignoring in 1947 (having in 1945, under different ideological conditions, won the Stalin prize for the novel which, to complete the circle, he then rewrote in line with the film's corrective in 1951). The sequence demonstrates the pertinence to Stalinist culture of W.J.T. Mitchell's contention that the word–image border is a key site of cultural tension, the point at which the battle for what Mitchell calls 'propriety rights' over nature comes to a head, and of our own suggestion in the Introduction to this volume that the screen adaptation should be placed squarely within the framework of Mitchell's theory. With the conflict between a universal human spirit and the uncompromising intentionality of the ideological word reaching a new peak in World War II art, we have every reason to assume that the Soviet film adaptation of the 1940s was key to the shape of the emergent war mythology.

In the context of the close relationship between the screen adaptation and war mythology's role in consolidating Soviet power, *ekranizatsii* of children's literature are, for several reasons, of particular interest. First, with its pedagogical function (that of inculcating collectivist values within the receptive minds of the youngest members of society), children's fiction of the Stalin period reveals the ideological tendencies driving the mythologization process more starkly than works of adult fiction. But, second, the use of spontaneously innocent child heroes is concordant with the naturalization necessary to authenticate such tendencies. Thus, if war is the great universalizing authenticator, then war children redouble that authenticating effect, rendering children's fiction paradigmatic of wartime art. Third, precisely because it is unsullied by 'treacherous' adult consciousness, the world of children can be separated off from society at large and made to model it from a distance as its metaphor, whilst at the same time aspiring, orphan-like, to be adopted into it. Fourth, the screen adaptation of children's wartime fiction draws on differences in aesthetic logic, target audience and inscribed subject positions between film and literature in order both to reinforce the functions of the literary sources and to add to them a new dimension: that of the adult viewer, the suspension of whose consciousness between 'objective' parent and 'subjective' child plays out the tensions between individual and collective, bodily reality and abstract ideology, particular and general, by which Stalinist society is beset. In this way, it is not just the *fact* of war mythology's authenticating function that is modelled within the *ekranizatsiia* of children's literature, but the very *processes* by which that function is put to work.

Numerous adaptations of children's literature were made during the 1940s and 1950s, the majority of which, however, were animations of fairy tales from the various Soviet republics (including Russia). The Ukrainian tales of Gogol found particular favour with Stalin's animators, since they bridged two important divides: that between folk tradition and serious literature, and that between Russian culture and the culture of the non-Russian republics. This trend matched shifts in official wartime ideology away from themes of class conflict and towards nationalistic celebrations of folk tradition, and of the unity of the multi-ethnic Soviet superstate, though the fairy tales of Hans Christian Andersen also featured. A version of *Robinson Crusoe* was screened in 1947, however, and the popular humour of Kornei Chukovskii's children's tales was a frequent inspiration for the animation studios.

The only 1940s screen version of children's war literature proper is the 1946 adaptation of Valentin Kataev's 'Son of the Regiment' ('*Syn polka*'). However, the film's legendary popularity outweighs the paucity of co-members in the category to which it belongs and it constitutes the focus of the second of the two close readings around which my analysis is based. Although not strictly a work of children's literature, of course, *The Young Guard* has affinities with *Son of the Regiment* in that its heroes are adolescents suspended between the world of children and the world of adults. I will refer to it in this context in my conclusion. My first main object of analysis, however, is an adaptation of a work that predates the commencement of the war, albeit by a few months. Apart from having children as its subjects, its legendary fame, and its militaristic ambiances, the 1940 version of Arkadii Gaidar's 'Timur and His Gang' ('Timur i ego komanda'), published in the same year, establishes many of the principles incorporated into *Son of the Regiment*. I therefore treat the two as a pair. My focus is the role of the mini-genre to which I am assigning both films in authenticating Stalinist power through its contribution to the emergent war mythology. Methodologically, I proceed by highlighting differences between page and screen versions of the two works since it is these differences which reveal the relationship of word–image tensions to the representation of the war in Stalinist ideology, and thus to the enactment of Stalinist authority. I introduce the two films at the centre of my study in the chronological order in which they were made.

Tmur and his Gang: the mystification of Stalinist power

Gaidar's 'Timur and his Gang' was one of the few crude, propagandistic texts littering the Soviet school curriculum which held genuine appeal for its intended audience. Its now legendary fame owes much to the 1940 cinematic version of the story, which followed within months of the original book and for which Gaidar, who commanded a Red Army regiment during the Civil War and died a war hero at the front in October 1941, contributed his own scenario. Although set before the Nazi invasion of the Soviet Union, the action takes place against the background of growing military tension and, thanks partly to Gaidar's fate and partly to the story's highlighting of the theme of vigilance, which, as Peter Kenez notes, was central to early war movies (Kenez 1995: 169), it became inextricably associated with war mythology.

Gaidar began his writing career as a journalist, and even after turning to children's literature his plots journalistically reflected his own military experiences; another of his children's adventures is entitled 'A Military Secret' ('*Voennaia taina*'). Although the symbiosis of journalism and war literature characterizing fiction of the period owes much to pragmatic reasons (writers could better be armed with pens than with guns), it also reflects the ties linking fiction with official discourse under Stalin. Louise McReynolds underlines the role of Soviet war journalists as 'principal transmitters of the culture of the shared experience of war – a culture that kept the populace together in a way that the official culture of state and party could not' (McReynolds 1995: 41).

Gaidar's story is set in a dacha community for children with fathers serving in the Red Army and features a young girl, Zhenia, and her older sister, sent to live at the community. It soon transpires that a gang of boys, led by the precocious Timur, has made itself responsible for the maintenance of order in the community. With his military-style tree-house base and rituals, and his gang of acolytes, Timur metes out punishments to a rival gang of vandals and offers support to the Red Army families. Enthralled, Zhenia joins Timur in his exploits, to the dismay of her older sister and her fiancé, who see Timur as a hooligan. Eventually the sister is won over when Timur drives Zhenia on a motorbike over a long distance to see their father, who has returned on leave for one night. The story ends with Zhenia herself organizing a celebration (turned into a large parade in the film) for the military call-up of her sister's fiancé.

The screen version, made by Soiuzdetfilm and directed by A. Razumnyi, followed the book swiftly, indicating a clear intention to exploit the work's propaganda potential for the inculcation of correct attitudes in children, but also ensuring that the Timur legend emerged from a synaesthetic amalgam of cinematic image and literary word. The screen's role in establishing Timur's popularity points up a difference between book and film signalled immediately by the title credits scrawled, graffiti-style, on a fence, then by a carefully posed photograph of the gang, with Timur at its centre, and an accompanying image of the Red Army star. The 'nostalgizing' effect which, as Barthes argues, photographs exert on their object (Barthes 1981), provides visual confirmation of Timur's pre-established mythic status, which is confirmed at the end when the photograph reappears, locating the film's framing images in eternal time, of which the intervening narrative is merely a transient, linear unfolding. The juxtaposition of graffiti-style title and Red Army star foregrounds an underlying tension in Gaidar's text between unofficial subculture represented by the gang and the official culture into which it is inducted. The posing of the gang for the photograph works to similar effect, suggesting the organization of an arbitrary, chaotic force into patterned conformity. Rosalinde Sartori notes such tension in *Zoia*, which displays a similar 'subconscious attachment to unofficial values and qualities' (Sartori 1995: 191).[1]

The tension is reflected spatially in the location of the gang's headquarters in a tree house, a semi-civilized natural living space located at the margins of the dacha community, and temporally through the plot in which, in order to fulfil his virtuous duties, Timur must break official protocol, much to the consternation of the adult world. Zhenia's sister is foremost amongst those suspicious of Timur with whom she forbids Zhenia from associating. Whilst, as the camera work stresses, Timur wears his red star with honour, it is only when Zhenia's father gives his blessing to Timur after the motorbike escapade that his status as an approved hero is confirmed and the apparently parent-less Timur (there is no mention in film or book of his parents) is 'adopted' into the official world of adult authority. But the fact that neither the Red Army itself, nor the source of power behind it, are ever represented on screen, reinforces the mystique of an elusive but ever-present authority to which even Timur can never gain full access. This pattern, which recurs in war films like *Ballad of a Soldier*, is crucial to the legitimation of Stalinist arbitrariness: the ultimate example of a representative of power that sanctions rule-breaking in the interests of strengthening the hidden principles on which those rules rest is the dictator himself.[2] In Timur, the pattern is emphasized through a layering of the obstructions encountered by Timur and Zhenia. Once he has won over Zhenia's sister, he must persuade her fiancé (Timur's uncle), who is only convinced when Zhenia organizes the parade to celebrate his departure for military service. Moreover, the obstructions from 'above' are matched by those below in the form of the parallel gang of vandals who are also persuaded to join the parade at the end. Meanwhile, by visually underscoring the children's touching naivety, Razumnyi represents their virtuosity as an innate sense of natural justice in keeping with the principle that, in Sartori's words, 'the most popular [heroes] were the ones whose deeds were stripped of their ideological connections' (Sartori 1995: 190). The principles at the root of Stalinist ideology are thus made to inhere in the souls of all good Soviet people.

The story's setting is well suited to the pattern, the dacha community with its loose chronotope of unregulated time and unrestricted space and its sanctioning of relatively free behaviour accommodating the clash of spontaneous non-conformity and rule-bound regulators. Moreover, by locating the action at the peripheries of Stalinist space, Gaidar is able to *model* the centre at which Stalinist power resides. (A plot situated close to the centre of power becomes metonymically contaminated by its effects and cannot achieve the required distance to represent that centre in its entirety).

In Razumnyi's version of 'Timur', the modelling function facilitated by the peripheral setting is enhanced through visual parallels drawn between Timur's gang and the Red Army that they emulate, parallels absent from Gaidar's original. The tree house headquarters, for example, are equipped with elaborate militaristic paraphernalia (including a mock-up two-way radio communications system). The gang relies on its invisible viewpoint above the settlement to maintain a constant vigil, identifying miscreants and those in need of assistance, in a sanitized version of the surveillance operation conducted within Stalinist society as a whole. Timur's initial absence from the screen is maintained for as long as possible, in imitation of the awe-inspiring mystical force of the Red Army itself. His fatherly attitude to his subordinates both reinvokes that of Stalin, the ultimate Father, and reduces its terrifying aura. Through the director's sentimental treatment of the child heroes, adult viewers (a crucial by-product of the page–screen transfer relevant to a number of screen versions of children's literature and recognized at the time)[3] encounter a palatable variant on the power source that, in circumstances beyond the comforting surroundings of the cinema, inspires only dread. Timur's reference to his activities as 'military service' (*'voennaia sluzhba'*) generates respect within its younger audience for which Timur now becomes a mediatory figure bridging the divide between the carefree children's world and the duty-laden adult realm (a function intimated by a contemporary reviewer[4]), yet adult viewers perceive in the gang's grand pretensions a naive ignorance of the true nature of military service; when Zhenia asks her departing father if he will be travelling 'in a soft-seated train compartment' (*'v miagkom vagone'*), he wryly answers 'yes, a soft-seated one' (*'v miagkom'*). The next shot shows him climbing into a hard, metallic tank, encouraging the adult audience for which it is constructed to adopt an ironic, patronizing attitude towards the children, who collectively model the paternalistic state of which those same adult viewers are cowed, childlike subjects.

The screen version gives much attention to Timur's role in inducting Zhenia into the rituals of his gang. When Zhenia organizes the parade for her sister's fiancé, an avuncular Timur looks on approvingly, just as Zhenia's father had in similar fashion sanctioned Timur's actions. The film thus visually fortifies Gaidar's adherence to a key socialist realist trope: the mentor's induction of a disciple into the Party spirit. The parade itself, absent from Gaidar's fiction and a standard feature of Stalinist film, brings model and modelled together. Timur's gang, now led by Zhenia, is joined by the new military recruit and by other soldiers, as well as (after Timur's intervention) by the leader of the rival gang of hooligans, now thoroughly acculturated to the Red Army cause. Official culture (the Red Army), subculture (Timur's gang) and counter culture (the rival gang) merge in a visual spectacle of the comforting authority offered by the Red Army whose presence is, as the *Literaturnaia gazeta* reviewer suggests, occluded, except in swift synecdochic snatches, and which is itself no more than a metonymic representation of the true centre of power whose inaccessible mystique is reinforced.[5]

Despite reservations expressed at the time about its occasional slide away from the magical and the mystical (presented, revealingly, as positive attributes) into photographic prosaicism, it is the film which better accomplishes the mystificatory representation of Stalinist power.[6] This is because, through its precise visual language, it can deploy its metaphoric modelling approach more extensively than Gaidar's text, and because, with its capacity to address both child and adult realms, it penetrates more deeply into the fabric of Stalinist society, using the sentimentalizing 'child effect' to naturalize Gaidar's propagandistic text and disseminate it to a wider audience. (Film's syncretic nature enables it to breach the divides between adult and children, and between high and low culture.) Although the film relies on the book to authenticate its status (the photograph framing the film marks the already mythologized reputation accorded to Timur by Gaidar's original), its colossal success resulted in Gaidar writing a scenario for a sequel to *Timur and His Gang*, signalling the shifting balance of power between literature and film under Stalin.[7]

Adopting the child/adapting the text: Pronin's *Son of the Regiment*

Tied to their urgent propagandistic function, Soviet films made during World War II were often grim affairs aimed at instilling patriotic fervour and hatred for the enemy, lacking the epic distance which myth-making requires. Towards the war's end, however, sufficient progress towards victory had been made for this distancing effect to come into play. Narrative literature's inherently epic function ensured that it played the leading role in shaping the emergent war myths. With its instantaneous appeal and universal reach, cinema was accorded the task of popularizing these myths. Thus, the Soviet film adaptation assumed new importance in the aftermath of the war and the swiftness with which the works of Simonov, Sholokhov, Kataev, Fadeev and other key socialist realist documenters of the war effort reached the screen confirms that the transition from text to film had become part of a planned process.

One of the first post-war narratives to undergo conversion to celluloid was Valentin Kataev's novella 'Son of the Regiment' ('*Syn polka*') published in 1945 and adapted by Soiuzdetfilm in 1946, with Kataev's scenario. It marked a shift from the standard war movie in that, as a reviewer put it, it involved 'no real battle-front action', adopting a human interest angle on the war (Alferov 1946: 4). The film's success quickly established the work in the Soviet school curriculum and at the heart of Soviet popular culture; to this day, the term '*syn polka*' is encountered in everyday speech to describe the child over-eager to impress in an adult environment.

Unlike Gaidar, a Stalinist career writer, Kataev had roots in the early Soviet modernist period. Even as ideologically sound a work as 'Son of the Regiment' is not without traces of modernist subjectivity. In this sense, Kataev's involvement in film adaptations belongs to a broader process by which previously marginal figures are assimilated into mainstream Stalinist culture. In common with Fadeev and Polevoi, Kataev's literary talents were co-opted by the war effort when he was recruited as a front-line journalist – a factor easing the passage of 'Son of the Regiment' from page to screen; war journalism functioned as a mediator between literature and cinema, lending the documentary authenticity of the camera to literary narrative, and to cinema the weighty authority carried by its location within verbal discourse.

The plot of 'Son of the Regiment' centres on the story of a boy, Vania, orphaned during the Nazi occupation. Vania thus bears affinities with Timur, and, to a lesser extent, with the members of the Young Guard in Fadeev's work, who are likewise effectively parentless, a factor significant for the symbolic system in which the young heroes are deployed. Discovered in the forests of occupied Russia by a reconnaissance party dispatched by an artillery regiment, Vania, who had recently escaped from the Germans, becomes so attached to the soldiers that he refuses to be sent back to the rear. It is not only in the choice of the child hero that 'Son of the Regiment' strikes a cord with 'Timur'; like Gaidar's story, and as recognized in an *Izvestiia* review, Kataev's war tale engages the reader through its hero's capacity for rendering ideological rectitude via the attributes of a 'charming boy whose soul is open to feelings like comradeship and loyalty' (Kriger 1946: 7), and through its hero's battle with the forces of protocol requiring such orphans to be removed from the front line. Such non-conforming conformity, particularly when embodied in the naive enthusiasm of youth (cf. the audacious escapades of Fadeev's Young Guard) constitutes one of the myths of World War II Soviet heroism which the *ekranizatsiia* brought to the fore.

Vania absconds during an attempt to return him to safety, and finally convinces the regiment to adopt him as their 'son', displaying the same urge to be co-opted into the authority-bearing realm of adult soldiers as Timur. His knowledge of the forest is exploited on reconnaissance missions, but on one such mission he is recaptured by the Germans and interrogated. He is rescued by a Captain Egorov who, having lost his own son to the Nazis, takes Vania under his wing. The captain later dies in action and Vania is left 'orphaned' for a second time. However, the regiment now assumes the paternal role and eventually sends Vania for military training to Moscow where, in a subjective sequence reminiscent of the earlier Kataev, he dreams of meeting Marshall Suvorov.

The film, directed by V. Pronin and also a product of the Soiuzdetfilm studio, makes several ideological 'corrections' to Kataev's original. In the interests of underscoring the Red Army's high moral code of discipline and responsibility, the soldiers responsible for losing Vania whilst on a reconnaissance mission are in Pronin's narrative threatened with court martial. The portrayal of the German captors is harsher than that of Kataev. Vania's interrogator is initially shown from behind and her cruel taunting of the child, characteristic of cinematic renderings of the Nazis, is absent from the book. Her false maternal attributes (Kataev is unspecific about gender) underscore the pathos of Vania's orphan status. Indeed, the film restructures the story along a rigid self/other (*svoi/chuzhoi*) axis typical of Stalinist war films. This is achieved from the outset in a lingering shot panning across the soon-to-be shattered calm of the native Russian birch forest, a visual trope common to many Soviet war films and described by Alferov as 'a typically Russian, Levitan-like landscape' (Alferov 1946: 4), and through vividly contrastive photography, applied not only to the German–Russian relationship, but, in a doubling effect, to relationships within the Russian collective. Thus, an early shot/reverse shot sequence alternating between Vania and the Russian reconnaissance officers establishes mutual hostility, until the divide is erased in a celebration of togetherness. This doubling effect strengthens the barrier between the Russian self and the truly alien Nazis. The subjective elements of Kataev's narrative are expunged. One passage in which Vania mentally repeats the words 'I serve the Soviet Union' to steel himself for the rough military company is replaced with a scene in which he recites the words out loud, to the soldiers' (and adult viewers') collective amusement.

The film demonstrates how adaptations draw simultaneously on two referencing systems, one cinematic and one literary. Most significant among the cinematic intertexts is the ending which, recalling *Timur*, replaces Vania's dream of meeting Suvorov with shots of a military parade on Red Square watched by a momentarily glimpsed Stalin.[8] The panoramas of sunlit, formation-marching troops shot from a universalizing distance seem an ill-fitting appendage to the intimate close-ups in the officers' mess and the tragic melodrama of the orphan theme. Moreover, in its attempt to suppress Kataev's subjective ending, the film version merely transfers the dream experience from the main character to the audience, so that Vania's idealized inner vision of Suvorov becomes our idealized outer vision of Stalin. Referring to cinema's subjectivizing, oneiric quality and the darkened solitude in which films are viewed, Paul Virilio describes how 'moving images are substituted for my thoughts' (Virilio 1989: 30). Accordingly, Pronin's film is characterized by a periodic re-subjectivizing of a text that, in the distortions perpetrated on its narrative line, is elsewhere extensively 'objectified'. Earlier, the camera lingers in subjective close-up over the blissfully sleeping Vania, about to be awakened by news of Egorov's death. Such blatant sentimentalization exhorts the viewing adult audience to identify with the parental role, an identification considerably bolstered by the fact that the actor Iura Iankin, who plays Vania, was himself an orphan adopted by the army (Kriger 1946: 7).

The oscillation between the viewpoints of child and parent, familiar from *Timur*, enables the film to access an emerging mythology in which a chain of associations link the motherland with the anxious mother awaiting her son, and with the viewing audience (a central trope in *Ballad of a Soldier*). This tie accounts for the prevalence of the adopted orphan theme, developed in later films like *Fate of a Man* (*Sud'ba cheloveka*), in which a grieving father adopts an orphan boy, and Tarkovskii's *Ivan's Childhood*, which reworks the son of the regiment narrative in a polemical response to Kataev's sunny optimism (the surname of Kataev's Ivan is, fittingly, Solntsev). In this sense I would query Elena Prokhorova's otherwise pertinent observation that the orphan trope featured primarily in transition periods like the 1920s and 30s and the Thaw (Prokhorova 2003: 523).

The persistence of the parent/orphan theme in Soviet World War II mythology is tied to a singular–general problematic bound up with the representation of authority in Stalinist culture. When Egorov is killed, the regiment takes on the nurturing role, activating the title's full metaphorical force: Vania is now 'son of the regiment' in both a ritualistic and a literal sense. By the end, with Vania dispatched to Moscow, the orphan is re-adopted by his motherland.[9] This switch is presaged in the words of the dying Egorov who refers to Vania as 'son of his motherland' ('*syn svoei materi rodiny*'). The sequence running from single father figure, to collective father figure (the regiment), to universal mother figure (the homeland) integrates singular with universal, rooting authority (located in the central spaces of Moscow through which the military columns march in the final scenes) within the local and intimate realm of the individual family. As Sartori puts it, 'Would not an orphan be much more willing to accept Stalin, homeland and army as his one and only father?' (Sartori 1995: 182). But the integration is never complete. Whilst Vania undergoes numerous initiation rituals (for example, donning a uniform and adopting military styles of address), neither he nor we are ever permitted access to the ultimate source of power, which, but for the oneiric glimpse of Stalin at the parade, remains screened from the viewer's familiarizing eye, located in what Paul Virilio calls a 'Beyond with the space-time not of ordinary mortals but of a single war machine' (Virilio 1989: 79), ensuring that it is childlike awe which prevails.

Adult viewers of adaptations of children's stories like 'Son' oscillate between infantile identification with the awe-struck child and identification with the awe-inspiring, universal parent for whom the object of love is, nonetheless, intimately familiar. The oscillation finds its visual apotheosis in the switch from the intimate close-ups of Vania in the officers' mess to the anonymous masses of parading troops in Red Square, a switch intended to unite all viewers in veneration of 'the great devotion to one's people, uniform for grown-ups and the young alike' (Kriger 1946: 7).[10]

That the work of a writer somewhat distant from the ideological centre should become a war classic accords with the nature of myth, whose narratives, as Lotman and Mintz show, highlight the anomolous in order to evoke the pleasure gained from seeing the anomaly folded back into the norm (Lotman and Mintz 1981). In *Son of the Regiment*, everything is 'off-centre'. The hero is outside of his natural locus – a loving family. And the plot depicts not front-line action but a sentimentalized encounter between an orphaned child and a bereaved father, illustrating Maia Turovskaia's observation that the war produced a 'noticeable privatization of demand' corresponding to Vasilii Grossman's notion of war fiction as 'the literature of the inner world of Soviet man in extreme conditions' (Turovskaia 1995: 50). Yet this far from politically orthodox tale won the Stalin prize for literature in 1945, establishing its place in the cultural hierarchy for which film provided the official seal.

Conclusion

Despite the rich semiotic potential offered to Stalinist propagandists by the screen adaptation of children's literature, the two films we have analysed were the only pure examples of the genre to have been made in the 1940s. However, other key war films of the same period share many of the attributes of the films we have examined, confirming the genre's importance in a qualitative sense. Aside from the earlier mentioned ideological corrective that, like the Kataev adaptation, it performed on its original, Gerasimov's adaptation of Fadeev's *Young Guard* mines its source for its deployment of subcultural micro-collectives in a manner similar to *Timur*. For all their deference to Party authority, the Young Guard form, like Timur's gang, a subculture with their own rituals. And, like both Timur and Vania, the young heroes of Gerasimov's film engage in an attenuated form of convention-flouting essential to their entry into popular mythology. The exploits undertaken (setting fire to buildings, deliberately obstructing the production of factory goods) are perilously close to the activities of wreckers demonized during the pre-war purges. (As with Tarkovskii's reaccentuation of the orphan motif, a shift in framing context transforms the meaning of an entire narrative sequence.) Like that of the previous films, the literary plot that *Young Guard* adapts centres on the attempt by worthy outsiders who in their efforts to gain admittance to an elusive site of power, metaphorically represent the power-imbued spaces that their elders occupy, whilst keeping them at a tantalizing distance. And, like its predecessors, *Young Guard* transforms its literary source by attaching phantasmagoric connotations to the desired-for union with the 'parental' power source. Gerasimov ends, as does Fadeev, at the gravesides of the young martyrs.

However, rather than the novel's extra-diegetic listing of the names of the heroes and heroines, the citation is, in the film, transferred to the intra-diegetic level; the Komsomol leader, Protsenko, who guides them throughout, reads the names out loud to an appreciative crowd as the salute is fired into the heaven-like sky. The voice of paternal authority passes from the literary author to a Party functionary, but through this gesture, the source of that authority (the Party) is deferred beyond the screen's spatio–temporal frame. A parallel is drawn between the youthful martyrs who now also lie beyond life's biographical frame, and the guarantor of all power, the paternal Word of Truth, into which, through death, they have finally been adopted and through which they achieve the 'eternal glory' celebrated by Protsenko.[11]

The unprecedented speed with which works like 'Son' and *Young Guard* were adapted for the screen points both to the urgency with which policy makers wished to secure the entry of these ideologically resonant texts into the socialist realist literary canon (each film employs standard mentor–disciple paradigms particularly effectively embodied in the world of children), and literature's continuing status as a carrier of cultural capital. But it is also associated with the propensity for writers to locate their narratives at a tangent to society's officially constructed centre. Film makers rapidly recognized the mythologizing potential of such narratives and the flow of *ekranizatsii* followed accordingly. Such potential determines the off-centre loci for the texts selected for adaptation (dacha communities, the haunts of aspiring young partisans, regimental messes), loci linked in turn to a metaphoric modelling function, and to the prevalence of subcultural groupings or other temporarily marginalized individuals struggling with protocol to gain access to the aspired-to centre of authority. At a further remove, this struggle reflects the need to reconcile individual with universal, a need intensified by the extreme acts that war requires from its heroes (self-sacrifice; the readiness of children to place themselves in mortal danger).

One means of managing the singular/universal tension was through the theme of the orphan, since the adoption of child by family mirrors the assimilation of individual by super-family. The repeated deployment of young characters serves the further purpose of naturalizing the moral ideology of the Stalinist war hero. But, if in this the adaptations merely underscore their literary originals, then by furnishing a means for accommodating the paternalistic instincts of their adult audiences (a corollary of cinema's cultural heterogeneity), the child heroes enable the films to transcend their sources. The oscillation of viewpoints (from identification with the orphaned child, to identification with the adopting state) ameliorates the contradictions of Stalinist society, as the repressed terror inspired by the Father is sublimated in paternalistic pity for the child. The genre of adaptation (particularly that of a narrative for children) and the theme of adoption (the taking under one's wing of a sentimentalised orphan) thus turn out to be inextricably linked.

The oscillation terminates when, as a corollary of cinema's oneiric mode, viewers – adult and child – attain unity with a deferred power source situated in an elusive Beyond. With war arguably totalitarian power's ideal condition, this phantasmagoric unity is expressed repeatedly, and paradoxically, as images of organized masses filmed from an objective distance in a gesture intended to expunge any lingering subjective tendencies harboured by the literary originals, which are finally and conclusively adopted, along with their youthful heroes, into the elusive realm of paternal authority.

Notes

1 The role of the unorthodox and subcultural in Soviet war mythology is epitomized in the eponymous hero of Tvardovskii's poem *Vasilii Terkin* who 'ignored Army regulations … dishing out wisdom and shag tobacco'.
2 In *Ballad*, it is the hero's willingness to breach railway regulations to ensure that he travels back from the front with the girl he has fallen in love with which constitutes the struggle with protocol. For a fuller analysis, see Barta and Hutchings (2002).
3 An early review of *Son of the Regiment*, in which, as we shall see, this phenomenon is also important, notes that the film 'was watched with pleasure by adults and children alike' (see Alferov 1946: 4).
4 A reviewer of *Timur* in *Literaturnaia gazeta* describes the cinematic hero as 'unlike the others, serious, adult-like, a romantic leader' (Smirnova 1941: 5)
5 She characterizes Zhenia's father's role in the film as remote and mysterious 'like an icon' (Smirnova 1941: 5).
6 See Kassil' (1940: 4).
7 The film, *Timur's Oath* (*Kliatva Timura*), directed by A. Kuleshov, was released in 1942.
8 The replacement of Suvorov by Stalin is in part connected to the post-war move to 'reinstall Stalin' after his absence from the screen and to 'efface the individual from the public narrative of Soviet life' (Brooks 2000: 205).
9 For more on the orphan theme in Stalinist culture, see Clark (2000a).
10 Susan Buck-Morss refers to 'the infantilization' of Stalinist culture (Buck-Morss 2000). Geller uses the same term, referring also to the 'mixing of age criteria' in socialist realism, and naming *Young Guard* as an example (Geller 2000: 442).
11 Sartori discusses Arnshtam's 1944 film, *Zoia*, which also treats a young martyred partisan whose 'hagiographic qualities of sacrifice ensure her eternal life in the collective memory', and which ends with pseudo-religious images of the sky (Sartori 1995: 183–6).

Part II

Literature and film in the post-Stalin period

The myth in retreat

4 Adapting foreign classics

Kozintsev's Shakespeare

David Gillespie

In 1971, Roger Manvell stated that in the silent period there were some four hundred adaptations of Shakespeare's plays, and since then fewer than fifty, 'some of the most remarkable in Russian and Japanese translations' (Manvell 1971: xv). In more than three decades since, film-makers have been extremely imaginative and creative in making the Bard both attractive and meaningful for a contemporary audience. This has especially been the case in the 1990s, although mention should first be made of Kenneth Branagh's 1989 *Henry V* which eschews the jingoistic nationalism of Laurence Olivier's 1944 version and concentrates on the pain and suffering of war. Branagh made the first ever film version of *Much Ado About Nothing* in 1993, a witty and lively affair with an international cast, and played the part of Iago in Oliver Parker's 1995 *Othello* (which cut up to two-thirds of the original dialogue to make more of a visual spectacle). Baz Luhrmann directed the teenage *angst*-ridden *William Shakespeare's Romeo and Juliet* in 1996, set in modern-day Florida, and Richard Loncraine's *Richard III* of 1995 re-imagined the play in a fascist England in the 1930s. Branagh's four-hour *Hamlet* of 1996, set in the nineteenth century, was the first to use the whole text of the play uncut; Franco Zeffirelli had made a more violent version in 1991, starring Mel Gibson of *Mad Max* and *Lethal Weapon* fame. Michael Hoffman's *William Shakespeare's A Midsummer Night's Dream* of 1999 followed the trend of *Much Ado About Nothing* by casting star Hollywood actors in the main roles. Julie Taymor's blood-soaked and often harrowing *Titus*, released in 2000, showed graphic violence as a clear metaphor for the twentieth century, and in that same year Branagh made *Love's Labour's Lost* (the first film version of that play) as a revival of the 1930s Hollywood musical. Manvell's words of 1971 remain even more apt today: 'The history of the adaptation of Shakespeare's plays for the screen is also the history of the adaptation of the screen to Shakespeare's plays' (Manvell 1971: 9).

Adaptations of literary works for the screen have been popular – both critically and commercially – since the early years of film. There have been many reasons for this, from downright commercial exploitation to high-minded artistic endeavour, and film adaptations can, indeed, bear little resemblance to the source material. Still, a degree of allegiance to the text is required for the purposes of audience recognition, but the film-maker is above all making a film, not simply translating a text on to the screen, and is empowered to take liberties with the text in order to create and give shape to his/her own creative vision, employing 'selective interpretation', in the words of screenwriter DeWitt Bodeen (Bodeen 1963: 349).

Grigorii Kozintsev's last two films are adaptations of Shakespeare for the Soviet screen: *Hamlet*, made in 1964, and *King Lear*, made in 1970 and released the following year. These films can be seen as the culmination of Kozintsev's abiding interest in Shakespeare that spanned decades. He had staged *King Lear* in the Leningrad Large Dramatic Theatre (BDT) in 1941, and *Hamlet* in the Leningrad Pushkin Theatre in late 1953. Kozintsev's production of *Hamlet* coincided with that of Nikolai Okhlopkov in the Moscow Maiakovskii Theatre, the first post-war productions of the play.[1] It seems fair to say that Kozintsev remained enthralled by the Shakespearean themes of social unrest and justice, and his diaries and notebooks are full of quotations and reflections. Kozintsev published a book in 1962 (revised and reprinted in 1966), *Nash sovremennik Vil'iam Shekspir* (*Our Contemporary William Shakespeare*), translated into English and published as *Shakespeare: Time and Conscience* in New York in 1966 and London in 1967. The book contains chapters on *Hamlet*, *King Lear*, and the figure of Falstaff, as well as diary correspondence extracts, and reads more like an academic monograph than a director's vision or interpretation. Throughout, he emphasizes the socio-political dimension of Shakespeare's dramas, namely, the end of the feudal period and the beginning of the Renaissance: 'Shakespeare saw not only the evil of the old order but also the savage essence of the new. He knew that the coin minted by the Renaissance had two sides: on one the faces of Romeo and Hamlet and on the other Iago and Edmund' (Kozintsev 1966: 118).

Shakespeare has been a popular dramatist on the Russian stage for over two centuries. His plays were first seriously discussed in Russian literary circles in the mid-eighteenth century, and they began to be translated into Russian (initially from French and German) at the end of that century and the beginning of the nineteenth.[2] Russian translations from the original English began appearing in the second quarter of the nineteenth century, namely those of Nikolai Polevoi and Andrei Kroneberg, and the latter's translations were still being used a century later by Soviet theatres. Shakespeare's complete works first appeared in Russian translation in 1865–68 (using various translators, and in three volumes that ran to five editions), then again in 1902–04, and in the 1930s and 1950s, where translators included Boris Pasternak and Samuil Marshak.

The success of Shakespeare, and especially *Hamlet*, on the Russian stage is in no small measure due to the writings of the critic Vissarion Belinskii and his championing of the actor Pavel Mochalov's portrayal of the Danish prince in the late 1830s. While being very appreciative of Mochalov's performance (described as 'brilliant' and 'splendid'), the critic was also quick to point out the play's social aspect, the 'main hero' of all Shakespeare's plays: 'This hero is life, or, better, the eternal spirit that manifests itself in the lives of people' (Belinskii 1977: 50). Moreover, Mochalov's Hamlet was 'no weak and uncertain ditherer, but rather a fierce and heroic avenger', 'someone full of vitality and energy', an interpretation that had obvious attractions for Soviet actors and directors a century later (Altschuller 1999: 108).

Two decades later, another influential radical critic, Nikolai Dobroliubov, in his highly influential article 'The Kingdom of Darkness' on the plays of Alexander Ostrovskii, commented on the social aspect of *King Lear* in the personality of the King himself:

> The strength of his character is expressed not only in his curses to his daughters, but also in his recognition of his own guilt before Cordelia, in the regret he shows for his own severe disposition, in his lament that he thought so little about the miserable poor, and that he set so little store by true honour'.
>
> (Dobroliubov, 1962: 52–3)

Soviet interpreters of Shakespeare would develop the socio-political aspects inherent in the tragedies, where death and madness are accompanied by social renewal.[3]

However, a major problem for Soviet critics was to reclaim Shakespeare for 'realism', especially after the furious polemic of Lev Tolstoi, in a famous article written in 1903–04. Tolstoi denied Shakespeare's 'genius', complaining about the 'boredom [and] confusion' brought about by his 'mediocre and bad' plays. Tolstoi's real fire, though, is directed at the sheer lack of 'believability', in particular, of *King Lear*, whose every act he dissects scene by scene, showing the play's lack of realism, its 'unnatural' and 'artificial' plot development, which is full of anachronisms and 'contrivances'. Shakespeare's plays 'not only do not serve as models of dramatic art, but do not even satisfy the primary, universally acknowledged demands of art' (Tolstoi 1950: 236).[4] Because these dramas contain 'the lie' and 'an immoral outlook on life', they are 'evil'.

To counter Tolstoi's rejection, Soviet commentators have consistently emphasized Shakespeare's credentials as a 'realist' writer standing between two epochs, feudalism and the 'revolutionary' Renaissance, a period 'near to our own time, an epoch that sees the culmination of mankind's pre-history and the beginning of history' (Nel's 1960: 45). The task of the Soviet theatre, armed by socialist realism's 'boldness of vision' and the 'truth of understanding given to it by the Marxist–Leninist world-view' is to 'reveal the social and philosophical meaning of Shakespeare's drama in the light of socialist consciousness' (Nel's 1960: 26). In other words, there may be minor inaccuracies of detail or discrepancies, but the essential 'truth' of Shakespeare lies in his depiction of the life of the people and the inexorable movement of history.

To be sure, Shakespeare has been consistently part of the Soviet theatrical repertoire. The tragedies, in particular *Hamlet*, *King Lear*, *Macbeth*, *Othello* and *Romeo and Juliet*, have been particularly popular, but comedies such as *Measure for Measure*, *Love's Labours Lost*, *All's Well That Ends Well*, *Twelfth Night*, *The Taming of the Shrew* and *As You Like It* have also been performed frequently, both in the theatres of Moscow and Leningrad and across the regions and republics of the Soviet Union. Some of the great theatrical actors of their day have lent their talents: the part of Hamlet has been played by Mikhail Chekhov, Evgenii Samoilov and Bruno Freindlikh, and that of Lear by Solomon Mikhoels and Vasilii Sofronov.

After Stalin's death, Shakespeare became relatively de-ideologized, and productions both on the screen and in the theatre became a barometer of the Thaw. Anatoly Smeliansky notes that Peter Brook's *Hamlet* with Paul Scofield as the Prince 'stunned' the Moscow theatre world when it visited in December 1955: 'This was one of those productions that made an indelible impression on all who were to decide the course of Russian theatre for decades to come' (Smeliansky 1999: 7). Brook emphasized Hamlet's cruel moral dilemma, driven by the need for revenge but unwilling to commit a murder as retribution. For Soviet audiences, brought up on the doctrine of 'the ends justifies the means' and unable to understand why Hamlet could not finish off his enemies, this was subversive stuff, soon to be reinforced by Vladimir Vysotskii's guitar-led performances in Iurii Liubimov's Taganka theatre.

The Thaw also saw Shakespeare produced on screen. *Twelfth Night* was directed by Ian Frid in 1955 to great popular and critical acclaim, and Sergei Iutkevich's *Othello*, made the same year and released in 1956, contains a powerful, affecting performance by Sergei Bondarchuk as the Moor. Moreover, Iutkevich's film follows standard Soviet practice in dealing with Shakespeare's tragedies as it highlights the socio-political dimension of the conflict. Thus, the emphasis is on conquest and violence from the outset, with Venetian society shown as beset by bigotry and racism, a feudal way of life based on primitive passions and intrigue, avarice, venality and debauchery. Still, its theme of honour, love and beauty destroyed by an implacable evil had a clear contemporary resonance in the immediate post-Stalin years.

We should recall that Grigorii Kozintsev was one of the giants of early Soviet cinema, directing, together with Leonid Trauberg, classic silents such as *The Adventures of Oktiabrina* (1924), *The Devil's Wheel* (1926), and *New Babylon* (1929). He and Trauberg were also responsible for the ideologically impeccable 'Maksim Trilogy' of 1935–39. Their last film together, *Simple People* (1945), about the reconstruction of an aviation factory in Central Asia during the War, was released only after Stalin's death (possibly because of the film's emphasis not on heroism and achievement, but pain and loss). Kozintsev (without Trauberg) directed two biopics in the late Stalin years. *Pirogov* (1947) is about the nineteenth-century Russian surgeon Nikolai

Pirogov, especially his work as a field doctor during the Crimean War and his use of ether as anaesthetic. *Belinskii* (1953) relates the life of the nineteenth-century Russian literary critic, with due weight given to his radicalism and social conscience. In the post-Stalin era he made three films, all literary adaptations, beginning with *Don Quixote* in 1957. We should not be surprised by Kozinstev's literary interests: back in 1926, together with Trauberg and FEKS, he made a version of Gogol's *The Overcoat* which is still regarded as a classic of Soviet silent cinema.

There are interlocking themes in all of Kozintsev's last three films, and I will begin with a brief discussion of *Don Quixote.* Cervantes's picaresque novel is presented by Kozintsev as a mixture of burlesque and political satire, as the Knight of the Sad Countenance sees himself as the righter of social wrongs, the defender of the weak and oppressed. But he ultimately achieves nothing and his help is spurned by all. His naivety and innocence are seen as a threat by the ruling aristocracy and church, the Duke himself says that Quixote's purity, loyalty and virtuous acts are comical, and his notion of love is a mere figment of a fevered imagination. Sancho's brief reign as Governor brings about a measure of justice based on sheer common sense and decency, but when he is evicted from his temporary grandeur he shows a social and political awareness of his environment. He attacks the aristocratic lackeys as 'parasites', and affirms his own place with the simple, working people.

Cervantes's novel intends to ridicule and satirize the literary conventions of the day. Kozintsev's film is a mixture of realism and comedy, about a deranged old man at the mercy of, and abused by, a venal society that cares only for superficialities, with a cynical disregard for spiritual values or love. Furthermore, Sancho achieves a measure of political consciousness not out of place in the mindset of the socialist realist positive hero who progresses from a state of political innocence to enlightenment. Ideological imperatives are juxtaposed with aesthetic concerns.

It is significant that for both *Hamlet* and *King Lear*, Kozintsev uses the Russian translations of Boris Pasternak, who spent much of the late 1940s and early 1950s working on translations of many of Shakespeare's plays (as well as Goethe's *Faust* and Schiller's *Maria Stuart*), and these renderings are still today considered to be masterpieces of poetic translation. This is all the more important in that the figure of Hamlet looms large in Pasternak's novel *Doctor Zhivago* (1957), and is also the title of one of Pasternak's most famous poems, included in the closing chapter of the novel as the first of Zhivago's compositions (and recited by Vysotskii in his Taganka role). Pasternak's article on translating Shakespeare was first published in 1956, and in it he asserts that Hamlet is a man who is chosen by chance to be 'a judge of his time and a servant of something more remote' (Pasternak 1990: 179). It should also be pointed out that Pasternak translated Shakespeare's seventeenth-century English into twentieth-century colloquial Russian, thus making the language immediately accessible and comprehensible to a modern Russian audience. The use of the contemporary idiom helps Kozintsev to achieve what Peter Brook, in a letter to him, praised in Akira Kurosawa's version of *Macbeth* (*Throne of Blood*, 1957): 'the liberation of the play from the Shakespearean text' (Kozintseva and Butovskii 1998: 325). With such licence, Kozintsev emphasizes not so much the personal act of vengeance as the motif of social justice, with the foregrounded ideological message that 'Denmark is a prison'.

In both his stage and screen productions, Kozintsev takes liberties with the original text, so much so that the play becomes distorted. The scholars Sof'ia Nel's and Alexander Anikst strongly disapproved of Kozintsev's 1953 theatrical version of *Hamlet*, in particular the omission of Fortinbras, who in the original play arrives after Hamlet's death to claim the now vacant Danish throne. In Kozintsev's version he did not figure at all, and the production ended not on the theme of continuity and regeneration, but death. Feudalism continues, and there is no sign that the lives of ordinary people will improve: 'simplified updating leads to anti-historicity' (Nel's 1960: 293). Similarly, the roles of Rosencrantz and Guildenstern were reduced, and Hamlet's final words were not the play's 'The rest is silence', but rather lines from Sonnet 146: 'Shall worms, inheritors of this excess,/Eat up thy charge? Is this thy body's end?' This is undoubtedly bold and innovative, but the ideological message is too thickly spread, even, it would appear, for Soviet critics.

In the film, Kozintsev restores both Fortinbras and Hamlet's childhood friends Rosencrantz and Guildenstern, but makes, nevertheless, some significant changes. Act 1 Scene 1, when the Ghost appears to Francisco, Bernardo, Horatio and Marcellus, is omitted, so that Hamlet (with Horatio) is the only character who does see it. Furthermore, it is Horatio who puts in Hamlet's mind the idea of the Ghost. Many speeches are removed, presumably for reasons of economy, and others (such as the 'To Be or Not To Be' speech) are rendered as internal monologues. Polonius's advice to his son Laertes on how to respect but also be wary of people is cut, and his advice to Ophelia to 'give words or talk with the Lord Hamlet' is cut in such a way that he positively and unreservedly encourages his daughter to get closer to the Prince. Both before and after his words Ophelia engages in a puppet-like dance.

Act I ends within a clear socio-political framework, as Hamlet complains that 'The time is out of joint. O cursed spite,/ That ever I was born to set it right'. The act closes with a shot of Elsinore's huge, forbidding walls ('Denmark is a prison'). Scenes I and II of Act 2 are severely curtailed to stress Hamlet's seeming madness, but Kozintsev also strongly suggests the sheer physicality of the relationship between Claudius, Hamlet's uncle and now ruler, and Gertrude, Hamlet's mother. Polonius talks of knowing 'the very cause of Hamlet's lunacy', but fails to mention the return of the ambassadors from Norway, with their reports of Fortinbras's claims to Danish territory. The Ghost does not make his second appearance in Gertrude's bedroom after Hamlet has killed Polonius, but his presence is suggested as a light reflecting on Hamlet's face. In Act 4, as Fortinbras lands in Denmark to march on Poland, Hamlet's words on 'Two thousand souls and twenty thousand ducats' emphasizes how in feudal (and capitalist) times a man's life is measured in financial terms, and thus the subsequent monologue on 'what is a man?' is omitted. The viewer, therefore, is persuaded that in this society a man is 'a beast, no more!' When Hamlet returns to Denmark from England for the final act, he is with the people, an embodiment of their ambition to do away with the old order, a remorseless agent of their will.

Kozintsev's *Hamlet*, therefore, foregrounds the socio-political conflict, to the detriment of individual conscience and psychology. There is, on the other hand, much that is aesthetically innovative in Kozintsev's film. Hamlet's sea voyage to England, where he arranges for the deaths of Rosencrantz and Guildenstern, is invented to good cinematic effect, and the filming of Elsinore as an oppressive and frightening fortress is impressive. Ophelia in her madness is filmed through the prison-like bars of a wooden staircase, or surrounded by soldiers and their shadows, all the while accompanied by harpsichord music that reminds us of her initial dancing lesson, a marionette used by both her father and the court for political ends.

In cinematic terms the transition from page to screen is enacted in ambitious and vivid ways. The most obvious feature is Ionas Gritsius's stark black-and-white photography, a clear indicator of the themes of good and evil, and particularly the sheer darkness at the heart of Elsinore. Kozintsev's *Hamlet* also impresses with its epic sweep, as much of the film is shot from a ground-level camera, giving both architecture and characters, especially Hamlet himself, heroic stature. Elsinore is situated at the foot of daunting cliffs and battered by crashing waves, with massive portcullises and threatening shadows, all suggesting passions and ominous events about to unfold. Symbolism features prominently from the start: shots of the sea open and close the film, with the stormy waters representing Hamlet's inner agitation as well as the coming political turmoil. The expanse of the sea and birds in flight suggest the freedom beyond Elsinore, and Hamlet's last act is to look upon the sea before he dies. Fires flickering in the castle herald the dangerous political intrigues that are soon to be ignited.

Visually the most striking image is that of the Ghost of Hamlet's father. The Ghost appears on the battlements as a physically huge presence, enveloped by a billowing cloak that seems to reach right out to the sea. This is a world that is doomed, and the film is above all about corruption, betrayal and death. By ideological analogy this is the death of the old, aristocratic ways, the sweeping away of an outmoded order with Hamlet as both a black-attired avenging angel, and the agent of social change. Innocence, in the form of the puppet-like Ophelia, is humbled, ridiculed and ultimately destroyed. Ophelia is a prisoner in both her own family and the court.[5]

But the film, like the play, hinges on the character of Hamlet, who has much of the 'positive hero' about him. He is aware of the baseness of the world ('an unweeded garden') before he learns from the Ghost of the circumstances of his father's death. Subsequently he becomes a resolute man of action, a solemn and focused righter of wrongs. Significantly, therefore, the 'To Be or Not To Be' speech is rendered as Hamlet's internal monologue and is used not to explain vacillation but to justify action. Not for him self-doubt and hesitancy, but rather active resistance to tyranny and evil. Although Hamlet in the end dies, he is identified with social justice, retribution and renewal.[6]

But Hamlet is not an unequivocal character. He may rail at the inconstancy of his mother, marrying Claudius less than two months after the death of her husband and Hamlet's father, but he also uses anyone and anybody to achieve his revenge. In particular, he callously exploits the feelings of Ophelia and just as callously abandons her ('Get thee to a nunnery!'). He is both avenger and victim, secretly being observed and spied upon in an environment strongly reminiscent of Stalin's police state. He does away with a corrupt and decadent order that can be identified with both feudalism and totalitarianism.

Is Hamlet dissembling, or is he, indeed, mad? Certainly, his hysterical laughter resounds through the corridors of Elsinore. It is his erstwhile friend Horatio, the only major character left alive at the end of the play, who instils in his grieving mind the idea of the Ghost, and no one else sees the Ghost apart from Horatio (Horatio's confederates Bernardo and Marcellus do not see it, but are bound to secrecy). Tellingly, the Ghost does not make its second appearance in Gertrude's bedroom, nor does it speak again, as it does in the play; the dead King is depicted only as a locket around Hamlet's neck. Is the Ghost not simply an invention of Hamlet's troubled mind, put there by a scheming Horatio?[7]

It is interesting to compare Kozintsev's film with that of Laurence Olivier, made in 1948, with which Kozintsev was well acquainted, and which he praised. Olivier's Elsinore is also set against crashing waves and storm clouds, and the camera makes good use of the castle's architecture, its hard, forbidding stone walls and steep spiral steps suggesting the oppressive nature of the court. The music is by William Walton, thus giving the film a similar gravitas accorded Kozintsev's version by Shostakovich's score. Significantly, the 'To be or not to be' speech is half spoken, half interior monologue, as Olivier's Hamlet looks down on the stormy sea from the battlements above. The Ghost's second appearance, in Gertrude's bedroom, is fully incorporated, seen and heard by Hamlet but not by his mother. Kozintsev's film, then, adopts some of Olivier's earlier conventions, but otherwise takes issue with it, emphasizing the socio-political dimension of the conflict. Hamlet is an idealist in a corrupt world, a man of conscience 'who does not wish to be reconciled with the baseness surrounding him'.[8]

What is important, therefore, is not the *text*, but the play's *themes*, interpreted within the remit of the Marxist–Leninist vision of historical progress. Both in words and visual images Kozintsev thus 'liberates' the play from the text, giving prominence to an explicitly political interpretation, as endorsed by the Soviet literary scholar Efim Dobin:

> Kozintsev's modern reading of *Hamlet*, and his original and innovative interpretation are dictated by the ideological position of a Soviet artist and thinker, and the breadth of the social and historical vision and high moral precepts which inspired the socialist revolution. Hamlet the fighter against evil, Hamlet the herald of moral purity and freedom through the centuries proffers his hand to millions of people today who yearn to be liberated from the oppression of the moneybag, the power of anti-popular rulers and the yoke of lies and hypocrisy.
>
> (Dobin 1967: 134)

The ideological updating of *King Lear* is even more pronounced. For Pasternak it is a play where the 'concepts of duty and honour are falsely mouthed by criminals', where 'logic and reason are the pharisaical basis to serve their forgeries, cruelties and murders'. The positive characters in the tragedy are 'fools and madmen, vanquished and doomed to perish'. The play and its subject matter are therefore written 'in the language of Old Testament prophets and relate to the legendary times of pre-Christian barbarity' (Pasternak 1990: 191). Kozintsev has little truck with any biblical allegory, but is attracted more by the visual possibilities of a drama of social justice, and of individual tragedy bringing about a new social order. In a letter to Peter Brook, he says 'I am trying to find a visual "Lear", to turn nature into the form of a chorus for the tragedy' (Kozintseva and Butovskii 1998: 327). In notes taken down in the post-Stalin 1950s, Kozintsev dismisses academic claims that Shakespeare is a writer only of *his own* time: 'The ideas of him as a mirror of his own age are naive. All these "feudalisms", "Middle Ages", "the crisis of humanism" and so on are the reflections of *any age*. Including my own. A mirror does not lose its power in the course of these three centuries' (Kozintsev 1994: 68). For Kozintsev the literary scholar, then, Shakespeare is timeless, 'reflecting' the crises and dramas of all ages. But Kozintsev the director shows how Shakespearean themes can be adapted and assimilated into the twentieth century, and into Soviet ideology.

The class-based conflict of *Hamlet* is developed further in *King Lear.* If Kozintsev's Hamlet embodied the ultimately victorious forces of history and progress, here the director's emphasis is on the wronged hero's identification with his people. Kozintsev saw Peter Brook's Royal Shakespeare Company production when it visited the USSR in 1967, and disagreed with Brook's cinematic concept (Brook's film with Paul Scofield appeared at almost the same time as Kozintsev's): 'He [Brook] wanted to film *Lear* in such a way that there would be no signs of history at all on the screen'. Indeed, Kozintsev saw Brook's adaptation as emphasizing the 'senselessness of existence, the absurdity of history'.[9] To Kozintsev, Lear's tragedy is not so much the product of his own individual misery, as the evil caused by unjust social structures, and this insight brings with it social rebirth:

> The human heart cannot contain the misery of all humanity. But it responds, this little lump in the breast, with every shuddering beat to the pain which is the lot of so many people whose existence its master had formerly failed to notice. At this point, man and humanity begin to be experienced as a unity. The experience of the identification of individual sorrow with the sorrow of millions. This is the experience of Lear. He has seen life as it really is. He goes out of his wits and becomes a wise man.[10]

Kozintsev explained his concept of the play back in 1941, as he was producing it for the Leningrad BDT, and his vision remained remarkably consistent over thirty years: 'A social order that has outlived itself and reached its bloody apogee falls apart, together with all manner of human bonds that have arisen in this order' (Kozintsev 1941: 17). So this is a world that is turned upside down, where a fool becomes wise, the king a beggar and a blind man finally sees the truth of the world. It is not at all a sentimental tale of a wronged father, but 'a tragedy of the ruin of a house founded on blood' (ibid.: 19). Lear's world is that of the Middle Ages, where power is gained through conquest and enslavement, and he sees the new world when he stops looking with the eyes of a king, and begins to look with the eyes of a man: 'The theme of *Lear* is the death of a king and the birth of a man. The struggle of "the time" and "nature". The struggle of the dying old world and the emerging new' (ibid.: 23).

Kozintsev's film generally stays a lot closer to the Shakespearean text than does his *Hamlet*, with verbal exchanges and monologues slightly reduced for reasons of economy. In one key scene, however, words are omitted that distort the meaning of the speech overall. In Act III Scene IV, Lear has been banished by his daughters and hides from the storm in the hovel. His words on 'filial ingratitude' are missing from his monologue, and instead he looks down with pity on the 'poor naked wretches' sheltering with him. This is therefore a speech not about an old man's self-pity, and burgeoning self-realization, but the awakening of his social conscience: 'O, I have ta'en/ Too little care of this! Take physic, Pomp;/ Expose thyself to feel what wretches feel'.

Again, the film is shot in black and white (the camerawork is once more by Gritsius), with dark interiors eventually replaced by bright, sunlit expanses suggesting the radiant future. From the earliest shots in the film the masses are portrayed in their silent suffering, victims of internecine strife and then foreign invasion, their miserable lot made even worse by the court intrigues set in motion by Lear's division of his kingdom among his daughters and his rejection of Cordelia. Indeed, it is clear from the outset that the people are destitute because of Lear's misrule. A recurring contrast is that of images of destitute humanity and the arrogance and opulence of the Court. The apocalyptic nature of the imagery in *Hamlet* gives way here to shots of riderless horses, wolves and fighting dogs. This is a world about to be torn apart, with symbols of loyalty and freedom now usurped by greed and ruthlessness. This is symbolically realized as Lear rips apart the map of his kingdom when Cordelia refuses to take part in the ritual servility demanded by her father.

The film's visual symbolism is striking, if a little predictable. Dressed in white and bathed in ethereal light, Cordelia is marked as tragic victim from the early shots, while the Court around her is caught in shadow, officials bedecked in black robes. Fire and smoke dominate the scenes when Lear divides his kingdom, and when he then addresses his people announcing his decision to retire. Storm clouds, lashing rain and wind also help pinpoint the themes of discord, madness, greed and murder. But individual tragedy is here given a clear socio-political dimension: Lear's madness is also that of his age, and his suffering is mirrored in that of his people.

Significantly, Lear's redemption comes less from insight gained through suffering, than through the reassertion of his link with his downtrodden people, firstly in the hovel as he shelters from the storm, and then in the final battle when he and Cordelia are captured. Yet social renewal is brought about not through Lear's gaining of insight and resolution, but through another, similarly wronged character. Edgar is the son of Gloucester and half-brother to the scheming and illegitimate Edmund, who plans to usurp the throne. Edgar is eventually victorious. It is not, however, when he confronts the sight of his tortured and blinded father, wandering alone in a desolate landscape, that he is fired to bring about justice and peace. Instead, it is the even more pitiful sight of the refugee masses fleeing from war which brings about this effect.[11] Edgar it is who gains true social and political insight through suffering, by feigning madness as 'Poor Tom', who overcomes personal loss and grief to right the wrongs of the people.

After the carnage, the Fool (a superb Oleg Dal') is left alone and grieving in a devastated and overturned world. Kozintsev's Fool is not the buffoon or jester in outlandish dress, but rather a Russian Holy Fool (*iurodivyi*), shaven-headed, in rags and chains, whose flute-playing brings down the final curtain on the tragedy. He is an image of 'the most intelligent and most perceptive person', seemingly mad but speaking the fundamental truth of the world, 'the bitter wisdom of the destitute people' (Kozintsev 1941: 28).[12] He is left alive at the end (in the play he is hanged), his sad and lonely music ushering in the new world that is born on the ashes of the old.

In his drive to extract the maximum realistic effect from the play, Kozintsev assaults the eyes with the dirt, rain and mud of this world. The director also does not flinch from showing scenes of harrowing violence, such as the blinding of Gloucester and the agonizing, convulsive death throes of Edmund. Lear's age is a brutal one where brother plots against brother, sister poisons sister, and fathers are betrayed by their children. Only golden-haired Edgar at the end offers hope for a brighter future.

Kozintsev's *King Lear* treats the Shakespearean drama of madness, blindness, betrayal and death as primarily a political conflict, one lauded by Soviet commentators, where Lear's personal family tragedy takes second place to the momentous historical changes occurring: 'The people, its sorrow and humiliation, the injustice of the social order – this is the theme that defines the production of this tragedy on the Soviet stage' (Nel's 1960: 45). The same could be said of Kozintsev's film version.

It should be emphasized that in purely aesthetic terms both *Hamlet* and *King Lear* are visually striking, with the landscape and architecture given epic dimensions and Shostakovich's music heightening the dramatic intensity. The acting, too, is excellent, with both Smoktunovskii as Hamlet and Iarvet as Lear giving the best cinematic performances of their careers. Soviet reviews were ecstatic. The director Sergei Iutkevich approved of *King Lear*'s socio-political stance:

> Kozintsev's film I saw not as the story of the majesty and fall of one king but as a multi-voiced symphony in which the fates of different people are intricately interwoven with the fates of the age, and where history without any contrivance becomes close to modern man.
>
> (Iutkevich 1971: 76–7)

Dmitrii Urnov was also positive, noting the historical theme as dominant, 'the collapse of family ties and the emergence of civil relations' (Urnov 1971: 125). Aleksandr Anikst was the most enthusiastic (rather ironically, given his reservations about Kozintsev's theatrical production of *Hamlet* in 1953), calling *King Lear* 'an outstanding phenomenon of cinematic art' and 'a genuinely artistic piece of work' that 'translates Shakespeare's imagery into the language of the cinema' and is 'profoundly poetic' (Anikst 1971: 4–5).

Both these adaptations assert the primacy of ideology over human drama, and in the post-Soviet age we are inclined to question the legitimacy of an approach that puts classic drama at the service of a ruthless, oppressive, and now discredited, world-view. Given that Kozintsev held consistent views on the modern relevance of Shakespeare from at least the 1940s onwards, are we entitled to judge and condemn aesthetic criteria, even socialist realist ones? Does Kozintsev merely interpret, in the spirit of his age and society, or is he seriously distorting Shakespeare's text for ideological purpose? As I have tried to show in this chapter, he does a little of the former, and a lot of the latter.

Kozintsev brings both a contemporary resonance and idiom to his adaptations of Shakespeare and a clear ideological underpinning. His use of the modern Pasternak translation certainly 'liberates' the play from the text, and enables us to seek out contemporary analogies: for instance, Hamlet's struggle against a recognizably modern totalitarian state. Kozintsev makes of Shakespeare a man for all seasons and all ideologies. We should also bear in mind, however, that Kozintsev's last two films will most likely be remembered by future generations not for an ideological thrust that reflected the twentieth century's political divisions, but for the imagination, wit and exuberance of their visual realization, complete with grand metaphors and symbols, and the faultless acting, from princes to grave-diggers, kings to footmen, jesters to assassins.

Notes

1 In a review of both productions, Aleksandr Anikst hinted at the difficulties the play presented to the Soviet theatre: 'the complexity of interpreting the tragedy is because it is unclear how the ideas of this work can be correlated to our present age' (see Anikst 1955: 62).

2 For further details, see Levin (1988), especially pp. 7–17.

3 An exception here can be made for Mikhail Chekhov's portrayal of Hamlet in the Moscow Art Theatre in the 1920s (until his emigration in 1928) as 'abstract' and 'mystic', a weak man, unable to act and longing for death as the only way out of reality (see Nel's 1960: 58).

4 The job of reclaiming Shakespeare for the 'realist' camp was most ardently carried out by Aleksandr Anikst, who praised the dramatist for the 'popular spirit' (*narodnost'*) in his plays, and their 'truth of life': 'The implausibility of some details takes second place to the certain truth of the real-life situation' (see Anikst 1974, especially pp. 24–34).

5 Shostakovich's musical score actively aids characterization in the scene that introduces Ophelia, as Kozintsev himself comments: 'The short piece (the dancing lesson, Polonius' daughter's first appearance) was to have been played on guitar, then Shostakovich suggested that it should be played on the violin and piano. Then a lute was brought from the museum of musical instruments, for a new tape-recording. And then one began to hear Ophelia's frailty, her artificiality, her tenderness, doomed to perish' (see Kozintsev 1977: 247).

6 In a gushing review, L. Pogozheva noted the 'contemporary' nature of the film in that it was a tragedy 'whose humanistic idea, the idea of freedom of the individual from the fetters of feudalism, are immortal.' See Pogozheva 1965: 71. The film was not so much an adaptation as 'an original creative work based on Shakespeare'.

7 Such an interpretation is reminiscent of the wickedly wry ideological gloss put on the play by the academic Ember in Vladimir Nabokov's *Bend Sinister*, who foregrounds not Horatio, but Fortinbras in the progressive role: 'Consciously or unconsciously, the author of *Hamlet* has created the tragedy of the masses and thus has founded the sovereignty of society over the individual. This, however, does not mean that there is no tangible hero in the play. But he is not Hamlet. The real hero is of course Fortinbras, a blooming young knight, beautiful and sound to the core. With God's sanction, this fine Nordic youth assumes the control of miserable Denmark which had been so criminally misruled by degenerate King Hamlet and the Judeo-Latin Claudius. … [W]ith the closing scene, the idea of mass justice impresses upon the whole play its seal of historical significance' (see Nabokov 1974: 97–8).

8 'O liudiakh, delavshikh "Gamleta" ', in Kozintsev 1982–6, II (1983): 495. In his published diary extracts, Kozintsev notes that 'Olivier cut out what is of most interest to me, the theme of statehood. I won't concede a single brush-stroke from this line' (see Kozintsev 1966: 286). At a discussion of the screenplay for his own film on 19 June 1962, Kozintsev noted that 'In Laurence Olivier's *Hamlet*, magnificent in its own way, I see the tragedy of a son, his mother and her lover,

the rest does not interest him'. See 'Rezhisserskaia ekspozitsiia fil'ma "Gamlet" ', in Kozintsev 1982–6, II (1983): 491.

9 'Prostranstvo tragedii', in Kozintsev 1982–6, IV (1984): 30, 32.

10 G. Kozintsev, 'King Lear', in Samarin and Nikoliukin (1966): 233.

11 The awakening of Edgar's social conscience through the sight of his destitute and oppressed people is very similar to the radical resolution of another character in an earlier film by Kozintsev, Vissarion Belinskii. In *Belinskii*, his film of 1951 (the title role was played by Sergei Kurilov), Kozintsev shows the nineteenth-century literary critic fired to revolutionary thoughts above all when he witnesses the peasant masses oppressed and beaten, but defiantly fighting against a tyrannical autocracy.

12 In a letter to Innokentii Smoktunovskii Kozintsev wrote that 'for Shakespeare always – in every play – being mad means obtaining the privilege to speak the truth, the ugly, cruel truth of people in power and of the baseness of careerists and flatterers' (see Kozintsev 1966: 308).

5 The sound of silence

From Grossman's Berdichev to Askol'dov's *Commissar*

Graham H. Roberts

Vassilii Grossman was born in 1905 in Berdichev in Ukraine, home of one of the largest Jewish communities in Eastern Europe (and the place where Balzac became engaged during his sojourn in southern Russia, as famously mentioned by Chebutykin in Chekhov's play *The Three Sisters*). He is best known in the West as the author of *Life and Fate* (*Zhizn' i sud'ba*), a monumental work of twentieth-century realist fiction structured as a family saga around the battle of Stalingrad. This novel was, of course, banned in the USSR for several years. It is generally held that this was because it suggested that the Bolsheviks had as poor a human rights record as the Nazis. Indeed, Grossman's harassment at the hands of the KGB is usually cited as an example of precisely what lengths the KGB were prepared to go to – when they raided his flat they took not just the novel's manuscript, but even the typewriter ribbon. (This is an anecdote cited on countless occasions over the years both by liberal Western academics discoursing on the Soviet regime's repression of free-thinking artists, and, since it was eventually published despite the KGB's best efforts, by those who subscribe to the Romantic Russian view that 'manuscripts don't burn'.)

There was little in Grossman's previous career, however, that presaged such a brush with the authorities. Discovered by Gor'kii in the 1930s, prior to *Life and Fate* he published two novels (*Gluchkauf* and *Stepan Kolchagin*), alongside several volumes of short stories, mostly on the Civil War and the lives of workers. 'In the Town of Berdichev' ('*V gorode Berdicheve*'), which was written in 1934, comes from this period. As Robert Chandler puts it, describing Grossman's earlier, pre-war output in his translator's preface to *Life and Fate*, 'despite an occasional vivid detail or slightly risky piece of philosophizing, these works are typical of the official Soviet literature of the time' (Chandler 1985: 7).

At first glance, it would appear that quite the opposite could be said about *Commissar* (*Kommissar*), Aleksandr Askol'dov's 1967 film based on Grossman's story. It was in no sense typical of official Soviet cinema of the 1960s since it was banned by the Party and not even released until 1987 (it shared an identical fate with Kira Muratova's debut full-length feature, *Brief Encounters* (*Korotkie vstrechi*, 1967)).[1] In terms of its narrative logic and structure, it clearly does not conform to the tenets of Soviet Socialist Realism in the way that 'In the Town of Berdichev' does. However, to suggest that this was the main reason for its banning would be to miss the point that by the mid-1960s no one knew what SSR was (if they ever had). Certainly by anybody's standards it would be difficult to argue that many of the films that *were* released in the mid- to late '60s, such as Gaidai's wonderful *Caucasian Captive* (*Kavazskaia plennitsa*, 1964) or Shepitko's *Wings* (*Kryl'ia*, 1966) held to the tenets of SSR, however defined. What can be said with greater certainty, however, is that a film-maker prepared to give Schnitke such a free hand in the composition of the soundtrack, and to use the kind of unconventional film and narrative techniques usually associated with the likes of Eisenstein and Dovzhenko – such as asynchronous sound and image, extradiegetic sequences, and dreamlike, surrealist imagery – was courting trouble. In fact, the official reasons for the Party's displeasure were, in order of significance, the positive representation of the Jewish community in the year (1967) that Israel was engaged in a six-day war with the Soviet-backed Arabs, and, conversely, the negative representation of the Bolsheviks and their Revolution.

Whether or not these charges were justified, the fact is that Grossman's story was considered politically correct from the point of view of official Soviet ideology of the time, while Askol'dov's film was regarded as politically very *in*correct in the very different domestic and international political climate of the mid-1960s.[2] So far, so simple. However, as Pierre Macherey and others have shown, any text (whether cinematic or literary) has 'silences', which may legitimately be exposed by reading 'against the grain' (Macherey 1978). So do Grossman's short story and Askol'dov's film contain such silences? And if they do, can these texts be read in such a way that these silences may be articulated? If they can, what might this tell us about the way we in the West read the texts – cinematic, literary or whatever – that constituted official and unofficial Soviet culture? And what might it reveal about that culture's relationship to the Soviet censorship machine? The purpose of the present chapter is to answer these questions.

Before we examine the ideological tensions that might characterize each of these works, let us pause briefly to consider the structure of each. From the narrative point of view, what they have in common is the pregnancy of Vavilova, a Red Commissar during the Civil War of 1918–21, her billeting at the house of a Jewish tinker and his family in the town of Berdichev, the birth of her son, and her subsequent return to the front. There are numerous differences, however, both in terms of the narrative elements themselves, and as concerns the weighting and perspective of each. As we might expect, Askol'dov's film represents an extension and elaboration of Grossman's story. 'In the town of Berdichev' contains fourteen distinct scenes, while *Commissar* contains twenty-three. Askol'dov's film contains more flashbacks than Grossman's story (the only one which Grossman presents, right at the end, is unconvincing). It also features extradiegetic elements, such as a kind of flash forward, in which Vavilova follows the tinker and his family as they enter what looks like a concentration camp, only to stop on the threshold, her new-born in her arms.

If we look more closely at the contents of Grossman's story, rather than its structure, it appears to contain many features which mark it as politically orthodox, ideologically closer to Dmitrii Furmanov's *Chapaev* (1923) than Isaak Babel"s *Red Cavalry* (*Konarmiia*, 1928). For one thing, the plot is far sparser and more compact in Grossman's story, which begins *in medias res* with Vavilova's announcement of her pregnant state to Kozyrev, her commanding officer. The focus is on the birth itself, and then, almost as an afterthought, her ideological dilemma, the tragic conflict between the love she feels for her newborn, and her duty towards the Revolution. These are the two poles that eventually mark the limits of her moral universe. As always in tragedy, whether Racinian or Bolshevik, the protagonist's sense of moral and civic duty gets the better of his or her romantic yearnings. Of course, we are not meant to see this victory, and the self-sacrifice and ultimate death through martyrdom which it implicitly entails, as a tragedy, but as another brick in the wall of the bright new future just over the horizon. This has to be presented as a happy ending, because there can be no room for an explicitly tragic ending, not in the year Gor'kii and Zhdanov (1934) were waxing lyrical about Soviet Socialist Realism at the First Writer's Congress. Indeed, the tone here is valedictory, grandiose, triumphal, heroic:

> And suddenly she remembered a vast square in Moscow. Several thousand workers who had volunteered for military service and were bound for the front had crowded round a hastily erected wooden platform. A bald man was delivering a speech to them, and waving his cap in the air. Vavilova stood close to him. She was so excited that she could only make out half of the words spoken by the man in his clear, slightly guttural voice. The people next to her listened, breathing heavily as they did so. An old man in a padded jacket was crying for some reason. She had no idea what had happened to her in that square, in Moscow. One night she had wanted to tell her silent lover about it. She thought he would understand. But the words wouldn't come. And as they walked from Theatre Square to Brianskii Station they sang the very same song.
> (Grossman 1958: 102)[3]

Vavilova's decision to return to the front is as sudden as it is unexpected, and with Lenin's (we assume it is he) Red Square speech and the crowd's song ringing in our ears, we are no more invited to grieve for Vavilova than we are for Chapaev, whose death at the end of the Vassil'ev 'brothers" film also heralds the radiant future. Indeed, our abiding memory of Grossman's heroine is of a woman infused with revolutionary ardour, just at the moment when the story appears to be petering out to a whimper. In one stroke of the pen, Grossman, it would appear, reimposes the public over the private, and the ultimate victory of ideology over morality (contrast this with the more recent efforts of Kieślowski and Kundera to reassert the supremacy of the private over the public, in such works as the film *The Double Life of Veronique* (1991) and the novel *The Joke* (1967)). Indeed, Grossman deliberately depersonalizes and de-individualizes Vavilova in the final scene, referring to her simply as 'a woman in a fur cap and greatcoat' ('*zhenshchina v papakhe i shineli*') (102). As the Jewish tinker so colourfully expresses it, when he watches this woman go towards the front and to a martyr's end: 'There go the real people, Beila. And we, are we people? We're just shit' ('*Eto nastoiashchie liudi, Beila. A my razve liudi? My navoz*') (103). How can we possibly censure this courageous woman, how can we possibly think that she has made the wrong choice, either morally or ideologically?

But is all as it seems here? Quite clearly it is not. For one thing, it is rather difficult to square this image of an active, public woman who abandons her baby (albeit for the noblest of causes), and the Party's revisionist, pro-family policy towards women as it emerged in the mid-1930s. In this sense, Vavilova belongs to a different era from the one in which 'Berdichev' was written – either the 1920s (cf. the 'proto-feminist' 1927 movie *Bed and Sofa* (*Tret'ia Meshchan'skaia*)) or the 1940s (when the Party once again favoured strong, active female characters in the face of the Nazi threat – for example, Ermler's 1941 classic *She Defends the Motherland* (*Ona zashchishchaet rodinu*)). What is especially interesting here is the way in which Grossman sharply contrasts Vavilova's death wish with the fatalistic maternalism of the Jewish woman Beila. It is the latter who is much closer to the Party's ideal woman, especially at a time when women were being encouraged not to go and get themselves killed, but instead to stay at home and have as many children as possible to ensure over-fulfilment of the Five Year Plan. Her priorities are indicated clearly in the closing scene of the story, when, in response to Vavilova's heroic departure and Magazinik's lament, she simply remarks that there are more urgent, pressing matters to attend to: 'Listen, the children are awake. Go and light the stove, we need to heat up some milk' ('*Slyshish, dite prosnulos'. Razvedi luchshe primus, nado nagret' moloko*') (103). The problem, however, is that by portraying two radically divergent modes of positive femininity, one public, one private, Grossman is trying to have his cake and eat it. Not surprisingly, this is not possible, and it is the Jewish mother Beila who emerges as the more positive character – by virtue of the fact that we hear her *after* we see Vavilova leave for the front – rather than her Bolshevik counterpart.

But Grossman has prepared us for this moral victory (and indeed, the victory of the moral over the ideological) from the outset. For from beginning to end this story mocks the Communists' ignorance of what really matters in life, and implies that they behave unnaturally. Kozyrev asks Vavilova about the birth 'as if talking about something shameful' ('*tochno govoria o stydnom*') (88), for example, and puts down on his report as the reason for her billeting 'po bolezni' ('by reason of illness'), writing and then crossing out the qualification 'for a woman's problem' (*'po zhenskoi'*) (89). At one and the same time, then, Grossman invites us to recoil at the Party's abnormal attitude towards that most natural of phenomena – childbirth – and also towards the thing that makes childbirth possible – sexual difference. Kozyrev's refusal to recognize gender difference is portrayed as part of his – and the Party's – misogyny (hence his attempt at mockery in the opening line).

Indeed, Vavilova, who is also an official representative of the Party (and one specifically responsible for propagating its vision of the world), is herself guilty of this 'sex crime', for she attempts to subjugate (sublimate?) her true identity for the sake of ideology. She tries at first to deny her femininity, threatening the doctor whom she asks for an abortion with a revolver, an archetypical phallic symbol. Grossman in fact emphasizes her feminine, maternal nature, by having her cry just after giving birth, and having the mid-wife observe to Beila that 'mine always weep after the birth' (*'oni u menia posle rodov vsegda plachut'*) (97). He is more convincing in this respect than Askol'dov, whose burly heroine attempts to rediscover a lost sense of femininity by wandering around the city ruins carrying her baby in her arms and dressed in a summer frock and headscarf (a sequence which is entirely Askol'dov's creation).[4] It is possible to read this story, then, as a tale about the need to obey one's true identity, one's real nature – 'nature gets its way' (*'priroda svoe beret'*), as the Party cadre ironically puts it on hearing of Vavilova's pregnancy (89).

Ultimately, however, Kozyrev and the Party which stands behind him do not understand this simple truth. For they do not understand the world – what Grossman calls 'the complex world' (*'slozhnyi mir'*) (93). This is why, when they come to visit Vavilova to see how her pregnancy is proceeding they are confronted with something completely beyond their comprehension, and all they can say is 'indeed' (*'deistvitel'no'*), which they mouth inanely and repeatedly (98). The point is also made succinctly and convincingly by Beila that the Bolsheviks' work – giving birth to a new society by means of violent revolution and bloody war – is nothing as compared to women's work – giving birth to children: ' "You think", she said, "that giving birth is as easy as going to war; one, two, three and it's out. Well I'm sorry, it's not that simple" ' (*'Rozhat' detei – skazala ona – vy dumaete, chto eto prosto, kak voina: pif-paf i gotovo, nu net, izvinite, eto ne tak prosto'*) (93), an observation to which Vavilova has no answer.

So the Party not only has an unnatural attitude towards life, it also fails to understand life in all its complexity. In this and many other respects the Party is starkly contrasted with the local Jewish community (to which Grossman of course belonged), which represents authentic, great, sacred time in contrast to the secular Communists. At one moment a blind beggar intones a prayer, 'as ancient as the Jewish nation' (*'drevniuiu, kak evreiskii narod, molitvu'*) (91). At another moment, Grossman refers to the town's Jewish market – 'bubbling with life' (*'utrom bazar kipel, kak vsegda'*) (100).

As this last quotation suggests, not only does the Jewish community represent great time, it also represents life itself, in contrast to the Communists who bring only death (Vavilova of course brings a life into the world but in order to be a true Communist, she has to abandon that life, and become once again an agent of death). This is clear from the fact that the Magaziniks have so many children, in contrast to Vavilova, for whom even one child is at one time too many (at the beginning of the story she tries to provoke a miscarriage). The vitality of the Magaziniks is underlined by Grossman in the description of their home, where 'the air was so thick with the smells of a place where people live ... Paraffin, garlic, sweat, goose dripping, unwashed linen' (*'tak gusto dokhnulo zhilem ... Kerosinom, chesnokom, potom, gusinym smal'tsem, nemytym bel'em'*) (90). It is also emphasized during the birth scene, which is interspersed with references to the local Jewish community (in contrast to the film, where this scene contains dreamlike images of war and barrenness). Unlike the Party and its foot soldiers, Jews such as Magazinik understand perfectly well the difference between men and women. As he puts it to his wife, who has commented that Vavilova is 'just like a good Jewish mother': 'Do you think ... that if a woman wears leather trousers it makes her a man?' (*'Chto ty dumaesh', ... esli zhenshchina odevaet kozhanye shtany, ona ot etogo stanovitsia muzhchinoi?'*) (97).

This comment is typical of the ways in which the story dramatizes the moral victory of the private, individual sphere over the public, collective. As if to underline this, the laughter (*smekh*) of the story's opening lines ('what are you laughing at?'; *'chego smeesh'sia'* (88)) turns to fear (*strakh*) towards the end – a narrative logic which is hardly that of Soviet Socialist Realism. The sudden attempt to defuse the atmosphere of foreboding, by reference to the stirring speech the 'bald man' (Lenin) gives in Moscow, fails to convince (101–2). This is partly because the story has nothing to say about the bright future, mentioning only the future of the war. The reference to Lenin's speech represents a golden opportunity for Grossman to look forward to such a future, but crucially he fails (refuses?) to take it, since he does not even attempt to quote Lenin's words. Lenin (if indeed it is he) is silenced both by Grossman, and by Vavilova herself, who, as we have seen, tries to tell her lover what Lenin said, but is unable to do so ('nothing came out of her mouth'; *'u nee nichego ne vyshlo'* (102)). The Party and its worldview is decentred, marginalized and ultimately silenced by Grossman in favour of other, 'centrifugal' discourses in what is a deceptively subversive piece of writing.

So Grossman's story is far more politically incorrect, more subversively heteroglot than we might assume. What of Askol'dov's film? The director may well have thought he was on safe ground with a story, and a writer, so indisputably part of the official Soviet literary canon. Or he may have had an exceptional ear for the text's multiple ideological 'silences'. Either way, *Commissar* was his first and last full-length feature film. Indeed, it is easy to see why the film might have displeased the authorities (even if we discount, as we must, the view prevalent in the West that anything of artistic merit which emerged from the USSR must by definition be anti-Soviet).

For one thing, Askol'dov's Vavilova, who stands metonymically for the Revolution itself, is initially a very negative character. This comes across quite clearly in a lengthy opening sequence which is not to be found in the original story, and which culminates in Vavilova mouthing revolutionary platitudes as she condemns a defenceless deserter to death. Her cruelty is emphasized by the way that she is more concerned about the fate of the deserter's horse than about the life of the deserter himself. Her complete lack of compassion is compounded by her rank hypocrisy; it is ironic that she accuses the deserter, who is guilty of the 'heinous' crime of going home to see his wife, of betraying the Revolution for the sake of a woman's bed, when she herself is shortly to withdraw from the fighting in order to give birth. Had the Soviet public been allowed to watch the film, they may also have found Vavilova's justification for executing the deserter – her faith in the 'bright future' ('*svetlee budushchee*') – richly ironic, given the political repression and economic stagnation that was to become such a feature of the Brezhnev era (Attwood 1993). Moreover, the fact that Kozyrev's laughing face suddenly and unexpectedly fills the screen immediately after the execution scene creates the impression that he and the entire Party is rejoicing at the deserter's death, rather than expressing amusement at Vavilova's predicament. The implication here is that all the bloodletting produced by the Revolution was futile, and therefore morally unjustifiable. Furthermore, the way the Magaziniks' children mimic the adults' war games and anti-Semitic cruelty, and the way they line up naked as the canons trundle past (none of which was in the original story) suggests that all the Revolution and Civil War succeeded in doing was engendering further cycles of violence (this would not have been lost on Party censors, precisely thanks to Khrushchev's de-Stalinization campaign and the subsequent wave of rehabilitations).

Unlike Grossman's story, Askol'dov's film contains no reference to Lenin making a rousing speech to volunteers in Moscow. The Party does lead the troops into battle in the final scene (Askol'dov's camera lingers over the Bolshevik flag), but this is ironic, since the young cadets are marching slowly but surely to their death, without any allusion to ultimate victory. As for the troops themselves, there is visually nothing to distinguish the Whites from the Reds, and the Jewish tinker himself claims that when it comes to terrorising the local populace, they are just as bad as each other (a charge also found – but explicitly refuted – in *Chapaev*).

The treatment of the Revolution was the second official reason for the film's banning. The first such reason was the positive representation of the Jewish community which, even if relatively toned down in comparison to

Grossman's story, spelt political suicide in 1967, when the USSR was officially supporting the Arabs over the Six Day War with Israel. The film foregrounds the Magaziniks' Jewishness more explicitly than the story (Rolan Bykov, who plays the Jewish tinker, was a very popular Soviet Jewish actor at the time). By itself this might not have been an issue. However, Askol'dov underlines far more explicitly than Grossman the ethnic tension between Jews and Russians. If the film stops short of actually accusing the Russians of persecuting the Jews, it is nevertheless significant that Vavilova is a passive, detached observer in the holocaust scene, watching the Jewish family as they enter the concentration camp, but doing nothing to help them.

Thematically and formally, then, Askol'dov's film is no *Chapaev*! But does that mean it is fundamentally anti-Bolshevik? It is perfectly possible to read the film in another way, one which emphasizes just how orthodox it in fact is (just as there are many ways in which *Chapaev* is politically *un*orthodox, as Marc Ferro has shown: Ferro 1976). Of course, no text is ever completely submissive or subversive. What is interesting to note, however, is that in many respects Askol'dov's film constitutes *less* of a challenge to the prevailing Party line than Grossman's story. One could argue, for example, that Vavilova (despite the association with Babylon that her name conjures up) is a far more positive character in the film than in the story. In the final analysis she is much more prone to self-doubt, and realizes that it is her fate to put ideology before biology, something which she does with both courage and conviction. She is portrayed in Askol'dov's film as so incongruous a mother, so unnaturally feminine (the choice of the physically imposing Nonna Mordiukova to play the part is significant) that we are invited to approve of her decision to give her child to her Jewish host to look after.

Also worthy of note here is that fact that Askol'dov chooses to call the Jewish woman Maria, rather than Beila. He also suggests, as Attwood and others have observed, that Vavilova's child is in some (miraculous, mystical) way the Magaziniks' own (Attwood 1993: 91–2). Immediately after the birth Maria tells her husband 'we've had a boy', and he replies 'I knew it' – an exchange conspicuous by its absence in Grossman's story. This could be meant as a contrast between the false religion of Bolshevism and the true (Judaeo-Christian) path to enlightenment. However, the allusion to the holy family could also be interpreted as a justification of the suffering caused by the Revolution, since it draws an analogy between Christ's Revolution which eventually brought a better world, and the legacy of the Bolsheviks (shades of Blok's poem 'The Twelve' here). The most important thing, it would appear, is to make the 'leap in faith', as Vavilova herself almost literally shows by abandoning her baby and returning to battle at the end, despite the impossible odds. Read in this way, *Commissar* constitutes a rallying cry to the troops at a time when they are beginning to lose the faith (the first half of the 1960s), in the wake of Stalin's Terror, Khrushchev's secret speech and Brezhnev's return to repression. If Vavilova can undergo a Pauline conversion from a bad, violent, vindictive, anarchic, spontaneous (*'stikhiinyi'*) Communist to a good, self-conscious, life-giving one, then so can the Party as a whole. Viewed in this light, she embodies not just Marx's and Lenin's spontaneous proletarian mass, but also the Soviet Communist Party itself, and the Party's (putative) transformation from a bloodthirsty terrorist outfit to a force for good in the world. The Bolshevik cadets certainly undergo such a change over the course of Askol'dov's film, which they begin by cowardly sacrificing an innocent individual, and end by heroically and altruistically sacrificing their collective selves.

But what of the scene (also absent from the story) where the shot from the young scout's rifle echoes menacingly around the town's various places of worship, which might be interpreted as a clear evidence of the destructiveness of Bolshevism? Well, it should be remembered that this scene, too, comes at the beginning of the film. Moreover, the young, excited scout who fires his rifle is hardly presented as the embodiment of an evil, destructive force. True, the scene is accompanied by some rather eerie music by Schnitke, supplemented by some dizzying camera work. But might that not serve to reflect the boy's trepidation as he enters an apparently deserted town all alone? At the very least there is a fundamental ambiguity about this entire sequence.

However, Askol'dov is not really very interested in the Revolution, or the Bolshevik Party that gave birth to it. Neither does he dwell very much on the fate of Berdichev itself, unlike Grossman. Originating from a different place (although he shares Grossman's Jewishness), and working in a different time, his interest inevitably lies elsewhere. His lack of interest in the Party explains why he silences so many of the dissenting voices which he tantalisingly gives us glimpses of. Just as Grossman omits Lenin's stirring speech, so Askol'dov prevents us from hearing practically any voice which might cause us to question the righteousness of the Bolshevik cause – either the deserter, or the broader Jewish community in Berdichev, or the priest who comes across Vavilova as she walks her baby through the town, or indeed the ironically dissenting narrative voice of Grossman's original story. Indeed Kozyrev, Vavilova's superior in the Red Army, has less to say than in Grossman's story, and therefore is not provided with so many chances to come across as an idiot. (Even *Chapaev*, the archetypical Soviet Socialist Realist civil war film, gives the Whites some kind of voice – literally as well as metaphorically.)

The question is, then, if Askol'dov silences opposition in this film, what is he really interested in? His focus is, I would suggest, the emotional conflict between two archetypical images of femininity, the mother and the whore (Askol'dov emphasizes Vavilova's nature as whore by showing us her liaison with the father of her baby, something which Grossman omits altogether). In suggesting that the Jewish mother is by far the happier of the two, and by associating her with Mary, the 'mother of all mothers', whose statue we glimpse in the film's opening shot, Askol'dov is perfectly in tune with the

Party's gender politics of the time and subsequently. The Party line was predicated upon an intrinsic association between femininity and maternity, which meant that womanhood and motherhood were seen as one and the same thing.

It is surely here, and not in the treatment of the Bolsheviks or their legacy, that this film's main focus lies. And it is very possibly this that made the film so unpalatable for the censors. For what the tension between Vavilova and Maria does is articulate a truth first found in Grossman's (apparently orthodox) story, namely that the scientific laws of Marxist–Leninist economics notwithstanding, life is complicated. Being good and being happy – as Vavilova learns to her cost – may be mutually exclusive. Askol'dov's film dramatizes that existential dilemma so terribly articulated by Jean-Paul Sartre and others that in an attempt to give our life meaning, we may end up having no life to speak of at all (either figuratively or literally).

In conclusion, this chapter has attempted to highlight some of the silences in Grossman's story, on the one hand, and Askol'dov's film, on the other. It is perhaps easier to argue convincingly for Grossman as a subversive writer than it is to defend the image of Askol'dov as a political conformist. Indeed, we would maintain that the question of Askol'dov's views on the Bolsheviks is in many respects a 'red' herring. For him, Grossman's story was an apparently safe vehicle to explore existential issues of personal freedom and identity. The problem for Askol'dov was that while Khrushchev's thaw implied that these issues could be de-politicized (as they were, for example, in Kalotozov's 1957 classic, *The Cranes are Flying* (*Letiat zhuravli*)), in Brezhnev's USSR they very definitely could not be.[5]

The problem for *us*, of course, is that by attempting to challenge received wisdom on these texts, we may well have raised as many questions as we have answered. Just why was Grossman's story accepted for publication in a decade when even writing for children did not guarantee an author immunity from arrest and imprisonment (Zabolotsky 1994)? Conversely, why was Askol'dov's film banned for so long? With Grossman, it may have been the allusion to Lenin and his ability to inspire even young mothers to ignore their maternal feelings for the sake of the Revolution that pleased the censor(s). In the case of Askol'dov, the film's opening sequence, with the silent deserter brutally executed may have been enough to convince the authorities of the director's political incorrectness. On the other hand, it may just be that Soviet cultural policy was far more arbitrary and contradictory than Western academics have hitherto supposed (Caute 2003).

Of course, to ask these questions is in a sense to miss the point, since the very distinction between dissident and non-dissident art will depend on the context of their reception, as well as that of their production. The real lesson from our attempt to read these texts politically is, I would argue, that we need to stop reading Soviet cultural products as political texts, and look at other ways of approaching them. This is because children, rather like the

Magaziniks' sadistic offspring in Askol'dov's film, always end up saying things that their progenitors would rather they didn't. *'Priroda svoe beret'*. Ultimately this is a truth that Grossman and Askol'dov both had to learn the hard way.

Notes

1 Aleksandr Askol'dov was born in 1937 in Moscow. He studied directing and screenplay writing between 1964 and 1965, and made *Commissar*, his first and only full-length film, between 1966 and 1967. Between 1976 and 1985 he directed musical theatre. With the exception of two documentaries for television, *Commissar* was his last film.

2 The film's rehabilitation and release in 1987 was hailed as a triumph for Gorbachev and a sign that his liberalising reforms were genuine, on a par with the publication of Pasternak's *Doctor Zhivago* and Zamyatin's *We*.

3 All references are from this edition. The author would like to thank Mr Martin Dewhirst for making this text available to him.

4 It should be noted that there is a certain ambiguity surrounding Askol'dov's representation of Vavilova in this scene, created by the tension between the visible awkwardness with which she assumes her new role, and the obvious tenderness with which she contemplates her child. This ambiguity is heightened by the fact that the actress who plays Vavilova, Nonna Mordiukova, was already known by this time for her portrayal of a number of more conventionally feminine characters.

5 On Kalatozov's film, see Woll (2000: 73–9).

6 Film adaptations of Aksenov

The Young Prose and the cinema of the Thaw

Julian Graffy

The period in Russian twentieth-century history known as the Thaw is primarily remembered – as the metaphor indicates – as one of political and cultural relaxation.[1] On closer inspection it turns out to be a time of contradiction. Within its short span there were several occasions, most notably at the time of the Cuban missile crisis of October–November 1962, when the Soviet government seemed to be lurching away from liberalization. As always in the Soviet period, political developments were reflected in the arts, and, specifically, in Russian cinema. Thus the cinema of the Thaw is a cinema of contradiction, a phenomenon that can be examined in microcosm in two films made that year from early novels by the writer Vasilii Aksenov, Aleksei Sakharov's *Colleagues* (*Kollegi*) and Aleksandr Zarkhi's *My Younger Brother* (*Moi mladshii brat*). Though they were made in the same year, at the same studio, Mosfilm, and released within months of each other, they take very different approaches to the treatment of conventional themes of the Thaw period.[2] A comparison of the differences between the two novels, between the two films, and between the novels and the films may shed some light on the contradictory evolution of the Thaw, a period of course characterized by dramatic changes, but also by continuities which have hitherto attracted less attention.

Thaw cinema was, like the other arts in these years, motivated by a desire to reject the so-called 'lacquering' (*lakirovka*) of reality of the late Stalin period and to re-establish the greater 'truthfulness' of the immediately post-revolutionary years. This led, particularly in the early Thaw years, to the making of a number of cinematic adaptations of works of early Soviet literature, including Alov and Naumov's *Pavel Korchagin* (1956, a version of Nikolai Ostrovskii's novel *How the Steel was Tempered* (*Kak zakalialas' stal'*)), Chukhrai's *The Forty First* (*Sorok pervyi*, 1956, taken from a story by Boris Lavrenev that had already been filmed by Iakov Protazanov in 1926), Gerasimov's *Quiet Flows the Don* (*Tikhii Don*, 1957–58, from Mikhail Sholokhov's epic novel) and Kalik and Rytsarev's *The Youth of Our Fathers* (*Iunost' nashikh ottsov*, 1958, based on Aleksandr Fadeev's story 'The Rout' ('Razgrom')).[3] Gradually, though, filmmakers also turned their attention to the new Thaw generation of poets and prose writers. Perhaps the most celebrated example of this phenomenon is the inclusion of a poetry reading at the Moscow Polytechnical Institute by Evgenii Evtushenko, Boris Slutskii, Robert Rozhdestvenskii, Bella Akhmadulina and Bulat Okudzhava in Marlen Khutsiev's film *The Il'ich Gate* (*Zastava Il'icha*), finally released in truncated form as *I Am Twenty* (*Mne dvadtsat' let*) in January 1965, but already attacked by Nikita Khrushchev in a speech of 8 March 1963 for failing to 'personify our wonderful youth'.[4]

Vasilii Aksenov sprang to prominence with his first novel, *Colleagues* (*Kollegi*), written in 1959 and published in June–July 1960 in the new journal *Iunost'* (*Youth*), which had itself been set up in 1955 as an outlet for young writers. His second novel, *A Starry Ticket* (*Zvezdnyi bilet*),[5] was written in 1961 and appeared in the same journal in June–July 1961. He became closely associated with the 'Young Prose' movement and joined the board of *Iunost'* in November 1962. But he would come under attack in one of the periodic campaigns against young artists in early 1963, and would be forced to publish a recantation of his 'excessive' attitudes and behaviour in *Pravda* on 3 April of that year.[6]

Colleagues is set in the symbolic year of 1956, the year of Khrushchev's famous 'Secret speech' attacking Stalin's excesses. It tells the story of three 24-year-old doctors, Aleksandr (Sasha) Zelenin, Aleksei (Alesha) Maksimov and Vladislav (Vlad'ka) Karpov, completing their studies in Leningrad, and embarking upon their first jobs. It shows the hopes and disappointments, the trials and the triumphs of their early careers, and also traces their difficult love affairs, that of Sasha with a young Moscow student, Inna, and, in a more indirect way, that of Alesha and Vlad'ka with Vera Veselina, the wife of a research student. *A Starry Ticket*, on the other hand, is both written and set in 1961, and is the tale of 17-year-old school-leavers, who have not yet begun to work and are resistant to the very notion of study. It too tells the story of a trio of friends, the central figure Dima Denisov and his class mates Alik and Iurka, all of them to a greater or lesser degree in love with their school friend Galia. The four embark upon a trip west, to Tallinn, and their adventures are contrasted with the tribulations of Dima's elder brother Viktor, born almost a decade before Dima, and the 'older brother' of the film's title, who relates much of the story. Viktor is a research scientist who has begun to doubt the validity of his own research, and who wonders whether he should settle down and marry his girlfriend Shurochka. Thus both within *A Starry Ticket* and through the contrasts between the two novels, Aksenov draws readers' attention to the very different experiences, attitudes and desires of two Thaw generations, one born before the Second World War and marked both by the War and late Stalinism, the other having conscious experience of neither.

It is perhaps unsurprising that films drawn from two texts which, though superficially familiar, in fact tell very different stories in very different tones should themselves turn out to be different in their moods. This difference is even encapsulated in the different ways in which the titles of the stories were treated by the makers of the film versions. *Colleagues* the novel becomes *Colleagues* the film. In the novel, the word, redolent of the Soviet stress on worker solidarity, is also a section heading in the penultimate chapter. In the film it takes on even greater significance, since it is the very last word of the film, spoken to camera by Aleksei Maksimov after he and Vlad'ka have saved Zelenin's life by operating on him in remote Kruglogor'e. The words *A Starry Ticket*, which refer to a patch of sky Viktor Denisov watches from the window of the family's Moscow flat, are almost the very last spoken in that novel, articulated by the hero Dima. They suggest both a continuity with his now dead brother and the beginnings of an understanding of Viktor's complex character and fate. But these words were not destined to remain the film's title, and were replaced by the phrase *My Younger Brother* (*Moi mladshii brat*). This title is ambiguous. On the one hand, it heralds a far greater role for Dima than the one he plays in the novel, and signals that the film will be a conventional story of the new Thaw generation, but, on the other hand, it draws attention to the role of Viktor as narrator of the younger generation's fate. Yet Zarkhi's film greatly underplays the role of Viktor, leaving viewers bemused by a title which draws attention to an aspect of the novel the film director has eschewed.

It is interesting to speculate as to why the fates of the titles of the two novels should be so different, and useful to turn to the testimony of Aksenov himself. In the half-page introduction to Volume 1 of a 1990s collection of his writings, Aksenov reminds his readers that, though the novels were written consecutively and published in consecutive years in the same journal, there is actually a huge gap in their political moods. If *Colleagues* is, in his words, a 'completely conformist piece' ('vpolne konformistskaia veshch'), then *A Starry Ticket* is 'not completely conformist' ('ne vpolne konformistskaia'), and 'between these "completely" and "not completely" the distance is greater than between "not completely" and "completely not" ' (Aksenov 1994: 5). Thus the contrast between the works provides some indication of Aksenov's own maturation as a writer and the increasing complexity of his vision. He also reports, in an interview broadcast on the main Russian television station before a showing of the film in the mid-1990s, that it was censorship that forced the filmmakers to change the title of the second film, and that this amounted to a downgrading of the 'cosmic' questions raised in the story.[7] These elements are associated specifically with Viktor, the experimental scientist elder brother, and the film also downgrades his role and that of his science. *Colleagues* was considerably more successful at the Soviet box office, attracting 35 million viewers in its initial release, making it the second biggest box-office hit of 1963. It is also much more orthodox and conventional, particularly in its attitude to the Communist Party and its rhetoric, and in its treatment of the key contemporary theme of science. In the first work Sasha Zelenin, a man of science, almost dies, but is saved by the efforts of his friends; in the second, Viktor Denisov, a man of science and Zelenin's contemporary, does die, in a mysterious research accident.

An initial assessment, therefore, would suggest that the more conventional earlier story, more conventionally filmed, was the greater success; the other film, taken from the less conventional later story, encountered difficulties, harsh criticism and less success at the box office. Yet on closer inspection of what links and what distinguishes the two films, our reading of the situation must become more complex and contradictory.

Both stories have a central male trio (and a girl for love interest) and both films transfer this structure to the screen, thus placing themselves in a strong tradition of Soviet films about a trio of male or female friends, going back to such classics as Kozintsev and Trauberg's *The Youth of Maksim* (*Iunost' Maksima*, 1934). The tradition was flourishing in the early 1960s, finding expression in such works as *The Il'ich Gate*, Daneliia's *I Walk Around Moscow* (*Ia shagaiu po Moskve*, 1963) and Kalik's retrospectively set *Goodbye, Boys* (*Do svidaniia, mal'chiki*, 1964).[8] Josephine Woll has drawn attention to the model, describing the protagonists as 'one idealist, one "cynic" and a cypher' (Woll 2000: 155), and the formula applies here, though more crudely in both the novel and the film version of the earlier *Colleagues*.[9]

The three doctor heroes of the novel *Colleagues* are 24, having all been born in 1932. They joined the Komsomol in 1947, and, in the novel's present, they are just graduating as doctors, in Leningrad, in the momentous year of 1956. Aksenov himself was born in 1932, lived in Leningrad from 1950 and graduated from the Pavlov Medical Institute in 1956. He was assigned to work first in the quarantine service in Leningrad, and then in a hospital on Lake Onega, in the Russian north.[10] These facts of his biography are shared among the characters in the novel, in which Alesha Maksimov and Vlad'ka Karpov work in the quarantine service of the Leningrad port while hoping to get jobs as ships' doctors, whereas Sasha Zelenin, the central figure, takes up a post as a village doctor in the northern village of Kruglogor'e, near Lake Onega.

The novel is imbued with the spirit of 1956, combining the questionings of post-War youth with a very strong remaining belief in the values of 'true' Communism and the need to return to it. While Aleksei distrusts 'lofty words' ('vysokie slovesa'), which he also refers to punningly as 'talkology' ('trepologiia'), Sasha, the central hero, remains the embodiment of these values. Indeed Sasha, with his 'going to the people', his desire to serve the simple inhabitants of a north Russian village as a doctor, conforms to the conventional type of Russian intellectual ready to serve the people, a point emphasized by references both to zemstvo doctors and to Chekhovian texts. Another traditional concern of Soviet society and of its artists reflected in the novel is the cult of sport. Sasha is a volley ball player, and sport is shown to promote health, to develop a capacity for teamwork – and to offer the chance of an encounter with a beautiful young woman.

Figure 6.1: The trio of friends in *Colleagues* before Sasha departs for Kruglogor'e. From the left: Vlad'ka Karpov (Oleg Anofriev), Sasha Zelenin (Vasilii Livanov), Alesha Maksimov (Vasilii Lanovoi)

Source: From the personal collection of Julian Graffy

Figure 6.2: Alesha and Vlad'ka (third and fourth from the left) arrive for work in the quarantine service of the Leningrad port.

Source: From the personal collection of Julian Graffy

The habitual importance Soviet art ascribed to building, and to construction, is displayed in the stress on the construction work being carried out near Kruglogor'e at Stekliannyi mys. Sasha sees bulldozers and new roads, and learns of plans to merge the village and the construction site into a new town. This is just one of the ways in which the continuities of the Thaw with the late Stalin period are made apparent.[11]

The new mood of frankness which the Thaw had ushered in is apparent in the novel's admission of the existence of (petty) crime in Soviet society (a theme it shares with such landmark Thaw films as Iosif Kheifits's *The Rumiantsev Affair* (*Delo Rumiantseva*, 1955), and of the system of forced labour camps. A petty official in the Leningrad port, Iarchuk, is involved in theft and the bribery of a Komsomol doctor, Stolbov (but is resisted and exposed by Maksimov), while the hoodlum Fedor Bugrov and other inhabitants of Kruglogor'e are revealed to have spent time in the camps. Aksenov's mother, Evgeniia Ginzburg, had served for many years in labour camps and he had spent the years 1948–50 with her in Magadan (Ginzburg 1981: 259–80). The camp theme came absolutely into the spotlight a month before the release of the film version of *Colleagues* with the publication in the November 1962 issue of the journal *Novyi mir* of Aleksandr Solzhenitsyn's story 'One Day in the Life of Ivan Denisovich' (*'Odin den' Ivana Denisovicha'*). The changing mood of the time is also alluded to by the novel's raising of the problem of the generation conflict (something whose presence in Soviet society Khrushchev explicitly rejected).[12] The young men are interested in jazz, in clothes,[13] and in the new dances, and at the start of the novel they clash with the invalid war veteran Sergei Egorov, who is in Leningrad on a visit. Nevertheless, it is typical of the novel's relative timidity that in due course Sasha comes to regret his mocking treatment of the elderly village medical orderly Makar Ivanych, and that by its end the very same Egorov has turned into a conventional Soviet paternal mentor figure both for Sasha and for his friends.

One of the least successful aspects of *Colleagues* is Aksenov's treatment of the love stories. None of the women, not Inna, the beautiful Moscow student and talented pianist who becomes Sasha's wife, not the northern beauty, the *komsomolka* nurse, Dasha, not mixed-up Vera Veselina, admired by Alesha and Vlad'ka and married to a conventional postgraduate student, is drawn in sufficient detail, and their relationships with the heroes are thin and scarcely credible. This, too, is a feature common to the art of the period and it has been suggested that Aksenov had written a more truthful version of the sexual relationships which did not get past the censors.

Aleksei Sakharov, the director of the film version of *Colleagues*, was born in 1934, two years after Aksenov, and was one of a new generation of Thaw directors. His film version of Aksenov's story combines overall fidelity with significant elisions. He preserves the novel's sententiousness, its idealistic speeches, its sense of duty and faithfulness to Communist ideals. He underlines Sasha's Chekhovian heritage by hanging a portrait of the writer on the wall of the 'doctor's flat' in Kruglogor'e. He keeps the trio at the centre of the film, making some attempt to develop the 'cypher' figure Vlad'ka. He keeps the sport, the cult of Soviet construction and the criminality in the Leningrad port. But he makes no allusion to the existence of a criminal gang in Kruglogor'e, totally removing references to the camps, and excising the figure of Ibragim Enaleev, who in the novel plays the role of the criminal who reforms.[14] Thus Fedor Bugrov is reduced to a simple village thug, jealous of Sasha because of the attention he pays to the nurse, Dasha, whom Fedor himself intends to marry.

The unsatisfactory love interest is further attenuated in the film. The figure of Vera Veselina is entirely removed, and Sasha does not marry Inna, who becomes an even more marginal and unbelievable figure. On the other hand, the role of the nurse, Dasha, is developed, to the extent that she becomes a real, if undeclared, rival for Inna. The outcome of these changes is to produce a very conventional Soviet film, which stresses the positive values of work and acceptance into the community, and idealizes male friendship in a way that is reminiscent of the films of the 1930s, such as Ivan Pyr'ev's 1939 musical *Tractor Drivers* (*Traktoristy*), which opens with a scene of a train journey shared by a carefully contrasted trio of demobbed soldiers. Visually, too, the film is conventional, though two sequences, one in which Sasha dances for joy upon receiving a telegram from Inna, and another in which he is knifed by Fedor Bugrov, seem explicitly based upon similar sequences in Aleksandr Dovzhenko's *Earth* (*Zemlia*, 1930), one of the most visually ambitious of early Soviet films. Here, perhaps, is a continuity of a different kind.[15]

The film ends with his friends saving the hero's life and declaring themselves to be his 'colleagues'. This final sequence, in which the ideologically exemplary hero is brought near to death but saved in the nick of time by the love and skill of his comrades, exemplifies the fascinating continuities of Soviet cinema. The motif of the hero brought to his bed of pain by illness or accident had been used in a number of Thaw films. In Fridrikh Ermler's *An Unfinished Story* (*Neokonchennaia povest'*, 1955), the worker hero, played by the charismatic Sergei Bondarchuk, is bed-ridden and despairing after illness, but at the end of the film takes his first steps without crutches, encouraged by the love of his female doctor. There is a similar sequence in Aleksandr Zarkhi's *Height* (*Vysota*, 1957), in which the construction worker hero falls from the top of the blast furnace he is building but is nursed back to health by the love of a female colleague and even manages to make his way, leaning on his crutch, to the ceremonial site opening. Particularly fascinating comparisons can be made with Sergei Paradzhanov's film *A Flower in the Stone* (*Tsvetok na kamne*, 1962). In this film, too, the worker hero, Grigorii Griva, a brigade commander at the Komsomol'skaia mine, is beaten up by hoodlums who are opposed to the values of hard work, discipline and solidarity he has come to represent. The film opens and closes with Griva on his hospital bed and consists of a long flashback recording how he got there. Coincidentally it was released exactly a week before *Colleagues*, on 11 December 1962. But the motif of the fallen hero reduced to his bed is also a recurring trope of late Stalinist cinema.[16]

The text which best shows the continuity of the motif in the Stalin and post-Stalin periods is, of course, Nikolai Ostrovskii's autobiographical novel *How the Steel Was Tempered*, set in the immediate post-Revolutionary period, written in 1932–34, and filmed, as *Pavel Korchagin*, in 1956, by the young directors Aleksandr Alov and Vladimir Naumov. Korchagin (who, in a further continuity, is played by Vasilii Lanovoi, the actor who in *Colleagues* plays the part of Aleksei Maksimov, the doctor required to perform the life-saving operation at the end of the film), is perhaps the most extreme example of the hero brought to his bed by illness or injury and yet not destroyed by what he has to endure. After suffering a back injury during the Civil War, and a later attack of typhus, he is eventually laid low by paralysis and becomes blind. From his bed he writes his stirring memoirs, and even when the only copy of the manuscript is lost in the post he finds the strength, sustained by his belief in the Party and his mother's love, to begin the seemingly impossible task of writing them again from the beginning. Thus the treatment of Sasha Zelenin in *Colleagues* places him in a gallery of tenacious Soviet heroes who suffer grievously in the course of their ideologically directed activity. While the recurrence of serious injury in works set during wartime is understandable, the continual recourse to this motif in films set much later is a fascinating and ambiguous phenomenon. It seems that these men must be physically and emotionally punished for their own heroism, suggesting the presence of a deep-seated masochism in Soviet culture and in the psychology of the Soviet artist.[17]

But the film's foregrounding of work, comradeship, maturation and sacrifice clearly struck a chord with Soviet critics. Their praise of the film was conventionally cast in terms of the human warmth of its characters and plot. The *Pravda* reviewer found the film to be 'imbued with a profound love of our young people' and the heroes themselves to be attractive in their pureness of heart (Lukin 1962). In the same vein the critic for the newspaper *Komsomol'skaia pravda* thought that the heroes were 'genuine fellows' (Rubanova 1963) and the writer in *Moskovskaia kinonedelia* detected that behind their irony and wit they were concealing 'very serious reflections about life' (Chernenko 1962). One of the most extensive critical engagements with the film, a review by V. Frolov in the leading cinema journal, *Iskusstvo kino*, is notable for its concentration on moral values. It suggests that the film shows how cinema can 'answer the fundamental questions of life' and proves that young people do still possess 'civic feeling' ('*grazhdanskii pafos*'). Frolov also exaggerates the degree to which the protagonists already know their path in life (Frolov 1963: 97, 98). All of these qualities found success with viewers, and its trio of young leading actors would go on to have important cinematic careers. Most notably Vasilii Livanov, who plays the central figure of Sasha Zelenin, would gain phenomenal popularity as Sherlock Holmes in a series of hugely successful television adaptations of Conan Doyle's stories made in the 1980s by Igor' Maslennikov. *Colleagues* is traditional, melodramatic and heart-warming, and its success at the box office was assured.

A Starry Ticket is also a novel about three young men and a girl, but it has an alternative centre of intellectual and existential gravity in the story of the central hero Dima Denisov's elder brother Viktor, a research scientist. Its trio of young men are 17 in 1961 and were born in 1944. If the trio in *Colleagues* were born before the Second World War and started their college education under Stalin, *A Starry Ticket* represents a crucial generation shift, embodying the first Soviet generation not to have conscious experience of the war. The mutterings in *Colleagues* about the flatulence of lofty Party rhetoric are set against a background of unquestioning commitment to study, gaining a qualification and the worth of their service as doctors. Here, neither higher education nor work is even aspired to; what the protagonists want is relaxation and travel, and they want it now, not later. Significantly, too, they travel west, not east, to Tallinn, the capital of the (then) Soviet Republic of Estonia, which they call 'our little Europe' (*'nasha malen'kaia Evropa'*), thus neatly reversing the recurrent Soviet motif of the journey east, into the heart of the country, in order to make a contribution to the epic endeavour of Soviet construction.[18] Dima and his friends are unequivocally open to Western influence, and in this they are prototypical bearers of the spirit of the young people of the Thaw who experienced a vertiginous cocktail of new Western influences in the Khrushchev years.[19] They consistently call Galia, an aspiring actress, Brigitte Bardot, and refer to *La Dolce Vita*, to Ionesco and Camus, Beckett and Sartre, to Existentialism, Neo-Realism and Rock Music. Their lexis is peppered with English words.

This sense of newness is also carried through the references at the beginning and end of the novel to the destruction of the Moscow apartment house, the 'Barcelona', in which Dima and his brother have lived all their lives. The Khrushchev years were characterized by a frenzy of new construction, particularly of enormous, uniform apartment blocks, and the destruction of old Muscovite buildings. Their replacement, viewed without qualm as a sign of Soviet modernity, is a recurrent motif in films made around this time, including Andrei Tarkovskii's diploma film at the State Film Institute *The Steamroller and the Violin* (*Katok i skripka*, 1960) and *I Walk Around Moscow*, in which the young friends boast of Moscow's reconstruction to a Japanese tourist. But for all the heroes' rebelliousness, the novel ends with the beginning of their reintegration into Soviet society. In this respect it remains a typical Soviet story of maturation, of reclamation through labour (the young people work on a Baltic fishing collective farm)[20] and the wise influence of older mentors, of an increasingly sober attitude to love (each of the trio settles down with a girl) and even, by the end, of a readiness to embark upon a university education.

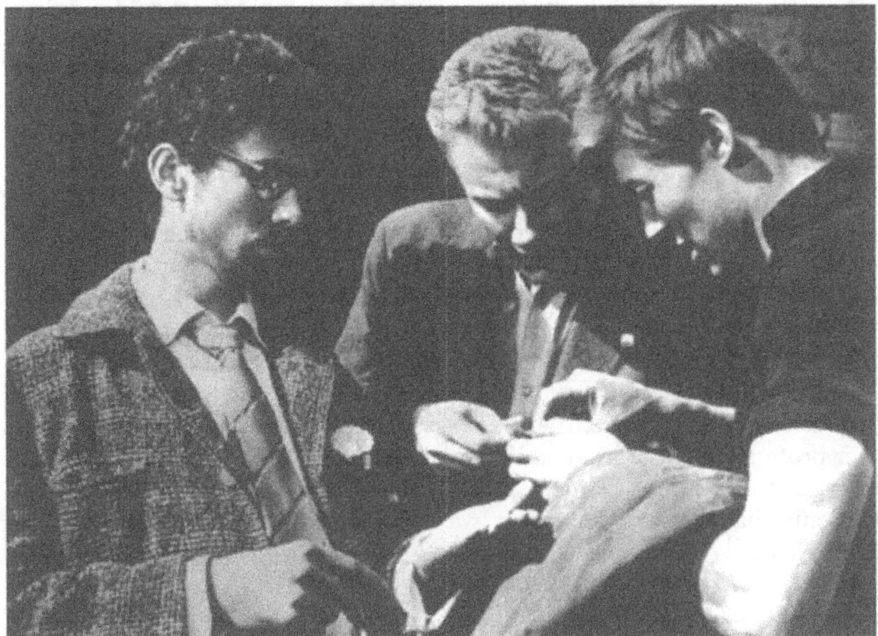

Figure 6.3: The trio of friends in *My Younger Brother* in Tallinn. From the left: Alik (Oleg Dal'), Iurka (Andrei Mironov), Dima (Aleksandr Zbruev)

Source: From the personal collection of Julian Graffy

Figure 6.4: Dima and Iurka in the fishing collective farm

Source: From the personal collection of Julian Graffy

Nevertheless, an equally important, and considerably more subtly drawn figure in the novel, his role underlined by the fact that the 'starry ticket' is his term for the area of sky he watches from the window of the family's flat, is Viktor, the research scientist elder brother. We are told that he is 28, which means that he was born in 1933, making him almost the same age as the doctor heroes of *Colleagues*. Crucial to the novel's ambiguous tone is the fact that Viktor is beset by doubts about the validity of his almost completed dissertation. The novel thus raises the troubling question of scientific research as a battleground between truth-seeking and careerism. Viktor is ready to abandon his dissertation since a paper he has recently written seems to negate its conclusions, and he is also prepared to engage in risky new experiments. His accidental death while carrying out this work at the end of the novel is shrouded in mystery. Though the trio of *Colleagues* were also men of science, they were never moved to doubt the validity of their profession. But a more ambiguous treatment of Soviet science and the experience of Soviet scientists, ready to acknowledge the dangers and the accidents that marked their lives, was also emerging in the fiction of the Thaw years.[21] The subject was addressed in other films of the period, notably in Mikhail Romm's *Nine Days of One Year* (*Deviat' dnei odnogo goda*, 1961, released in March 1962), in which the hero, Gusev, a researcher at a nuclear physics institute, embarks upon a series of pioneering but dangerous experiments. Though he gets a lethal dose of radiation, and he knows that he is doomed, he continues his work, and makes a major scientific discovery.

Thus *A Starry Ticket* differs from *Colleagues* both in the characters of its young heroes and in its treatment of Soviet science. Its complex, experimental narration also marks a considerable advance on the earlier novel. *A Starry Ticket* is told both by Dima and by Viktor, both in the first and the third person, with narrated thoughts and occasional uncertainty about the narrative voice. In this respect, above all, it can be seen as a transitional work for Aksenov.

The director chosen to film *A Starry Ticket*, a novel about uppity youth, was the veteran (born 1908) Aleksandr Zarkhi, who had first come to prominence with the ideologically driven films he co-directed in the 1930s with Iosif Kheifits – *Baltic Deputy* (*Deputat Baltiki*, 1936) and *Member of the Government* (*Chlen pravitel'stva*, 1939). This unlikely alliance is only superficially paradoxical – the use of an ideologically reliable veteran would calm the authorities' fears about the treatment of a 'difficult' subject, and in his Thaw films *Height* (1957) and *People on the Bridge* (*Liudi na mostu*, 1959) Zarkhi had shown that he could combine a relatively fresh treatment of the intimate lives of young people with a conventional Soviet construction film. According to a recent interview with the actor Aleksandr Zbruev, who played the title role in the film, there was a major battle to get this innovatory work filmed at all, and he confirms that the choice of the veteran director was itself a compromise aimed at getting the film passed. In

Zbruev's words, 'I do not think that he could have made the film as sharp as Aksenov's story, many things have simply been smoothed out in the film. But the very fact that he got it through was quite something for the time' (Kriukova 1998).

Nevertheless, what Zarkhi produced led to widespread dissatisfaction. Though V. Popov repeated the cliché a colleague had written about *Colleagues*, that the film was made by people 'who sincerely love our young people and look at them though the kindly eyes of friends' (Popov 1962), more perspicacious critics found less cause for satisfaction. V. Sokolov insisted that Dima Denisov's tense and complex inner life had not been treated sufficiently seriously (Sokolov 1962). The most acute reservations are expressed by Vera Shitova in her review in *Iskusstvo kino*. Calling the film an 'imitation' rather than a 'screen version' (*'ne ekranizatsiia, a imitatsiia'*), Shitova insists that it utterly fails to capture the spirit of the novel, rendering the complex straightforward, calling it an 'uncle's film' (*'diadin fil'm'*), which, exuding an 'unyouthful good-naturedness' (*'nemolodaia dobrodushnost''*) renders these difficult young people safe. It makes the heroine Galia more glamorous and interesting than she is in the book, reduces the mutually influential relationship of the two brothers to one of benign fraternal advice from the elder, Viktor, and surrounds the young trio with a plethora of kindly and wise mentor figures. The heroes are profoundly changed, becoming 'more malleable, softer, more naive, more pleasant'. She accuses Zarkhi of a desire to 'smooth everything out', and finds him guilty of 'timidity in the face of complexity. A tendency to explain the unfamiliar through the familiar' (Shitova 1962: 65–7).

These are serious charges, and they are born out by Aksenov himself in his 1990s television interview. Speaking from thirty years' distance, he is able to look on the whole episode with a good deal of nostalgia, but he does contend that his novel had, however tentatively, registered the presence in the Soviet Union of a protest generation, a generation that was unconsciously resisting Soviet norms. The Central Committee of the Komsomol had sensed this, telling the filmmakers that 'if the film turns out to be like the book, we shall be against it'. Zarkhi, defending the film against such a potential fate, had, in Aksenov's words, made a film that 'isn't quite what I wanted to say in the novel'. He also noted that young people, who had embraced the work when it appeared in the summer of 1961 in the journal *Iunost'*, felt that 'their' novel had been betrayed. When the film had its premiere at the Moscow University Humanities Faculty Club on Mokhovaia Street, students, desperate to see the film, which had been delayed and already subjected to critical attack, were shocked at the 'outrage committed against our novel' (*'nadrugatel'stvo nad nashim romanom'*).[22]

Though there is enough youthful irresponsibility left in the film to infuriate the arch-conservative critics of *Nash sovremennik*, who are provoked into a heavily sarcastic diatribe about the trio's alleged 'tiredness' and a hymn of praise to their more high-minded 'elder brothers' in *Colleagues*

(Zalesskii and Kuznetsova 1963: 183–6), it is certainly true that the young characters of *A Starry Ticket* have been tamed in Zarkhi's film. Their rebellion is never threatening, always measured and reasonable, and the film turns it into a natural stage in the maturation of three charming and sincere young men. The contagion of generation conflict, which was so important to Aksenov, and which Soviet society was so anxious about catching from the West, is stifled in the embrace of a series of understanding adults. The thematic elaboration of the young people's concerns is also expressed through the traditional Thaw themes of sport (ball games on the beach), an encounter with small-scale crime (they resist the invitation to pilfer from the Estonian furniture warehouse in which they briefly find work) and reclamation through labour. The ending of the film combines the episode with which the novel ended, of Dima thinking of his dead brother Viktor and his 'starry ticket', and realizing that he is finally mature enough to take up his proffered moral baton, with an invented scene reuniting the four friends in the half-destroyed Barcelona on a summer Moscow evening.

But perhaps the most profound way in which the film negates what the novel was attempting to say is in the treatment of the older brother Viktor. Zarkhi's film marginalizes him and his concerns, failing to engage with his ethical doubts or to investigate his character and the motivation of his death. The character of his fiancée, Shurochka, is removed and, with her, his uncertainty about whether to marry. His role in the film is reduced to four sequences, two of them at work, which raise but do not develop his scholarly crisis, and two in which he gives concerned and conventional advice to his younger brother. His dangerous cosmic searching is consistently downgraded, which is reflected in the change of title. Viktor is as underwritten as Inna in the film of *Colleagues*, but he is a far more crucial figure in the original and his elision is concomitantly more disabling.

The complex narrative of the novel is also considerably simplified, substantially reducing the film to a straightforward narration of the adventures of the three young men and a girl. Yet here lies another paradox. By his timorous reductionism Zarkhi has, almost by accident, made a prototype for the considerably more ambitious and probing 'youth' films of the next few years such as *The Il'ich Gate*, *I Walk Around Moscow* and the historically set *Goodbye, Boys*.

So two films, made the same year from works by the same writer, hint at the paradoxes of Thaw cinema, as expressed both through the aspirations of its filmmakers and through the preferences of its audiences. *Colleagues*, the more conventional story, makes a more conventional film, more formally achieved as melodrama. Directed by a neophyte director, it paradoxically supports positive, Soviet 'Thaw' values by looking backwards in order to reclaim and reinterpret Soviet models of plot and character. It makes its audience feel safe and uplifted, and consequently it is a huge box office hit. *My Younger Brother*, made the same year, is taken from a less conventional story narrated in a less conventional way, which makes it far less easy to transfer to the screen. An awareness of its greater subversive charge leads to its being handed over to a 'reliable' veteran, who out of an unconscious sense that the work needs protection turns it into a lame 'imitation' of its true self. Yet though the second film is less successful, both artistically and commercially, its very compromises hint at the increasing ideological and generational complexities of Soviet society. In its wary engagement with its young protagonists, it suggests the emergence of a new Soviet generation, and of a new cinematic theme (the 'youth film'). The trio of young actors who emerged in this film, Aleksandr Zbruev, Oleg Dal' and Andrei Mironov, would all go on to become major stars, beloved by Soviet cinema audiences, but perhaps none of them would ever again play a character with such symbolic significance for a generation and for the evolution of a cinema.[23] A comparison of the two novels shows Vasilii Aksenov to be a young writer in rapid evolution, and a comparison of the two films shows 1962 to be a cusp year for Soviet cinema, enriched by its contradictions, proving that the Khrushchev period had more than one 'young generation' and half opening the door on the confused decade to come.

Notes

1 The term 'Thaw' has been used to designate periods of varying length. In its narrowest usage it refers to the time of political and cultural relaxation following on the death of Stalin in March 1953, symbolically expressed by the publication of Il'ia Erenburg's eponymous story in the journal *Znamia* in May 1954, and reaching a high point in Nikita Khrushchev's so called 'Secret Speech', partially denouncing Stalin, delivered on the last day of the Twentieth Congress of the Soviet Communist Party, 25 February 1956. Other scholars have used the term in a broader sense, to cover the entire Khrushchev period, 1956–1964. In this article I shall use the term to cover the period in Soviet cinema from 1954 to 1967, as demarcated by Josephine Woll in her influential study of the cinema of the period (Woll 2000).

2 According to the main annotated catalogue of Soviet films, *Colleagues* was released on 18 December 1962, and *My Younger Brother* on 20 August 1963 (Piotrovskii and Glagoleva 1968: 477–8 and 489–90). There is nevertheless much evidence to suggest that *My Younger Brother* must have been released in the late summer of 1962. The reviews listed by Piotrovskii and Glagoleva (ibid.: 490) are all from the autumn of 1962. The authoritative *Iskusstvo kino* review appeared in the November 1962 issue. And the assessment in *Nash sovremennik* states definitively that *My Younger Brother* appeared before *Colleagues* (Zalesskii and Kuznetsova 1963: 183).

3 That this backward glance was still in operation at the end of the Thaw period is evidenced by Mikhail Shveitser and Sof'ia Milkina's film *Time, Forward!* (*Vremia, vpered!*), taken from Valentin Kataev's novel, and not completed until after Khrushchev had been removed from power, in 1965.

4 For Khrushchev's March 1963 attack on the film see 'Khrushchev speaks again', Johnson and Labedz (ed.) 1965: 153–5. For the original Russian text, see Khrushchev 1963 and Fomin 1998: 131–2.

5 I use here the title of the English translation of the novel by Alec Brown, published in London in 1962. The novel also appeared in New York in 1963 as *A Ticket to the Stars*, in a translation by Andrew MacAndrew.

6 For the text of Aksenov's recantation, see Johnson and Labedz 1965: 206–9.

7 Information taken from an interview with Aksenov shown before a screening of *My Younger Brother* on Channel One of Russian television in the mid-1990s. Copy of the film held in the Library of The School of Slavonic and East European Studies, University College London, Call number V-393.

8 The model was reapplied with enormous popular success in the Brezhnev years in Vladimir Men'shov's Oscar-winning tale of the lives of three young women, *Moscow Doesn't Believe in Tears* (*Moskva slezam ne verit*, 1979), and continues to be an effective vehicle to this day in films such as Aleksandr Surin's *Flowers from the Victors* (*Tsvety ot pobeditelei*, 1999) and Roman Kachanov's *Demobbed* (*DMB*, 2000).

9 Aksenov asserted in an interview given in emigration in December 1980, days before he would be deprived of his Soviet citizenship by an order of Leonid Brezhnev, that he had engaged in self-censorship and placed next to the 'image of the rebel Maksimov, who rejected Stalinism ... the image of the idealistic little fool Zelenin' (Aksenov 1981: 434). Though the element of self-censorship, present in all Soviet writers, was of course of fundamental importance, the perception from twenty years after the writing of the novel that he had found Zelenin to be 'an idealistic little fool' is at odds with the fact that Zelenin is clearly the central character in the novel and his conventionality and earnestness are treated with affection and sympathy. An assessment based upon the evolution of Aksenov's own attitudes, both to the society he lived in and to his own possibilities as a writer, an evolution from 'completely conformist' writing to 'not completely conformist' and beyond, seems more persuasive.

10 These details of Aksenov's biography are taken from the 'Interview with V.P. Aksënov Washington, D.C., December 1982', an interview given to Inger Lauridsen and Per Dalgård (Mozejko (ed.) 1986: 14–25).

11 Compare, for example, the transformation of the Kuban' village of Ust'-Nevinskaia in Semen Babaevskii's 1947–48 novel *The Chevalier of the Golden Star* (*Kavaler Zolotoi zvezdy*), which in 1950 was made by Iulii Raizman into a film which came to be seen as the epitome of the 'lacquering' of reality by Stalinist art.

12 In his March 1963 speech, with specific reference to *The Il'ich Gate*, Khrushchev insisted: 'In Soviet socialist society there are no contradictions between generations. There is no 'father-and-son' problem in its old sense. It has been invented by the makers of the film and artificially inflated with not the best of intentions.' Johnson and Labedz (1965: 155).

13 On Aksenov's own interest in fashionable clothes as a young man and his reputation as a '*stiliaga*', see his memoir (Aksenov 1995).

14 There is one significant change to this generally sanitizing activity. The forester who suffers a serious accident, and whom Sasha and Dasha save after a perilous helicopter flight in Chapter 7 of the novel, dies in the film.

15 *Colleagues* of course differs from *Earth* in that Dovzhenko's hero does not survive the attack. Sakharov studied at the State Film School (VGIK) in the studio of another classic Soviet director, Sergei Iutkevich.

16 Among the Stalin period films in which this theme is present are *Fighter Bombers* (*Istrebiteli*, 1939, directed by Eduard Pentslin); *Mashenka* (*Mashen*'ka, 1942, directed by Iulii Raizman); *Wait For Me* (*Zhdi menia*, 1943, directed by Aleksandr Stolper and Boris Ivanov); and *The Celestial Sloth* (*Nebesnyi tikhokhod*, 1945, directed by Semen Timoshenko. The most notable example of the trope occurs in Stolper's 1948 film *The Tale of a Real Man* (*Povest' o nastoiashchem cheloveke*), based on Boris Polevoi's 1946 story about the exploits of a real-life heroic pilot, Aleksei Mares'ev. After he is shot down and loses both legs Meres'ev (his name changes by one letter in the film) spends a long time in

hospital and is reduced to despair. But with the support – and the ideological guidance – of his comrades and the medical staff he not only rises from his bed but, amazingly, manages to return to his flying. I am grateful to Susan Larsen, with whom I shared a panel entitled 'Flight patterns: Daring, Discipline and Domesticity in Aviation Films of the Stalin Era' at the 33rd National Convention of the American Association for the Advancement of Slavic Studies, Washington, 15–18 November 2001, for drawing my attention to the prevalence of this motif in the flier films of the Stalin period.

17 It is of course highly significant that this motif is parodied in the treatment of the hero of Sergei Livnev's emblematically titled 1994 film *Hammer and Sickle* (*Serp i molot*). Set in the Stalinist period it tells the story of a record-breaking female tractor driver, Evdokiia, who in the service of the state undergoes a sex-change operation turning into the model worker Evdokim. Later he is paralysed by a misfired shot by a Young Pioneer and put on display as an exemplary, bed-ridden figure, in a museum.

18 As Aksenov recalled: 'This novel changed the wind direction from East to West' (Aksenov 1994: 5).

19 Notable examples of this phenomenon are the 'Week of French Cinema' held in October 1955; an International Festival of Young People and Students held in August 1957; and an American exhibition in Moscow in the summer of 1959.

20 The work of the collective farm (*kolkhoz*) was, of course, a favourite and officially encouraged theme of Soviet cinema. Earlier films set on a fishing *kolkhoz* include Boris Barnet's *By the Bluest of Seas* (*U samogo sinego moria*, 1935) and Vladimir Batalov's *The Women* (*Baby*, 1940).

21 For a fascinating analysis of the increasingly subtle treatment of science in the prose of this period, see Marsh (1986: 163–235).

22 See Aksenov's interview on Russian Television, Note 7. For another memoir of the enthusiastic reception of the novel and the warm reaction shown to the actors by tourists during filming in Tallinn, see Aksenov 2003.

23 A biographer of Oleg Dal', who played Alik Kramer in the film, suggests that both for him and for Aleksandr Zbruev, the parts they played in their later careers were dictated by the character established for them in *My Younger Brother* (Galadzheva 1991: 6). Andrei Mironov, playing the part of the 'cypher', Iurka, was more able to escape from the context of this first role.

7 Screening the short story

The films of Vasilii Shukshin

John Givens

Vasilii Shukshin knew better than most filmmakers the difficulty of bringing literature to the screen. Prolific author (three novels, over 130 short stories, ten works for stage and screen), active director (five films in 14 years) and busy actor (roles in some 20 movies, including two of his own), Shukshin not only pursued three careers, but, to a large extent, synthesized them in his work. His first three movies were film adaptations of short stories he had already published, while in his last two movies, he not only wrote and directed the script but also acted the main role. 'I began to write under the influence of the cinema and to make films under the influence of literature', he declared in a 1973 interview (Shukshin 1973: 3). Shukshin defined this influence, however, in a very straightforward way: his short stories, like movies, are dialogue driven, while his movies, like short stories, eschew long sequences where nothing happens (what Shukshin called 'pure cinematography') (Shukshin 1973: 3). Later, Shukshin likened his creative persona to that of the 'folk storyteller' (*narodnyi rasskazchik*) whom he remembered from his childhood – village tellers of tales who were 'both playwright and actor, or, more likely, a whole theater in one person' (Fomin 1976: 296). Such was Shukshin's reputation – he was a 'jack-of-all-trades' and his success in three careers made him something of a phenomenon in Soviet culture.

Yet, Shukshin's tri-fold identity as an artist was as conflicted as it was harmonious. Shortly before he died, he vowed to give up the cinema, move back to Siberia and devote himself to his writing, which had suffered from his film career (Shukshin 1981: 234–5). This tension between literature and cinema expressed itself in different ways throughout his short career and, indeed, was bound up with not just one, but two split identities: celebrated author and successful film *auteur* on the one hand, and Siberian peasant and Muscovite intellectual on the other. For Shukshin, the two were linked. Siberia was the locus and the inspiration for his writing, while Moscow was where he became an intellectual and a filmmaker. Thus it is not surprising that Shukshin's attempt at screening his short stories should involve not only questions about his artistic identity, but personal identity as well. When Vasilii Shukshin set about bringing his own short stories to the screen, he was faced both with the problem of self-translation and self-presentation, for the image he would project of his characters on film would also be the face he put on his very heritage and his split identity. And while Shukshin is typically characterized as a filmmaker who favoured an aesthetic of 'maximum popular accessibility' (Faraday 2000: 98), his attempts to screen his own short stories in his first three films also reflect the more subtle issues of *auteur* cinema in the Soviet sixties, in which film was reasserted as both a distinct art form and a product of an artist's personal vision.[1]

The resources of literature and the resources of cinema

'The resources of literature and those of cinema are not equal', Shukshin wrote in 1967. 'The point is, it's *impossible* to make a film which in all respects is equal to a work of literature' (Shukshin 1981: 136). Literature, Shukshin argues, is a richer, longer-lived medium than movies, which are in danger of being forgotten as soon as the next advance in film technology makes them look dated (ibid.: 237). Indeed, Shukshin goes as far as to say that 'true, serious literature cannot serve as a basis for cinema' (ibid.: 139). As an example, he discusses the difficulties that would face any director wishing to make a movie of Leo Tolstoi's 1859 story 'Three Deaths' ('*Tri smerti*'). The story's first part, Shukshin argues, would by itself be impossible to film. How, Shukshin asks, could one convey the sick noblewoman's irritation at the fact that everyone around her is hale and hearty? The coachman's robust voice, the maid's fresh face and corpulent body, the appetite of the woman's husband, even her own children's health are all unbearable reminders of her sickly state. The endless muddy roads that lie between her and the foreign spas where she hopes to convalesce underscore the hopelessness of her condition. How can one convey all this on film? The maid will simply look fat, the roads will look like any other one sees in movies set in the nineteenth century, and the young lady's exasperated 'Again!' at every brush of her maid's cloak will on film simply be 'a minor supplement to the suffering grimaces of the actress' rather than the powerful linguistic means by which Tolstoi works his literary estrangement (ibid.: 141). So why bother, Shukshin asks, when the only result is that the film version will be somehow inferior to its literary basis? Worse still, 'in our busy age', Shukshin warns, 'we'll watch the movie and not read the story' – the most harmful outcome of all (ibid.: 143).

Here Shukshin is but repeating apprehensions raised by the film critic André Bazin in 1948. Are not all film adaptations of literary works, he asks, simply 'condensed versions, summaries, film "digests"?' (Bazin 2000: 21). Do not most films based on novels 'merely usurp their titles?' Yes, Bazin answers, and yet he warns against a cultural elitism and an 'idolatry of literary form' that would privilege the 'individualistic conception of the "author" and of the "work" ', an idolatry established in the nineteenth century and which, post-structuralism notwithstanding, persists to this day.

Such a 'subjectivist notion', Bazin reasons, no longer fits in 'with an aesthetic sociology of the masses in which the cinema runs a relay race with drama and the novel and does not eliminate them, but rather reinforces them' (ibid.: 22–3). Bazin's point is that once we do away with our overly reverential attitude toward the author and the text, the act of adaptation is greatly clarified.

According to Bazin, 'adaptation is aesthetically justified ... because the adapted work to a certain extent exists apart from what is wrongly called its "style", in a confusion of this term with the word *form*' (Bazin 2000: 25–6). In Bazin's theory of adaptation, 'faithfulness to form, literary or otherwise, is illusory: what matters is the *equivalence in meaning of the forms*'. Filmmakers must have 'enough visual imagination to create the cinematic equivalent of the style of the original' and critics must have 'the eyes to see it' (ibid.: 20). Thus Tolstoi's linguistic devices – the sick lady's 'Again!' – must find their non-verbal, cinematic reflection. As Bazin alludes in his article, you cannot film Camus's present perfects, though they 'are inherent in the metaphysical drama of *The Stranger*' (Bazin 2000: 20). In each instance, cinema must 'transform' the 'voltage' of literature while preserving its 'aesthetic energy' (ibid.: 25).

Unlike Bazin, Shukshin remained sceptical about the need for filmed literary adaptations, let alone their prospects for success. 'The cinema is the eighth wonder of the world; it doesn't need to chase after literature', he asserted. What is needed instead is for cinema to acquire its own literature (Shukshin 1981: 143). At the heart of Shukshin's objections to literary adaptations is precisely his inability to get beyond the 'individualistic conception of the author'. For Shukshin, the main difference between literature and film is that literature is a solitary undertaking, while a film is, in a sense, 'co-authored' by everyone working on it.[2] This co-authorship is virtually impossible to achieve when you are adapting one of the great writers of world literature for the simple reason that you cannot truly be a co-author with Tolstoi or Dostoevskii. 'With the likes of me, you can', Shukshin allows, but not with one of the classics (ibid.: 144).

Shukshin's categorical stance is understandable. Even in adapting his own works for cinema, he experienced a whole host of problems, many of which in his later judgment he failed to overcome. In particular, Shukshin laboured against two biases. The first came from his own peasant heritage, which held that the 'meaning of the song lies in the words'; the tune 'exists only to emphasize the words' and 'comes of itself' (Figes 2002: xxv). This bias in turn found its reflection and reinforcement in the Soviet film factory, where, since the days of high Stalinism, content (film scripts, character dialogue) was privileged over form (innovative camera work, visual experimentation). A heavy emphasis on scripts and an impossibly cumbersome editorial process that involved several layers of committees and departments whose chief task was to ensure ideological correctness relentlessly emphasized the verbal, often at the expense of the visual.

As a writer, Shukshin understood the power of the word. But as a director, Shukshin also understood that literature and cinema are two different languages. Therefore, screening his own short stories, he acknowledged, was 'also translating from one language to another'. On the one hand, writers must understand that the very lines they insist should make it onto the screen will change in emphasis and meaning depending on the actor reading them and what the camera shows at that time. Directors, on the other hand, 'often do not feel that a word can also be an image', according to Shukshin, and therefore do not exploit the visual potential latent in words (Shukshin 1981: 169). Shukshin himself grappled with these questions in his own attempts at filming his stories.

Obviously, for Shukshin, literature and cinema were linked in ways that went beyond self-adaptation. Author and *auteur* were mutually dependent faces of one creative persona. Even so, the idea of making movies from his own short stories meant subjecting them to a different kind of judgment. When asked why a writer should aspire to the screen, Shukshin answered: 'What author would refuse to appear with his program in front of an audience of millions? ... In bringing my stories to the screen, I can check the correctness of my artistic method' (Shukshin 1981: 168–9). This 'validation process', however, brought its own unexpected outcomes. The rural/urban dialectic that drove Shukshin's fiction proved to be difficult to translate to the silver screen. The visual quality of movies literally meant putting a face on his creative programme, and Shukshin seemed uncertain who exactly should appear before that 'audience of millions': the Muscovite filmmaker or the Siberian writer?

Before the 'audience of millions'

Shukshin's mentor at the film institute in the late 1950s, Mikhail Romm, taught him to film what he knew, advice that meshed well with the cultural atmosphere of the post-Stalin period, when the search for authenticity was uppermost on artists' minds. Influenced by Romm, Shukshin set out to make his first film a tribute to the big-souled people of his native region in Siberia. He succeeded beyond his wildest dreams. *A Guy Like That* (*Zhivet takoi paren'*, 1964) won prizes at home and abroad, including the prestigious Golden Lion Award at the 1964 Vienna Film Festival. Audiences were charmed and amused by the film's big-hearted hero, Pasha Kolokol'nikov, at once a prankster, a dreamer and something of a knight in shining armour. Driving his truck in picaresque fashion along the famous Chuiskii Tract highway in western Siberia in search of his 'ideal' (the perfect woman), Pasha alternates comic stunts with good deeds, ultimately failing in his quest but winning over audiences and critics. The role, played to acclaim by Leonid Kuravlev, is one of Shukshin's most memorable cinematic creations.

Loosely plotted, shot largely on location, employing non-actors in bit roles, and pointedly devoid of any message, the film was as studiously artless as the Italian Neo-Realist movies Shukshin saw at the film institute, whose influence his movie clearly betrays. It is based in part on two short stories, 'A Classy Driver' ('*Klassnyi voditel"*') and 'Grin'ka Maliugin', both published a year before the film's debut in the spring of 1964. They comprise the film's opening and concluding episodes, thus serving as an important frame upon which the rest of the movie is hung. The picture begins with Pasha's falling head over heels in love with a village librarian who is already spoken for and ends with his saving a gas station from a burning truck. In between are scattered encounters with other women: a new arrival from the city who lectures Pasha on culture, a single parent female acquaintance depressed over her lot in life, and an old woman who tells Pasha a supernatural story. There are also brief dream sequences and a longer vignette in which Pasha plays matchmaker between his Aunt Anis'ia and his elder friend and fellow driver, Kondrat.

Shukshin's skill as a storyteller does not fail him on screen. *A Guy Like That* feels very much like Shukshin's short stories: simple in its narrative form, propelled by catchy, authentic dialogue, and dynamic in its movement. Though episodic, the ubiquitous presence of the Chuiskii Tract roadway along which Pashka travels and the charismatic figure of Pashka himself link and unify the otherwise loosely connected series of dreams and encounters. While some critics complained about the movie's fragmentariness (especially with regard to the dream sequences) and its weak ending,[3] Shukshin seems more concerned, both as a filmmaker and a short story writer, with capturing in dynamic fashion select moments of his hero's life rather than creating a well-rounded story. In an article written shortly after *A Guy Like That* debuted, Shukshin states 'The cinema and the short story are different phenomena. But the laws by which good films and stories are made is the same'. 'The main thing', he writes, 'is motion'. Accordingly, a story or a film is good if it 'by some miracle has preserved this motion, has not destroyed life but somehow "transplanted" it, unharmed, into the reader's [or viewer's] consciousness' (Shukshin 1981: 115, 114, 117). From its opening sequence to its final frame, *A Guy Like That* relates its story the way Pasha drives his truck: at top speed. Indeed, it does not conclude so much as come to a halt, and only then because Pashka breaks his leg during his heroic stunt in the film's final episode. Thus immobilized, he is unable to continue either his journey or the stories we have been watching, both of which depend on Pasha's movement along the Chuiskii Tract highway. This outcome is, in its own way, ingenious and imparted to the movie and its audience a sense of the vitality and energy of the film's impetuous hero.

And yet, Shukshin was unhappy with his adaptation, dissatisfied that viewers and critics considered it a comedy. Something obviously got lost between story and screen, he complained in an 'afterword' published in the industry journal *Iskusstvo kino.* 'I wanted to make a film about the beauty of a pure human heart, capable of kindness', Shukshin wrote in his article. 'We wanted to infuse it with the truth about life'. [4] If we are to judge by

Shukshin's other works, the proximity between the concepts 'kindness' and 'the truth about life' and the film's Siberian setting is intentional, something hinted at in the film's opening shot of a map of the Chuiskii Tract and all of the villages that dot its length. Siberia is not so much 'exotic' as 'other', that is, set in opposition to Russia proper. 'Kindness' and the 'truth about life' are to be found here, and Shukshin is (literally) giving us the roadmap. The cultural critique implied by this opposition (kindness and truth are not to be found in Moscow) is clear and speaks to the artist's own experiences as a rural immigrant and transplanted Siberian in the capital of the Soviet Union. On screen, however, this polemic is largely invisible.

Perhaps Leonid Kuravlev's utterly charismatic performance as Pasha took the movie where Shukshin did not intend it to go. In the film, he is somewhat of a sanitized hero, a cinematic jester first and a truck driver second. Here, Shukshin the director betrays Shukshin the writer, for in the story we glimpse a darker side to the character, who is vaguely described as being somewhat nasty (*zloi*) and whose actions – particularly his nocturnal attempt to kidnap his librarian love – are more ambiguous. Other controversial aspects of his life – such as his Old Believer parents – are nowhere in evidence in the film, nor do we feel in the movie the very real sense of rootlessness that lends his literary character a distinctly melancholic colouring, where the ambiguous symbol of the truck, shuttling between the collective farm and the city, symbolizes the consequences of mixing technology and agriculture in the countryside. Yesterday's peasants have become today's itinerants, a fact hinted at in the film by Pasha's profession as well as his constant quest for his ideal and his failure to find her. She and a sense of a permanent home and stable identity remain elusive. The film's dynamic movement masks this problem, which significantly comes to a head when Pasha is immobilized by his accident and must confront his failed quest.

The film's humour also interferes with Shukshin's more serious message. Whereas the humour in the story offsets the very real desperation just beneath the surface of Pasha's personality, the film's comic aspects on the contrary emphasize a light-hearted, affirmative attitude toward life, summed up in the movie's closing line, uttered by Pasha: 'Znachit, budem zhit'' (almost untranslatable, something between 'life is good' and 'there's always tomorrow'). As Shukshin laments in his 'afterword', viewing the movie as a comedy displaces its serious themes.

Partly to blame for the mistranslation from page to screen is Shukshin's failure to find a visual language capable of elucidating the movie's deeper themes. In his first time out as a director, Shukshin was clearly unsure what he wanted to accomplish visually in the movie. Thus the film with its fantasy and dream sequences, which could have afforded a wonderful opportunity for the director to be more visually playful or daring,[5] nevertheless consistently subordinates image to word. Dream and fantasy sequences are shot as simple visual illustrations of their underlying stories and are hardly differentiated from the film's 'real life' scenes. Indeed, at times Shukshin's rapid cuts between dream and reality make for abrupt, confusing transitions. While Shukshin succeeds in capturing 'with sensitivity and without sentimentality' the movie's Siberian setting and subtly treats the peasant hut interiors familiar to its director since childhood as neither 'quaint, ethnographic objects' nor 'fetishes or icons to be venerated' (Woll 2000: 171), most of the time, his self-adaptation betrays its creator's literary bias. Indeed, it is hardly surprising that one of the scenes added to the movie version – the travelling fashion show that visits the village where Pashka is working – appeared as the basis for a short story published three years later.[6]

Though Shukshin, true to his word about the collective undertaking of cinema, did invite his actors to be co-authors with him by urging them to improvise certain parts of scenes, relatively little of this improvisation actually made it into the movie's final version.[7] Similarly, Shukshin seems to have kept his cameraman, Valerii Ginzburg, on a short rein, for the camera is rarely allowed to indulge in any visual expression that is not directly connected with the movie's plot. At least in his first film, Shukshin did not rely on his 'visual imagination to create the cinematic equivalent of the style of the original' (to use Bazin's words) so much as the verbal resources of the movie's literary basis and the verbal skills of his actors. Many viewers, of course, did not see this as a bad thing and, indeed, for some, this outcome was even to be desired. Thus one critic, in an otherwise positive review, notes that 'when his direct, personal, writer's intonation disappears [from the movie] … Shukshin falters' (Pogozheva 1964: 3).

With his next movie, *Your Son and Brother* (*Vash Syn i Brat*, 1965), Shukshin dramatically changed his approach to how he would screen his own prose, for the first time exploring strictly visual resources for telling his tale even as he makes much plainer the movie's basis in three separate short stories. *Your Son and Brother* premiered only eighteen months after the release of *A Guy Like That*, an indication of the frenetic pace at which Shukshin worked throughout his brief career. The film's opening announces Shukshin's new-found interest in what he called 'pure cinematography', those long, silent takes he so often criticized in others. Extended shots of the ice breaking on the river Katun' in Shukshin's native western Siberian homeland provide a background for the movie's credits and serves as an introduction to another visual essay, this one showing a village coming to life in the springtime. Following the words 'It was Sunday' (*Bylo voskresen'e*), we see a series of shots apparently taken of real people in a real village: kids play on the riverbanks, young women stroll the muddy streets, rugs are aired and beaten, boats are repaired and readied for the summer, farm animals are fed, dogs and cats enjoy the outdoors, a tipsy *muzhik* staggers home to his displeased wife, and a village barber trims his clients' hair right outside his *izba*. Accompanying this montage are the lyrical strains of the soundtrack, which pick up on a melancholy folk song the young women are singing, imbuing the sequence with an unmistakable affection and intimacy. Though muddy, austere and somewhat dilapidated, the village in spring is nonetheless clearly being held up as an ideal of sorts and indeed it is not long before we understand why: these are the much-longed-for sights and sounds to which Stepan, in the film's first segment, wants so badly to return. These are also the images which in the next vignette haunt Stepan's brother Maksim, working in distant Moscow, and to which the third brother, Ignatii, is so conspicuously indifferent in the movie's concluding story.

Your Son and Brother is based on the stories 'Stepka', 'Snake Poison' ('*Zmeinyi iad*') and 'Ignakha's Come Home' ('*Ignakha priekhal*'), all of which appeared in the journal *Novyi mir* in 1963 and 1964. In his movie adaptation, Shukshin is even looser in his narrative forms than in *A Guy Like That*, relying on three nominally linked episodes with separate central protagonists. He is in essence telling three different stories here, each with its own rhythm and conflict, and yet the movie is remarkably unified in theme, style and content. Making the protagonists all brothers from one family certainly helps Shukshin minimize any disjointedness that might have arisen from the film's structure, and yet it is really Shukshin's attention to the visual grammar of the movie that makes its separate parts relate so well to each other. To put it paradoxically, the film holds together so well because of the way its visual components 'talk' to each other.

In the first segment, Stepan returns home three months early from serving a five-year sentence in a labour camp for brawling. We find out later that he has escaped because he could not bear being away from the village in the spring, hence the segment's prologue described earlier. Stepan, it turns out, has also been watching the springtime activities in his village from a rise on the other side of the river. Thus he, too, becomes inextricably inscribed into the village topography we have been viewing – he is as much a part of it as it is of him. By the time Stepan puts in his appearance at home and before a single line of script has been pronounced on camera, we are already drawn into Stepan's longing for his native village. As word spreads of his homecoming, the village begins to arrive, neighbour by neighbour, to bid Stepan welcome and join in the celebration. Any discernible dialogue fast becomes inaudible in the din of the joyful merrymaking, during which Shukshin's camera scans the hastily assembled table now groaning under the food and drink brought to mark the occasion. While exchanges between characters punctuate the glad activities, Shukshin is more concerned with filling our eyes and ears with the drinking, singing and dancing that Stepan's return has occasioned than with having characters talk in front of the camera. Words, Shukshin implies, are inadequate in such situations. Stepan himself discovers as much when he tries to explain to the local police officer, who soon arrives on the scene, why he escaped. It is, significantly, Stepan's deaf-mute sister Vera who brings this point forcefully home when she, alone of all the celebrants, realizes what is happening. Her weeping, stumbling figure returning home from the police station is the last we see and it expresses all the dashed joy and pain awaiting Stepan's entire family. Thus,

Shukshin relies heavily on non-verbal means to convey the emotional content of his first segment, which is told as much through the opening shots of spring in the village, the merrymaking at Stepan's house and Vera's weeping flight as through any of the dialogue from Shukshin's short story.

The film's second segment tells the story of Stepan's brother, Maksim, who lives in a worker's dormitory in Moscow and labours at construction sites. The abrupt transition between the two segments, figured by a shot of a train moving thunderously across the steppe, prepares us for a quite different topography – that of the 'human anthill' of the nation's capital. We first see Maksim in his dormitory, reading a letter from his sick mother, who is asking him to find medicine (snake poison) for her lumbago. As Maksim reads, Shukshin's camera pans the dormitory room, so familiar to him from his own years working at odd construction sites in and around Moscow in the late 1940s. Some are playing guitar and singing, others are listening, some are reading, others smoking and playing cards, while the inevitable magazine pictures can be glimpsed taped to the wall. This is Maksim's surrogate family, and we immediately feel the difference between it and his real family back home. A montage sequence follows as Maksim – a mere bit of human flotsam bobbing in a sea of harried, care-worn Muscovites – undertakes to fulfil his mother's wish, scouring pharmacies for the medication but meeting with failure and indifference at every step. He next decides to enlist the aid of his brother Ignatii, a famous wrestler who works with the Moscow circus. Again, Shukshin's camera discovers a meaningful contrast. From Ignatii's kitsch-filled apartment and fashionable wife to scenes of circus performers rehearsing their routines, a picture of the big city emerges that clashes dramatically with the movie's visual tribute to the village in the first segment. Moscow is atomized, the domain of false, low culture (the circus) and homelessness (figured in institutions like the workers' dormitory) where people like Ignatii marry for the sake of a residence permit (he recommends Maksim do the same with a friend of his wife's). Indeed, Shukshin would return to this question of how to 'set oneself up' in life ('*ustraivat' byt"*') in his next movie. Only connections can procure the medication, and Ignatii uses his to do just that. As it turns out, he and his wife are leaving themselves for their first visit to see his parents since he got married, so he can take the medication personally. Maksim accompanies them to the train station at the episode's conclusion. Thus the same train motif transports us back to Siberia.

Having been well prepared by the contrast established in the film's first two segments, the viewer is ready for the final resolution of the city/country opposition in the film's concluding episode. It has been five years since Ignatii has been home (significantly, almost the same length as Stepan's prison sentence). The visit does not go well. Ignatii has become proud and boastful. He brings everyone expensive presents and reads his father lectures on drinking and 'physical culture'. For his part, his father keeps goading the fourth brother, Vas'ka, who has stayed in the village and works as a carpenter, to wrestle Ignatii, hoping to prove in the contest of strength the superiority of the countryside. Here the tension between the city and the country, which up till now has been established almost exclusively on the visual plane, is finally made literal in the movie's plot, only never to materialize. All the same, the viewer is left in no doubt which side Shukshin is on. Just before the movie's final scene, another visual essay is inserted, this time of the river Katun' in its full summer glory, with herds of horses watering themselves and cattle being driven out to pasture in the verdant Siberian landscape. When we learn in the final scene that Ignatii has single-handedly pulled out a fence post the previous night as a show of strength, it appears as nothing more than a circus stunt in the context of the beauty and might of the Siberian countryside glimpsed just moments before. Indeed, Vera's appearance in the dress Ignatii bought her – both here and earlier in the episode when she parades about the village, joyously showing off her gift to her neighbours – only reminds us of her mournful walk from the police station which concluded the film's first episode. Vera's appearance at the end of each segment in its own way subtly defines Stepan and Ignatii without recourse to a single word (a fact underscored by Vera's deaf mute state). Here Shukshin's use of the visual to allow scenes to illuminate each other is deft and understated. Stepan's foolish flight home brings pain but is also indication of his profound love for the village, while Ignatii's homecoming is as showy and, in the end, superficial as the store-bought dress. Indeed, Shukshin's experiment with 'pure cinematography' is largely responsible for the movie's more controversial reception among critics. Whereas the stories themselves failed to create a stir when they appeared in *Novyi mir*, on the big screen the opposition implied in the film between the profane space of the city and sacred space of the country is provocatively foregrounded in the movie's cinematography and generated a minor firestorm in the critical press. Shukshin was accused of creating a village idyll and promoting uneducated and, in the case of Stepan, even criminal heroes.[8]

Though Shukshin, the actor Vsevolod Sanaev (who played the father) and cameraman Valerii Ginzburg were awarded the 1967 Vasil'ev Brothers Prize for their work in *Your Son and Brother*, the film was not a success at the box office. This is an unfortunate outcome, for both as a film and as a literary adaptation, *Your Son and Brother* is actually a better movie and a bolder treatment of the artist's conflicted Siberian/Muscovite identity. Three unrelated stories are more successfully stitched together (despite the fact that the stitches are made to show more in the transitions between vignettes) than the separate episodes that make up *A Guy Like That*. Moreover, these stories are far more interesting aesthetically and deeper thematically than those that formed the basis for his previous movie. Most importantly of all, Shukshin frees his visual imagination and his cameraman to create a cinematic style that achieves what good film adaptations should: he provides not just a film equivalent of his stories, but discovers in those stories through the mechanism of his adaptation a depth and truth that reveals them anew to his movie audience.

By the time we get to *Strange People* (*Strannye liudi*, 1969), conceived and shot three years later in 1968 and 1969, Shukshin is both more visually daring and experimental in his literary adaptation and more provocative in his treatment of his private history. The movie's subtitle – 'Three stories' – announces its structural innovation: three separate stories are told which do not relate to each other at all except in the broadest sense of the film's title. As Shukshin later explained, the idea was to reproduce in cinema what he held in high esteem in literature. 'In literature, I've always been most interested in the anthology', he states in a 1971 interview. 'The way I see it, you can be the author of a story, a novella, or a novel, but to be the author of an anthology is the difference between being a writer or not. I thought it was the same in the cinema, but it's not. Viewers have next to no experience with anthology movies'. Shukshin's experiment did not work. 'Hardly anyone saw it', he acknowledged. 'People even walked out of theatres in the middle of it' (Shukshin 1981: 170).

Strange People marks the last time Shukshin would attempt to screen his own short stories, in this case 'Oddball' ('*Chudik*'), 'Mille Pardons, Madame!' ('*Mil' pardon, madam!*'), 'Thoughts' ('*Dumy*') and 'Sten'ka Razin'. The movie also marks the culmination of Shukshin's desire – progressively more evident in his first three films – to emphasize the short story genre as a distinct cinematic unit. At the same time, as if to compensate for the film's heightened literary structure, Shukshin takes more risks as a director, experimenting with the movie's cinematic frame, the screen versions of the stories themselves, and the actors' address to camera.

By *Strange People* Shukshin had shifted his argument and his technique. Gone is Siberia as a necessary background. Instead, a more neutral image of the countryside is cultivated (the film was shot near Vladimir and Suzdal'). The background is no longer as important. What is important is what is in front of the camera in the foreground, and it is announced in the film's title: strange people. The countryside is no longer the repository of kindness and truth – it is the realm of eccentricity. The urban–rural polemic has been modulated and recast. His country protagonists are cranks and eccentrics, at once signs of deformity and protests against conformity. Kindness and goodness have been folded into a quirky, high strung eccentricity that lashes out at a world lacking in such qualities, a world dominated by the vagaries of urban consumer culture, fad and fashion. Shukshin's rural heritage is no longer idealized, but turned into a polemical tool. The opening credits announce this theme as well as the new film language through which Shukshin seeks to depict it.

As the credits for the film roll by, shots of Soviet citizens going in circles on an amusement park ride are interspersed with those of a man pacing aimlessly on the paving stones of some square and another of a young man in fashionable dark glasses bobbing slowly up and down on a ride that is ending. Over all this, we hear a couple (Shukshin and his wife, Lidiia Fedoseeva) singing the folk song, 'Dear One' ('*Milen'kii ty moi*'). The song creates a meaningful dissonance. While a woman sings of being abandoned by her lover returning to his wife 'There, in a distant land' (*'tam, v kraiu dalekom'*), we see Shukshin's pointedly disharmonious and slightly absurd illustrations to the song (the riders are all dressed in suits, hats, and ties, and one of them is reading a newspaper). Only the man in the dark glasses – who looks unconcernedly at the camera – seems at ease in his element. As the credits disappear, we are given a brief visual prologue in which we see a grassy hill along which a baby is taking a few hesitant steps. Then the title and acting credits for the first story begin to roll by, shot partially against a background of a wall of glass bricks back illuminated to reveal a staircase upon which people can be detected walking up and down. This title and credit sequence is the same for all three stories. When the movie concludes, we return to the shot of the baby on the grassy hill, who finally manages to lose her balance, and the end title appears.

These sequences framing the movie and the separate stories are clearly meant to be symbolic. The problem is, none of the images – the park ride, the pacing man, the baby, or the stairwell – obviously relate to any of the stories they frame. Only the song is heard again, in the movie's first vignette. Critics were quick to fault Shukshin for 'fashionable director's tricks' and 'pseudo-intellectual' filmmaking' (Levshina 1970: 49). For many reviewers, the film was an occasion to address the split in Shukshin's artistic identity. One complained that *Strange People* was decidedly 'below the level of Shukshin's prose' (Levshina 1970: 42) and blamed Shukshin's inability to handle the visual medium of cinema as deftly as the verbal medium of literature. 'Shukshin has become here the prisoner of his own prose' (Kulinichev 1970: n.p.) another complains, while yet another critic asserts that Shukshin's literary anthologies hold together better than his film anthology (Semenov 1970: n.p.).

Part of Shukshin's problem lay in translating the potent image of his village cranks for the movies. Shukshin acknowledged that eccentricity is much easier to control and depict sympathetically on the printed page than on the widescreen. 'The literary Oddball [from the movie's first story] turned out to be simply impossible on film, as impossible as Bron'ka Pupkov [from the movie's second]. I lost them in *Strange People*', Shukshin lamented. Neither Oddball nor Bron'ka are comprehensible, he said, without 'authorial mediation' (Shukshin 1981: 172). Shukshin anticipated this problem before shooting, rewriting 'Oddball' entirely for the screen. Oddball still leaves his distant village to visit his brother in the big city, but instead of focusing on his misadventures, as in the story, Oddball's brother is centre stage (hence the segment's title: 'Brother' (*'Bratka'*). Thus, instead of a study of Oddball's naive country idiosyncrasies, 'Brother' becomes an exposition of the petty, materialistic nature of Oddball's brother, who hopes to improve his living space by marrying a woman with a big apartment. Rather than a celebration of eccentricity focusing on Oddball, we are given a grotesque parody of the petty bourgeois in Evgenii Evstigneev's brilliant interpretation of the role. Oddball, dismayed at what his brother has become, leaves after only two nights, shielding his brother from censure back home by telling everyone that he lost his travel money and never made it to his destination. This last fact we learn from a voiceover narrator (Shukshin himself), an attempt by the director to emphasize the story genre of the etude (he narrates the opening to the next segment as well). Thus, in a subtle inversion, the segment's 'strange' hero has been relegated the story's secondary role and the quite ordinary (and repulsive) brother put centre stage. Goodness has become mere eccentric aberration (in the form of the powerless country bumpkin, Oddball); cynical calculation (the urban 'sellout', Bratka) rules the day.

In the movie's second story, 'The Fateful Shot' ('*Rokovoi vystrel'*, based on 'Mille Pardons, Madame!'), rural eccentricity is seemingly exposed as empty buffoonery. Its central hero is Bron'ka Pupkov, whose strangeness consists in his inexplicable need to tell the outlandish story of his alleged attempt on Hitler's life to groups of hunters whom he serves as a guide. Indeed, the story is the centrepiece of the segment, and Shukshin entrusts all of the scene's drama – and absurdity – to Bron'ka himself, who convinces the movie audience of his tall tale as much as the hunters. After scanning the listening faces of the assembled hunters, the camera settles on Bron'ka alone, who, in Evgenii Lebedev's riveting performance, pours out his bizarre confession with such emotion and remorse that it is impossible not to believe his tale just a little. With individual takes as long as 38, 39 and even 88 metres of film – almost unthinkably long takes for a scene where the actor is doing nothing but reciting a monologue (Tiurin 1984: 165) – Bron'ka's narrative is the film's most innovative moment, one paradoxically achieved through the verbal medium. In rejecting an earlier idea to illustrate Bron'ka's story with actors (complete with dwarfs playing the part of Hitler's generals), Shukshin places Bron'ka and all of his 'anguish [*toska*], wretchedness and grandeur' right in the viewer's lap (Shukshin 1981: 187–8). For some, the acquaintance was too close. I. Levshina calls Lebedev's performance 'a clinical depiction of an idée fixe' and describes the scene as 'unpleasant, pathological, on the border of what is aesthetically allowable on the screen' (Levshina 1970: 44). Shukshin, she complained, had lost control of his actor.

Shukshin disagreed. The problem, he explained later, lay in the difficulty of film adaptations. When the verbal becomes visual, there are unexpected consequences, even in such verbally intense scenes as this one. Lebedev conveyed in his interpretation of Bron'ka everything that Shukshin describes in his story: his 'high-pitched whisper, tormented shrieking, the nervousness of his speech, his soul-rending cry, his teeth-gnashing'. But *seeing* Bron'ka's histrionics rather than reading about them amplified their already shrill register and made them less sympathetic to viewers, who reacted more to the image before them than what lay at the heart of Bron'ka's self-slandering: his own failed life (Shukshin 1981: 174). Two years later in another interview

Shukshin complained, as if still smarting from the criticism levelled at the Bron'ka episode: 'We worry too little about the inner state of the image, the character. The visual nature of cinema is killing us. We can't shake the notion that cinema means spectacle' (Shukshin 1981: 186).

Ironically, Shukshin was criticized for just such spectacle in the movie's third story, 'Thoughts'. Though the piece was uniformly praised for Vsevolod Sanaev's performance as the collective farm chairman Matvei Riazanov, critics had grown tired of the fantasy sequence device by which Shukshin, as in *A Guy Like That*, illustrated Riazanov's meditations on his life, especially the sequence in which the chairman witnesses his own funeral and even answers a reporter's questions about what it feels like to be dead. The episode's secondary plot line, based on 'Sten'ka Razin', was marred by Shukshin's casting of a non-actor (fellow writer Iurii Skop) as Vaseka the sculptor and by the pedantic figure of Vaseka's mentor, the village teacher, who assumes 'narrator' duties at one point by addressing the camera and inviting viewers to follow him as he hurries to lecture the villagers about the Cossack rebel, Sten'ka Razin. These direct addresses to camera, which begin in the final frames of the Bron'ka episode and are sprinkled throughout the last segment, are another of Shukshin's innovations in *Strange People* that, according to Iurii Tiurin, neither viewers nor critics were ready for in 1969, when the movie was released. Like the mock funeral scene and the long 'word-as-image' takes of Bron'ka's monologue, they were too new to be appreciated (Tiurin 1984: 177, 169–70).

Though he defended parts of the movie, Shukshin considered *Strange People* a failure (Shukshin 1981: 170). As such, the movie became a turning point in Shukshin's film career. Never again would he experiment so boldly in the style, structure and visual grammar of his cinema. Never again would he experiment with the filmed short story genre or attempt any further literary self-adaptations. Whether Shukshin was right to have done so, of course, is open to debate. For all of its shortcomings – its clumsy framing device, the uneven quality of the first and third episodes, its awkward use of voiceover narration – the movie is nevertheless the first in which Shukshin really takes any risks as a filmmaker. Some of these risks – such as Bron'ka's compelling monologue, which has since become a set piece for Russian film students – were worth taking, even though they were only appreciated with the passage of time. At the 1976 Venice Film Festival, for instance, the film attracted 'huge interest', evidence perhaps that Shukshin was ahead of his time (Tiurin 1984: 158). As late as 1988 *Strange People* was still being shown in film festivals, when it was included in a tour of Soviet films travelling around the United States.

Viewed strictly as a literary adaptation, though, the film is more problematic. The movie's first story is not an adaptation at all, but a total rewriting. The three works comprising the last two stories are in and of themselves interesting screenings of their original versions, but do not relate to each other or the first story in an obvious a way, as had the separate stories of

Your Son and Brother. In this sense, the film's status as an anthology is, at first glance, questionable. If an anthology is meant to make up a larger, more meaningful and aesthetically significant whole than its constituent parts, as Shukshin implies, then *Strange People* failed as a film anthology for the vast majority of viewers and critics. This failure, however, should not distract us from its importance for Shukshin, who, in many ways, found in *Strange People* the ultimate expression of his quest for synthesis on both the aesthetic and biographical planes. A bold literary structure is proposed for a movie whose film grammar is equally daring in its risks. At the same time, Shukshin, following Bron'ka Pupkov's example, simultaneously 'slanders' his rural heritage in order to use it as a means for his sharpest cultural critique yet, one aimed not only at *both* the city and the country, but also more broadly at the ideological impulses that drive Soviet society. If, for instance, Oddball exposes urban materialism and cynicism, Matvei Riazanov in the film's final segment unmasks rural distrust of the city as he makes peace with his past and urban culture by accepting the introduction of rock and roll into the village. And while Bron'ka Pupkov playfully 'distorts history' in his fanciful story about Hitler and punishes himself for it, Vaseka the sculptor subtly battles the (Soviet) falsification of history by burning his own overly heroic sculpture of Sten'ka Razin. Thus, Shukshin manages to point an accusing finger in all directions, levelling the distinctions between urban and rural, privileged and marginalized within the context of a film that blurs the boundaries between film and literature. Admittedly, these connections are not obvious on a first viewing. Read in this way, however, *Strange People* emerges as Shukshin's most interesting – if least 'successful' – adaptation and his most provocative treatment of his conflicted identity as an artist and a transplanted rural immigrant in Moscow.

After *Strange People*, Shukshin turned away from literary adaptation, complaining of the need for *kinoliteratura* or 'literature for the cinema' (Shukshin 1981: 137–8, 185–6). His solution was to revive the so-called *kinopovest'* (cine-novella), something between a screenplay and a novella: literature expressly written with filming in mind. His last two films were based exclusively on his own *kinopovesti*, including his biggest film success, the phenomenal *Red Kalina Berry* (*Kalina krasnaia*, 1974), published as a *kinopovest'* a whole year before the movie came out.[9]

Looking back at his work as a filmmaker in 1974, Shukshin went so far as to limit his achievements in cinema to his last two films, the only ones originally conceived and written for the screen, *Peasant Stoves and Benches* (*Pechki-lavochki*, 1972) and *Red Kalina Berry*. 'All the others', he noted, 'were just part of mastering the craft, just part of surviving' (Shukshin 1981: 242). Ultimately, the problem lay, perhaps, as much in genre as in the act of adaptation itself. The short story, on which Shukshin's reputation as a writer is based, proved to be a difficult literary genre to translate to film for the simple reason that it takes more than one story to equal a feature-length movie. The harder Shukshin tried to overcome this difficulty, the less success he met with. When the more sophisticated film grammar of his second and third movies made his film anthologies more 'authentic' (as in *Your Son and Brother*) or 'aesthetic' (as in *Strange People*), the screen adaptations resonated less with viewers and the film establishment. Shukshin, too, understood that his attempt to work in the movies in the same genre as in literature had brought him to a dead end. If he ever wanted to win approval for the screen adaptation he most hoped to make – the film of his novel on Sten'ka Razin – he would need to prove himself in larger genres. Though audiences and critics liked the least sophisticated of his first three films best, it is really his second and third movies that anticipate the mature film style of Shukshin's last two pictures. Moreover, Shukshin's move from author to actor in those movies became a clarifying moment. Here the actor-writer-director of Shukshin's last two films merged with the folk storyteller of his prose. By using his role as actor in these movies to negotiate the gap between author and *auteur*, Shukshin managed to make storyteller and filmmaker one. Self-adaptation became self-enactment. Film *auteur* became folk storyteller, resolving – at least in the short run – the conflicting sides to his artistic and personal heritage. A peasant tradition enabled the urban filmmaker to find the winning formula that was to produce the movie for which he would be known in Soviet cinema history, *Red Kalina Berry.* But Shukshin could not have reached this point without his attempts at screening his short stories, which enabled him to test the limits and possibilities of marrying his literary and film careers and ultimately to discover how best to achieve a true synthesis of his artistic interests. In the end, the 'meaning of the song', Shukshin discovered, depended on far more than the words alone.

Notes

1 See Woll for an excellent critical treatment of these issues from 1953 to the late 1960s.

2 See Shukshin (1981: 169–82), where he discusses cinematic co-authorship at length.

3 See Furnkov (1964: 4), Pogozheva (1964: 3) and Kuznetsov (1965: 142).

4 See '*Posleslovie k fil'mu "Zhivet takoi paren"*' in Shukshin 1981: 111–14. The article originally appeared in *Iskusstvo kino* 9 (1964).

5 One thinks of Andrei Tarkovskii's *Ivan's Childhood* (*Ivanovo detstvo*, 1962) with its remarkable dream segments or Mikhail Kalatozov's fantasy scenes from *Cranes are Flying* (*Letiat zhuravli*, 1957).

6 'Inner Content' ('*Vnutrenee soderzhanie*') was published in the March 1967 issue of the journal *Moskva.*

7 Shukshin mentions one such improvisation with the actress who played Aunt Anis'ia, Nina Sazonova. See '*Pered mnogomillionoi auditoriei*' in Shukshin 1981: 179. Sazonova relates a different instance in her reminiscences of Shukshin, '*V kazhdom slove–sud'ba chelovecheskaia*', see Fedoseeva-Shukshin and Chernenko (1979: 281).

8 For a representative sampling, see Kriachko, Bleiman, Orlov, Anninskii and Klado.

9 *Kalina krasnaia* appeared in *Nash sovremennik* 4 (1973).

Part III

Re-viewing Russia

Myth and nation

8 The Mikhalkov brothers' view of Russia

Birgit Beumers

Screen adaptations have historically occupied a prominent place in Soviet cinema. In the silent era, the new medium of film primarily served to tell stories, drawn largely from classical Russian literature. The first Russian-produced movies presented the plots of short stories or derived their motifs from nineteenth-century novels. As Tarkovskii noted, in its early days cinema was a means of illustrating classical literature (Tarkovsky 1986: 63). In Russia, the approach to screen adaptation was therefore from the outset governed by a desire to capture as exactly as possible the qualities inherent in the novel. Moreover, film could offer a precise representation of real space through settings, costumes and the physiognomy of characters – elements that could only be verbally sketched in a novel and had to be fleshed out by the readers' imagination. Film illustrated the narrative, offering an accurate depiction of reality as setting for the fictional plot. The cinematic image thus conveyed reality with a degree of accuracy that exceeded the possibilities of the narrative. In this sense, film allowed the illustration, and thus perfection, of literature to the level of a seemingly 'objective reality'. In this lay both cinema's greatest attraction and its grandest illusion: the filmmaker could henceforth manipulate images and enliven the setting of a novel. While it was clear that actors played the characters, the illusion of reality was always present in the space, notably the nature shots taken on location.

Furthermore, early cinema relied on facial expression to render emotions before the word – in the form of intertitles – could support the narrative. With the advent of sound, characters could be portrayed through words and intonation, so that by the mid-1930s film could do the same thing as literature: tell a story with words, and more – illustrate and duplicate the world (Izvolov 2001). The use of an authentic setting was an important feature of Russian sound film (mostly shot on location with sound recorded later in the studio). At the same time, European film studios tended to reconstruct places of action (streets, houses, interiors) in the studio, which enabled them to record the sound on the set. Russian cinema adhered to the authentic representation of space that stemmed from the silent era rather than embracing the artistically designed re-creation of space that was common practice in the European studios such as Albatros, Epinay, UFA, and Denham.

This chapter explores the use of space, specifically nature, in the post-Thaw period to create, through Russian literary heritage, a national identity for Russia. The filmmakers chosen for this investigation are the Mikhalkov brothers, Nikita Mikhalkov (b. 1945) and his elder brother Andrei (Mikhalkov)-Konchalovskii (b. 1937), who belong to a family with allegiances both in Russian traditions of the nineteenth century and in the Soviet *nomenklatura*. Their father, Sergei Mikhalkov, wrote children's stories and the text of the Soviet national anthem; their mother, Natalia Konchalovskaia, was a poet; and their grandfather, Petr Konchalovskii, was a well-known painter and member of the 'Knave of Diamonds' art movement.

In a way, both Mikhalkov brothers show pride in their genealogy: Andrei was his mother's favourite and adopted her name, while Nikita traced his family tree back to Surikov, Pushkin, and the Romanov dynasty on the maternal side, and Tolstoi, Odoevskii, and Suvorov on the paternal side. Yet while Konchalovskii experienced problems with the censors (*Asia's Happiness* (*Asino schast'e*) was banned in 1967), Mikhalkov never had serious censorship problems with his films and was even allowed to film in Italy at a time when the same was held against Andrei Tarkovskii. Konchalovskii emigrated to the US, while his younger brother remained in the USSR.

When exploring the representation of nature as aesthetic and/or national space, the artistic circle – and not just the family background – of the Mikhalkov brothers needs to be borne in mind. Andrei Konchalovskii studied at the Film Institute with Andrei Tarkovskii, for whom he had written the screenplays for the first three films.[1] Tarkovskii later employed Konchalovskii's director of photography, Grigorii Rerberg,[2] for *Mirror Zerkalo*, 1974). Konchalovskii, who had made his debut at Kirgizfilm, continued for several years a close collaboration with the central Asian studios, and co-authored with Fridrikh Gorenshtein the screenplay for *The Seventh Bullet* (*Sed'maia pulia*, 1972), directed by Ali Khamraev; the designer on the film was Rustam Khamdamov. Gorenshtein co-wrote the script for Tarkovsky's *Solaris* (1972) and for *Light Wind* (*Ariel*, 1972, banned). He also composed, with Konchalovskii, the script for *Slave of Love* (*Raba liubvi*, 1975), which was to be directed by Khamdamov before the project was closed and the film's production handed over to Mikhalkov. By 1974 this circle closes, and the paths part: Konchalovskii's collaboration with Tarkovsky came to an end, as did his work with Rerberg; Khamdamov did not return to filmmaking until 1990, although his influence on designs remains visible beyond *Slave of Love*. The aesthetic (not political or nationalist) interconnectedness between a group of artists, many of whom were dissidents, show similarities in their view of Russia. These similarities stem, in the first instance, from their collective work in the 1960s and early 1970s rather than from a common nationalist ideology that can be attributed to similar images with different aesthetic qualities.

Both Mikhalkov and Konchalovskii worked on literary adaptations, classical and contemporary. Konchalovskii's career began with *The First Teacher* (*Pervyi uchitel'*, 1965), adapted from the novella of the Kyrgyz writer Chingis Aitmatov. After the ban of *Asia's Happiness* in 1967 Konchalovskii returned to adaptations with a film based on Ivan Turgenev's 1859 novel *A Nest of Gentlefolk* (*Dvorianskoe gnezdo,* 1969) and Chekhov's play *Uncle Vania* (*Diadia Vania,* 1971).[3] Mikhalkov began his career as filmmaker (after having successfully started off as an actor) with experiments in genre, notably the Western and melodrama, with *At Home among Strangers, a Stranger at Home* (*Svoi sredi chuzhikh, chuzhoi sredi svoikh*, 1974) and *A Slave of Love* before turning to literary adaptations. These range from Chekhov's *Unfinished Piece for a Mechanical Piano* (*Neokonchennaia p'esa dlia mekhanicheskogo pianino*, 1977) adapted from the play *Platonov/Fatherlessness* (*Bezottsovshchina*, ca. 1878) and the film *Dark Eyes* (*Oci ciornie*, Italy, 1987), based on Chekhov's 'Lady with a Lapdog' and other stories, to Ivan Goncharov's *Oblomov* (1979), and extend to adaptations of contemporary texts such as Aleksandr Volodin's *Five Evenings* (*Piat' vecherov*, 1978) and Sofia Prokof'eva's *A Private Conversation* (*Bez svidetelei*, 1983).

Russia traditionally had a special relationship to literary classics. Soviet filmmakers were largely concerned with fidelity to the original and the political correctness of their interpretation. Soviet criticism tended to make the issue of the filmmaker's fidelity to the writer's intention a measure of his loyalty to the Russian classical heritage and, by extension, to the ideological correctness of his views within the value system of Socialist Realism. From this premise stems the common insistence by Soviet critics that the merit of a screen adaptation lies in its 'accurate' and 'truthful' rendering of the original; any omission or addition equalled a distortion of the work. The concern, almost obsession, with 'fidelity' is well reflected in the debates on literary adaptations for stage and screen in several leading Russian literary journals and newspapers in the 1970s.[4] After the Thaw, departing from the original became common practice. Artists sought to express the texts' significance for the present, while the return to nineteenth-century Russia frequently served as a backdrop for criticism of the present, albeit in a hidden and disguised form. This is particularly true for the theatre, where more liberal and lax adaptations of the classics found their way onto the stage in the productions of Georgii Tovstonogov, Anatolii Efros and Yuri Liubimov in the 1960s and 1970s. Mikhalkov's and Konchalovskii's adaptations neatly fall into the period where fidelity stood for an official view and departure from the original equalled a potentially dissident reading of a classical text. One way of exploring Konchalovskii's and Mikhalkov's films is by assessing the degree of liberty they take. Konchalovskii seems to adhere largely to the original, while Mikhalkov exhibits more licence in reworking the material, a fact that may be related to their difference in age. Konchalovskii's choice of material is more conventional (a play and a novel), while Mikhalkov embarked on an early, unfinished and unwieldy play by Chekhov that lent itself to interpretation in the light of the main corpus of Chekhov's later work; the voluminous Goncharov novel clearly required pruning even for a two-series (i.e. over 100 minutes) film version as opposed to a television serialization; *Dark Eyes* is based on themes from the stories rather than a single, clearly identifiable narrative. Therefore, while Konchalovskii chose to remain formally within the conventions of literary adaptations, Mikhalkov deliberately ventured into experimentation with form and imposed his own stamp on his adaptation. In formal terms Mikhalkov is more adventurous than his brother. However, the imagery used to convey Mikhalkov's and Konchalovskii's view of Russia tells a different story about innovation and convention in the work of the two brothers.

I am interested less in the issue of fidelity to the original, although the adaptation technique will be mentioned in this context where relevant, than on the brothers' adaptations of nineteenth-century literature as a means of assessing how the worlds of Turgenev, Goncharov and Chekhov are captured on screen in an attempt to produce a national space for Russia. Consequently, I focus on the imagery chosen to convey Russia's classical heritage, rather than on narrative techniques, or the transposition of narrative strategies onto celluloid. The nature imagery as viewed through the prism of the classical literary heritage is related to Russian national identity and placed in the context of nostalgia for the past.

The imagery of nature, or rather of the space that is associated with Russia, forms the core of this enquiry. For the historical reasons outlined above, it is essential to set apart authentic space (nature) from artistic space (setting, studio). Henri Lefebvre's distinction between 'representation of space' (the image, the depiction of space, for example by the camera) and 'representational space' (space as representative of something else, for example of Russia) (Lefebvre 1991: 233) helps differentiate between space as an image and space as a symbol. If we are looking for ways of creating national identity in film, we should expect to find primarily the use of space as a symbol, representative of Russia's character. The following analysis of the use of space and mise-en-scène demonstrates that Konchalovskii is concerned primarily with the creation of space as an artistic setting, while Mikhalkov depicts Russia as a symbolic space that is seen at a distance, thus underscoring the longing for a precise, historical past.

The space of memory

Konchalovskii's *Uncle Vania* hardly goes beyond a theatrical approach. It follows the sequence of events in the play, omitting merely a scene between Voinitskii and Elena Sergeevna (act I), Voinitskii's monologue (act II), and some of Astrov's speeches on nature. Konchalovskii set the entire film inside a house, an artistic space neatly designed by N. Dvigubskii. There is another world outside, which is visible through the windows and the open doors: the real space of the Russian fields. The characters thus have a wider view of nature than we (the spectators): in Chatman's terms, the story space is larger than the discourse space (Chatman 1978: 96–7). Spatially, Konchalovskii eschews the possibilities of cinema, choosing a static location. Instead, he concentrates on the emotional relationships between characters rendered superbly by the actors (Innokentii Smoktunovskii, Irina Kupchenko, Sergei Bondarchuk, Irina Miroshnichenko), and makes elaborate use of colour, style of costumes and decor. The film is a well-made melodrama without a trace of Chekhovian absurdity.

Uncle Vania would be of little interest as an adaptation (film equals literature) were it not for the use of documentary inserts. The film begins with a series of documentary photographs of scenes from Russian life in the 1890s. Images from Chekhov's photo-album show the writer in the company of friends and actors. Pictures that could have been taken on his travels to the distant and deprived regions of Russia foreground dying children. Historical photographs depict the tsar and his family, and on the hunt with a shot deer. Other photographs document the famines of 1891–92, revealing newspaper reports and images of a starving population, of barren fields and thinned woods. These photos form the film's introduction. They are interspersed with the titles for the film and accompanied by the cacophonous music of Alfred Schnittke, which integrates noises diegetic to the photographs (the crying of a child, a train, a chorus, march music, bells). Later in the film Astrov looks at these pictures and pins some of them onto the wall. He also shows them to an uninterested Elena Sergeevna, almost interrupting the film's narrative with these illustrations that accompany his speech on nature in act II. The pictures reveal Astrov's disillusionment: he may plead for nature, for the importance of flora and fauna, but he knows only too well the reality that surrounds the estate. The scenes of the exploitation of the earth shown on the photos foreshadow in an apocalyptic vision the end of an era, the end of the Romanovs, the end of nature, the end of mankind. Konchalovskii uses photos as a document of the real – as opposed to the artificial – world in the house, thus referring subtly to the absurdity of the situation that the play creates: the frivolity of everyday melodrama is set against a backdrop of the end of an era. The historical Russian reality of the photos is more tangible than the family's emotional reality; the aesthetic realities (set, nature) have a more serious quality than the trifles and psychological entrapments of the characters. Nothing changes for the characters, but Russia stands on the brink of an abyss.

The drama proper begins with black-and-white shots of the interior of the house, which gradually becomes inhabited. The arrangement of the rooms in the house creates the illusion of space. The corridor on the ground level seems to connect all the rooms into one common space, making privacy and seclusion possible only by closing a door, or retiring to Voinitskii's room on the top floor. The windows overlook the garden without ever offering a view. They serve, rather, to reflect the characters in the glass, or to let in the breeze or the chill of the rain. The windows, together with the oval mirror in the dining room, offer the main sources of light in the otherwise dark and gloomy interiors of the house. While Chekhov's play moves from the outside (the veranda) to the inside, Konchalovskii confines the entire action to the inside. Only once does the camera leave the house, following Astrov's carriage across a field that resembles the barren land on the photographs. Konchalovskii refers to a number of different images of space (maps, documents, pictures), while offering a final panning shot of the wintry Russian forests. Russia is frozen, literally covered under a layer of frost and snow.

Every act starts off with a black-and-white sequence before moving to colour, and even then colour is restricted to a blue-green-white palette. The film shifts to colour when the Serebriakovs arrive; when Elena has rejected Voinitskii's love; when Voinitskii catches Elena and Astrov in an embrace. In each act, the shift to colour occurs when the dull life acquires a different twist: the arrival; the refusal to rekindle an old love; the abortive seduction. All these scenes represent attempts – doomed to failure – to breathe new life into the dull existence on the estate. In the final act Konchalovskii operates the same principle in reverse. After the Serebriakovs' departure (in colour) the film switches back to black and white as Sonia, Voinitskii and Astrov carry on with their dull lives. Yet these characters are aware of the outside world. Astrov knows the photos, owns maps, travels to the outside world. Voinitskii is attached to measuring and information devices, such as newspapers, barometers, clocks, and the abacus. The dullness and boredom of their existence is associated with a warmly tinted black-and-white, while the unrest brought about by the Serebriakovs brings cold hues of colour into the house. Konchalovskii's use of black-and-white sequences and the documentary photos is a technique not dissimilar to the documentary footage combined with black-and-white flashbacks in Tarkovskii's *Mirror* (*Zerkalo*, 1974), which was shot by the same director of photography, Grigorii Rerberg.

The device of inserted photos used to underpin the narrative recurs in *Nest of Gentlefolk*, where etchings from European cities are shown in lieu of the history of Lavretskii's travels. The artistic images (not documents as in *Uncle Vania*) summarize his trip to Europe, culminating with etchings of Petersburg and Moscow to mark his return to Russia. Then watercolours offer artistic views of the countryside, gradually dissolving into a shot of nature. Konchalovskii here enlivens artistic depictions of space. He brings paintings of Russia to life, turning them into a real space that is of direct importance to the characters. This space contains, according to Lavretskii, the essence of Russia. When seeking to define Russia, Astrov comments on the documentary images while Lavretskii refers directly to nature.

Nest of Gentlefolk juxtaposes two estates: Kalitin's and Lavretskii's. The first consists of a cultivated and arranged garden and a Western-style mansion with elegant and light interiors, a lived-in space. The latter is a neglected and overgrown mansion, a museum space containing memorabilia, but not a living space. In Lavretskii's house objects bear symbolic meaning or trigger memories. The apples in the lounge speak of the wasted harvest. The cobwebs remind one of the long absence of the master. The portraits of Lavretskii's parents trigger a flashback, as does the old book Lavretskii finds in a window-frame.

Lavretskii experiences two kinds of flashbacks. First there are reminiscences of his life in Paris (both in black-and-white and colour) as he recalls his wife whom he has left because of her infidelity, but whom he clearly loves (otherwise he would not remember). Second, the flashbacks that are triggered by a portrait of his mother and by the old book prompt his visions of a little girl in the countryside. On both occasions it is the memory of Lavretskii's mother that generates his visions, which consists of a projection of his own daughter onto the way in which Lavretskii imagined his mother to be: a peasant girl, at one with nature, running in the fields with a bouquet of flowers. It is not until the final frame of the film that Lavretskii achieves his dream-vision: he appears with the girl in a field, uniting his hope for Russia with his own child, harmonizing the time and the space of his vision. It is significant that Lavretskii's wife Varvara returns to Paris according to the film version, while in the novel she remains in Russia on another of Lavretskii's estates. The Varvara of the film reproaches him for sustaining an imagined view of Russia that holds no correspondence to reality. Lavretskii is reunited with his vision of Russia, and projects the memory of his mother onto the little girl, underpinning her genealogy, which predestines her to be also at one with Russia rather than follow the subversive path of Varvara, spoilt by the West.

Konchalovskii makes ample use of the relationship between art and life. Instead of using a narrator, he makes Lavretskii's biography the subject of a welcome monologue of Lavretskii's manservant Anton. Lavretskii's travels are summarized through illustrations. His life in Europe is, as it were, artificial, worthy only of a sketchy reference. The final scene between Lavretskii and Liza Kalitina takes place in a storage space for paintings, and Liza stands before a painting with an angel, thus alluding to her retirement to a monastery. As a character she has lost emotion and individuality and is destined to withdraw from reality into representation. In the picturesque wilderness of Lavretskii's estate the pastoral coexists with the artistic. Cows graze next to classical sculptures. At the same time, the life of the Kalitins is almost caricatured. Their visit seems at first to take place only in Lavretskii's vision. The girls hop through the garden like animated characters moving at the wrong speed, and Maria Kalitina is an extravagant, if not eccentric, woman with a number of mannerisms. Russian country life is just as false as society life in Paris, while the truth rings in the shots of nature, the trees filmed from below, the views of the fields and valleys unspoilt by architecture.

For Konchalovskii, the estate is a zone of seclusion from reality, where characters choose to ignore the changes in the world that surrounds them. The images and memory of this other world protrude and create an absurd relationship between inside and outside. Astrov's awareness combined with his inactivity makes his existence no less frivolous than that of the Serebriakovs. In *Nest* there is the memory of a happy marriage, a happy childhood, that clashes with the reality of Varvara's infidelity. Lavretskii's memory of his own child is associated with his mother (rather than his wife) and he is reunited with his past and his child (future) in the final frames, which thus reunite space and time. Konchalovskii's images of nature are always clearly delineated as such. Maps and photos, etchings and watercolours offer documentary and artistic views onto reality. His reference to nature is purposeful: Russia is a barren field on the photos, frozen in the final frames of *Uncle Vania*. It is made abstract, prepared for a new potential meaning to emerge after a social upheaval such as the revolution. Artistically created space may be private (the house of *Uncle Vania*) or social (the ballrooms of Paris, the salon of the Kalitins). Real, authentic space has pastoral qualities: the fields in *Nest*, the barren landscape in *Uncle Vania*. The natural spaces (the fields) which are glorified by Lavretskii as harbouring Russia's identity are riddled with art objects (sculptures) and exposed as imaginary in Varvara's criticism. Lavretskii chooses to live with the illusion of Russia's national character rather than away from his motherland. Konchalovskii never glorifies Russia without criticism, without pointing at the ignorance of reality, or the imaginary vision. Russian nature is impressive, all-embracing and beautiful, but it is not a national space. Konchalovskii's Russia is a 'motherland' (*rodina*) with distinctly female qualities (barrenness, fertility) and therefore associated with the mother/daughter figures in *Nest*. Konchalovskii's characters remember a precise historical or personal past associated with this motherland (famine in *Uncle Vania*, a mother's youth in *Nest*).

The monument of nature

The device of picture animation used in both of Konchalovskii's films has also been employed in several of Mikhalkov's films. In *Oblomov*, etchings of Petersburg monuments are superimposed onto views of the landscape, suggesting that urban space is a flat reproduction as opposed to the three-dimensionality of nature, thus privileging rural over urban space. The etchings gradually subside to watercolours of Gorokhov Street, of Oblomov's apartment. The images gain colour before they are endowed with life. Moreover, Shtolz's flashback to his childhood that starts when Shtolz sits by the window of the bathhouse and looks out onto a snow-covered plain also begins with a drawing of a boy by a window. A series of paintings then show a boy at a desk, and a boy with his mother, until the narrative of Shtolz's childhood reaches the moment of his departure from the estate, when the flashback switches to an authentic setting with real characters.

In Mikhalkov's cinematic interpretation of Goncharov's novel Ilia Il'ich Oblomov is played by the cheerful and much loved Oleg Tabakov (see Figure

Figure 8.1 A scene from Mikhalkov's *Oblomov*: Oblomov (Oleg Tabakov)
Source: Photo by Anatolii Pashvykin. Courtesy of Birgit Beumers

8.1).[5] Oblomov is a lovable character, as is Shtolz, played by Yuri Bogatyrev,[6] who displays the positive attributes of a caring and concerned friend. Oblomov is funny in his social ineptitude and charming in his naive and infantile reactions, withdrawing into a corner to sulk when laughed at in Ol'ga's house, or cheating himself when having a secret meal in his own kitchen at night while dieting. Mikhalkov refrains from showing Shtolz's activity and Oblomov's lethargy as sharp, contrasting principles. Instead, Mikhalkov brings back the childhood of both protagonists in a series of flashbacks that explain their character. Oblomov's lethargy is apparently caused by his early childhood, when he was pampered by his mother and cherished by the servants. The flashbacks to the Oblomovka estate are juxtaposed with the image of a depressing city. Oblomov is a more cheerful person altogether in the countryside than in Petersburg. In this respect, Mikhalkov plugs into the nineteenth-century literary tradition of interpreting Petersburg as a depressing and gloomy city.

The shots of nature capture the vastness of Russia. Pavel Lebeshev's camera frequently lingers on the landscape (Kostroma), both in the Oblomovka sequences and the shots of the woods and fields surrounding the summerhouse. Oblomov's destruction of the lilac bush to offer a wider view of the fields occupies a prominent place in the film, revealing Oblomov's thoughtless conduct vis-à-vis nature to achieve a perfect view of a beauty spot. Oblomov here acts on Ol'ga's prompting. For her, the artistic impression of the landscape is more important than the chaos that nature offers. This vision of nature as a perfect image is replicated by the filmmaker Mikhalkov, who also seeks to elevate nature above pure representation in order to establish its monumentality. At the end of the film the camera pans over the vast space of a Russian valley, while a boy (Andriusha Oblomov) runs through the field toward a river. The scene is accompanied by Rakhmaninov's *Vespers*. The green fields and woods with a river quietly flowing through a valley represent Mikhalkov's ultimate symbol for Mother Russia. It echoes a view of his own childhood over the river near his home in Nikolina Gora.

The image of a child in the Russian plains encompasses nostalgia for a Russia of the past. Oblomov wants to return to his childhood, Mikhalkov to nineteenth-century Russia. The sequences suggest Russia's expanse, its vastness, but – through the association with a child – its immaturity and, in the context of the narrative, the inability of the characters to be at one with the present. The characters idealize a Russia of their childhood as they dream of a return to a sheltered past, not unlike Chekhov's Three Sisters associating the location Moscow with the past. The past is reconstructed in the final shots from a spatial and temporal distance that is not acknowledged, repeating the past in the here and now. The boy Andriusha could just as well be Iliusha; the past therefore equals the present and time is frozen, without a possibility for change. Mikhalkov offers a restorative view of the past without recognizing the temporal and spatial displacement (Boym 1994: 293–1, 2001: xii–xix). When Russia is viewed from a distance, the degree of idealization increases: Oblomovka is a childhood memory as well as an estate at a distance. While Tarkovskii transposes his image into the here and now (Gorchakov is both in Italy in the present and in Russia in the past in the final frames of *Nostalghia*), Mikhalkov deludes himself and the spectator into believing in a perfect Russia of the past.

Mikhalkov's two Chekhov adaptations reflect the changes in his attitude to Russia between the 1970s and the 1980s. *An Unfinished Piece for a Mechanical Piano* departs considerably from the original, a little-known play by Chekhov, written in his youth and commonly known as *Platonov* (drafted 1878–79, completed 1881–83, published 1923), which presents many of the themes of his later plays in an uncondensed and unwieldy dramatic form. However, the film brought Mikhalkov international fame, winning the main prize at the San Sebastian International Film Festival in 1977. While Konchalovskii was more interested in the tension within the character (internal life), Mikhalkov dwells on the relationships between characters (external life), and therefore uses setting and space in different ways. If Konchalovskii starts from a specially designed empty space, Mikhalkov begins with a spatial composition, mixing nature shots with designed spaces.

The first scene of *Mechanical Piano* is set in the open. Triletskii is entertaining Anna Petrovna, the landlady of the estate. In the distance we hear the voice of Anna Petrovna's stepson Sergei, who is married to Sofia Egorovna. The opening immediately establishes Mikhalkov's favourite scenes: the open field bordering on a river; the old stone mansion with steps leading up to it; the stucco-decorated windows and the ornate stone banister of the balcony. The opening scene extends the interior comforts and decorations of the house out into the open space (see Figure 8.2). The farcical nature of the situation, with the characters pretending to be inside but seated in the garden, is underlined by a dialogue that is disjoined from the image.

The characters move from the open space on the veranda into the conservatory, and into the inner section of the house for a serious scene. Inside, there are wooden floors, rattan furniture, a wooden staircase to the top floor, and walls decorated with instruments of the peasants. Further inside the house there is a dark dining room, lit with candles and kerosene lamps later. The space is delineated: the inside is reserved for games (masking) and dinner-table conversation (unmasking), while the outside space accommodates both farce and melodrama.

Figure 8.2 A scene from Mikhalkov's *Unfinished Piece for a Mechanical Piano*
Source: Photo by Anatolii Pashvykin. Courtesy of Birgit Beumers

Mikhalkov consistently utilizes the farcical elements of the play (which Konchalovskii avoids), culminating in the finale, when Platonov runs after his former love, Sofia, reproaching her for marrying the idle Sergei. As the camera pans out, it emerges that Sergei has inadvertently been watching them. Upset and humiliated, Sergei decides to leave wife and estate, and requests carriage and horses. He is given only the carriage. Meanwhile Platonov attempts suicide by jumping into the lake, choosing its shallowest point. His wife comforts him, wrapping him in her shawl in a scene accompanied ironically by Nemorino's aria from Donizetti's *L'Elisir d'amore*. The film ends on a double absurdity: Sergei is asleep in his carriage without a horse, while Platonov stands in the shallow lake swaddled in a woman's shawl. The film's finale underscores visually the characters' inability to take meaningful action; all they are capable of is creating absurd and ridiculous scenes.

Of all the characters only Platonov realizes that he failed to make his ideals come true. He is honest to himself, yet he mocks those who speak about the fate of Russia without even being able of taking their own lives into their hands (Shcherbuk, Sofia, Sergei). Their lethargy stands in sharp contrast to their verbosity and their vibrant imagination, which allows them to reinvent themselves in different games. In many ways Platonov resembles Lavretskii (*Nest*), who knows that his idealized view of Russia may not match reality, but who nevertheless wishes to continue to see it this way.

In the 1970s Mikhalkov still shared with his brother Konchalovskii certain devices relating to the use of space. Their characters realize the utopian and illusory quality of their vision of Russia (Lavretskii, Platonov). Their longing for the past is honest, free from any attempt to rebuild it. However, the final shot of *Mechanical Piano*, the valley with a river and the sloping green hills, would be transformed into a symbol for Russia in Mikhalkov's subsequent films, including *Oblomov*. The estate in *Mechanical Piano* is a space containing the values of the past. Mikhalkov no longer pines for the past as time, but the past as location, taking the first step towards a nostalgia that has lost space rather than lost time as its object.

Having begun his film with various dissolving views of the estate, Mikhalkov ends *Mechanical Piano* with a shot in which the camera withdraws into the house and lingers on the boy Petia, asleep on the sofa. Petia (Shcherbuk's nephew) had featured before in the fields, flattening the grass and riding a bike. He never seeks the company of adults and never takes notice of their remarks about his conduct. Instead, he stands aloof from the trite concerns and grotesque behaviour that reigns in the adult world. Petia is at one with nature, like Iliusha Oblomov. As we saw with *Oblomov*, the child in the vast fields is an image that characterizes Mikhalkov's notion of Russia. Here, however, the child is protected inside the house, while chaos dominates the relationship of the characters (now outside), who have abandoned the fight for the estate and turned instead to their bonds with nature. Mikhalkov fills the space of Russia with the figure of a child that represents the future, but that child is here still blissfully asleep. Thereby, Mikhalkov implies a certain inactivity and somnambulism on the part of contemporary Russia.

Mikhalkov's second Chekhov adaptation followed almost ten years after his success with *Mechanical Piano*, and this time the film was made in Italy. In *Dark Eyes*, Mikhalkov uses several themes of Chekhov's stories, largely 'Lady with a Lapdog', and turns them into a melodrama.[7] *Dark Eyes* begins with a series of late nineteenth-/early twentieth-century cartoon drawings seemingly from old newspapers (the paper has yellowed), showing scenes of people boarding a ship and the ship's departure on a sea voyage. The final cartoon is brought to life when Pavel Alekseev peers through the window into the restaurant, where he sees the Italian waiter Romano. The artistic and comically distorted space on the cartoons becomes a real space, but only briefly. The enclosed space of the restaurant makes the minds of the protagonists wander, and another image – this time a documentary photo showing Romano's wife and her family – is animated.

Inside the restaurant Alekseev meets Romano (Marcello Mastroainni). Romano is the (unreliable) narrator of his life, and the film is an illustration of his narrative, during which the camera returns occasionally to the two men to remind us of the present. The starting point of the narrative is a photograph, a document of a past that comes to life. Romano tells his life in a series of flashbacks, endowing the film with a subjective perspective. Alekseev's brief narrative at the end of their meeting is not supported visually; only Romano's past has images. Yet while Romano has no images of the present, Alekseev lives in the present. Mikhalkov teases the viewer into a complicated game with time and images.

Romano's story harks back to his marriage with Elisa and his departure for Montecatini Terme when his wife encountered financial problems with her estate (the theme of *The Cherry Orchard* resonates here). The spa offers an outlet for repressed activities, encouraging the development of a carnivalesque atmosphere of playing roles and games, not unlike *Mechanical Piano*. In this setting, the Russian lady Anna (with a dog) attracts Romano's attention. Romano invents an absurd story about his 'weak' legs (a hereditary condition that is linked to the Vesuvio eruption) and pretends to be cured by the Russian word *sobachka* ('lapdog'). Yet instead of making Romano an absurd failure à la Platonov, Mikhalkov endows him with a sudden melancholy for a Russia that seems to lend a meaning to Romano's life which he lacks in Italy and hopes to find in Russia. Romano tells Anna a false and pitiful story of his life. He is a clown and pretender, never serious, but an excellent actor.

Romano projects his hopes for love and a happy life onto Anna at a time when Elisa can no longer offer him the luxurious lifestyle he has become used to. Under the illusion that he loves Anna, Romano uses the unbreakable glass his brother-in-law invented as a pretext to go to Russia. Or rather, failing to play a role in Italy, the actor Romano seeks his part in Russia.

Romano is more at home in Russia than in Italy. The fear of officials to reach a decision, and the shunning of action (the factory at Sysoev) is something that Romano shares with the Russians: he has escaped from solving problems and selling family property in Italy. Similarly, the superficiality and façades prevailing in Russia correspond to Romano's acting skills. The letter S of the station name falls off as soon as the welcome ceremony is over, and fences collapse. This façade suggests that Russia belongs to European civilization, while nature truly harbours Russia's spiritual values; most nature shots offer a view on a church. The local vet Kostia asks Romano not to build a factory as it would destroy nature and demolish the landscape of the little town located on a river. Kostia echoes the perennial concern with nature in Chekhov's work, but also Mikhalkov's obsession with forests, fields, and rivers.

Mikhalkov draws a fine distinction between, on the one hand, the style of the Italian villa with its rich interiors and its ascetic terracotta-colour exteriors and, on the other hand, the architectural opulence of Kalitin's or Lavretskii's estate in *Nest*, or even the mansion in *Mechanical Piano*. The Montecatini Terme are flanked by white marble columns and floors, enhancing the classical style of Italian architecture. Petersburg, by contrast, has a cardboard appearance with its empty streets and squares and flimsy facades, clearly not shot on location. If Italy provides a lavish theatrical setting, then Petersburg offers a flimsy cardboard décor.

In the final Russian frames of *Dark Eyes* Kostia takes Romano to the nearby station. They ride on a cart across the river and through a valley (see Figure 8.3). Romano dreams of his mother and remembers how he covered his ears with his hands when his grandma would sing the lullaby 'Ninna Nonna' for him, while the gypsies ride past singing their songs. Indeed, the scene of Romano riding through the Russian countryside is accompanied by the Italian lullaby and then only by a gypsy song. Romano believes that he has a Slavic soul and has more affinities with Russia than his native Italy. Mikhalkov offers two perspectives: the view on Italy seen through the eyes of a Russian director (himself) and the view on Russia seen through the Italian visitor. He also introduces two spaces of Russian life: the provincial town and the city, which are façade only, and the countryside, which is genuine. The emphasis on the national 'peculiarities' of drinking, dancing and singing (to quote the title of Aleksandr Rogozhkin's film, *The Peculiarities of the National Hunt* [*Osobennosti natsional'noi okhoti*, 1995]) turned *Dark Eyes* into a cheap 'kitsch' version of Chekhov for Western consumption.

At the end of the narrative we return to reality. Now Romano must lay the tables in the restaurant. Alekseev wakes up his wife Anna. Her face is lit by the sun, and the shot dissolves in the image of the Russian valley. The final image is that of a vast Russian field, the ultimate embodiment of the Russian soul with its quietude and width, with qualities that will never change in Mikhalkov's view. The artistic images (cartoons) have turned into a real space (restaurant), in which another real space (product of the director/set designer) is created in the minds of the characters (the past is re-enacted in a form of meta-film). Nature is filled with another meaning. The image of the Russian valley is frozen, void of human life. It is the space of a past irretrievably lost for the individual, but accessible to the entire nation as an artistic product created by Mikhalkov. Here Mikhalkov turns Russian nature into a symbolic image representing a past he wishes to resurrect.

The image of a child in the field represents for Mikhalkov a longing for a Russia of the past. There is the boy in the field and later asleep in *Mechanical Piano*. There are the flashbacks to Iliusha running across the fields towards the river and the final shot of Andriusha in the valley. And there is the final shot in *Dark Eyes* of a Russian valley with gypsy carriages in the fog. The sequences suggest Russia's expanse, its vastness, but also its immaturity and, in the context of the narrative, the inability of characters to be at one with the present. They idealize a Russia of their childhood, a cocooned existence, the dream of a return to a sheltered past.

Mikhalkov is prone to freeze images of Russian nature: the slope to the river in *Mechanical Piano* (frozen by the gaze of the camera from the house); the view of the valley, frozen as Andriusha continues to shout for his mother; the view of the valley with the gypsy carts in the rising fog. It is the act of freezing the frame that instils in the space a sensation of timelessness and monumentality. The space has a value as nature, harbouring pastoral values and traditions of the past. Yet the link to the past (the estate) has

Figure 8.3 A scene from Mikhalkov's *Dark Eyes*

Source: Photo by Anatolii Pashvykin. Courtesy of Birgit Beumers

been severed (the Voinitsevs' estate lost, the Oblomov estate run down, the Russian valley near Sysoyev lost through Anna having left her husband, the Mayor of Sysoev). These spaces of nature are always seen in the summer. The space is disconnected from reality, but they are neither imaginary nor artistic. These spaces are symbolic, and they are only filled by sound, which connects them to the film's diegesis (the *Vespers*, the lullaby and the gypsy song, the Donizetti aria).

The traditional content of nature has been destroyed by personal and social upheaval. Instead of facing up to this gaping abyss (as Chekhov did, and Konchalovskii after him) Mikhalkov artificially – and through means of his camera, artistically – creates a new meaning for this space: that of Russia's national and spiritual cradle. As such, this space becomes monumental, framed with a camera that pans out in order to grasp its scope, width and expanse. The aerial shot at the end of *The Barber of Siberia* (*Sibirskii tsiriul'nik*, 1998), which tells the story of the superior moral values of the Russian cadet Andrei Tolstoi over those of the Western 'invaders' into his life (Jane Callaghan) and into Russian space (the inventor of a tree-cutting device McCracken), merely crowns Mikhalkov's earlier shots of the Russian valley with the river, underlining the interconnectedness of all Russian spaces.

For both Mikhalkov and Konchalovskii the image of open landscape encapsulates Mother Russia. In Andrei Tarkovskii's films, too, Russia is rendered through the poetic image of a landscape with a country-house (*Mirror*), or a meadow with a hut by a little pond where past and present merge (*Nostalgia*). For Konchalovskii this image is always in real time (past), and is acknowledged as such by the characters in their discourse (through document or flashback), thus offering an authentic relation of time and space. For Konchalovskii, it is a barren, frozen land, or a summery field filled with characters in the present, choosing to continue a secluded life in the past. For Mikhalkov the image of the fields is both in the past and the present. He dissolves and blurs time and space, creating the illusion of a continuous past and, by implication, of Russia's permanence. For Mikhalkov the space of memory is the same as the space of the present, and here he differs from Konchalovskii and Tarkovskii.

Viewed from a distance, Russia is even more idealized. In *Dark Eyes* the image of the carriage travelling through the fields and crossing a river is not only in the past (in Romano's narrative) but also in a distant land (Romano is in Italy). Similarly, Oblomovka is a childhood memory as well as an estate at a distance. In *Nostalghia* the wooden house is not only in the past, but also in the distance, and it is simultaneously in the present and in Italy, surrounded by ruins. Tarkovskii transposes his image into the here and now, unifying the space of Italy and Russia while representing through this very same image the dichotomy of his character, split between Russia and Italy, past and present (Tarkovsky 1986: 213, 216). Mikhalkov deludes himself and the spectator into believing in a perfect Russia of the past without taking into account its negative sides (as Konchalovskii does with the documentary footage). Moreover, Mikhalkov transposes *himself* into this idealized Russia which is best illustrated in his role of the tsar in *The Barber*.

In conclusion, Konchalovskii offers a non-idealized view of Russia, choosing pictures of the past in *Uncle Vania* to point at the devastation of Russia's countryside, and admitting in the finale of *Nest* that Mother Russia is only a visual ideal, an empty phrase that does not hold up to reality and scrutiny by a Western eye. For Mikhalkov the image of Mother Russia (the child in the field with a river flowing quietly through a valley) is indestructible because it is timeless and symbolic. Konchalovskii portrays the past as a setting for relationships of eternal, and contemporary, significance. Mikhalkov returns to the past without connecting it to the present, but by making it feel like the present.

In her seminal studies on mythologies of the past and nostalgia, Svetlana Boym has drawn a distinction between an ironic, reflective relationship to the past and a restorative, utopian nostalgia that rebuilds a past that no longer exists. This restorative nostalgia dwells, in Boym's words, on the *nostos*, the place that is to be rebuilt, rather than the longing (*algia*), and therefore tends towards a nationalist revival. From the 1980s onwards Mikhalkov advances in his films a position of remembering the past with a view to restoring it. His inclination towards nationalist revival is most explicitly rendered in *The Barber of Siberia* which expresses a wish to return to a late nineteenth century grossly distorted through Mikhalkov's cavalier approach to historical accuracy (Kibirskii 2002; Sokolov 1999). Mikhalkov not only cast himself as the tsar, but in real life he toyed with the idea of standing for the presidential elections in 2000. It is, I would suggest, this move from the memory of the past as fiction, to its revival as a new national space that made *Dark Eyes*, *Burnt by the Sun*, and *The Barber* so controversial with Russian critics (Beumers 2004).

Konchalovskii represents space via clearly defined media (photographic documents, watercolours, etchings), substituting the filmic rendition of events through another medium. Mikhalkov starts with the animation of images more real than the filmic narrative, replacing this reality in the final shot with a nature frozen and made permanent. Mikhalkov fills nature with a meaning in the past and then elevates it as a monumental space representing the present of Russia's national space. This monumentalism rebuilds the home (*nostos*) as static.

Space acquires a different quality. In *Mechanical Piano* the camera pans the estate at the beginning and the valley at the end, having moved from an outside view to a view from the inside, reinforcing the permanence of nature. In *Oblomov* the artistic image of the city becomes animated, and the view of nature is frozen again at the end, thereby creating a superior artistic image. In *Dark Eyes* the cartoons telling the story of boarding a ship are animated, and in the end the return to Russia is marked by the reflection of the sunset in Anna's face, coinciding with the sunrise over the Russian valley. Nature becomes a monument of its own in a world where estates are not mastered, but neglected. The link between city and country is broken: Oblomov is dislocated from his estate, Anna separated from her world, the Voinitsevs strolling through the valley. Mikhalkov elevates nature to an artistic image of painterly quality in order to create a monument to the national past with its value system. His image of Russia, encapsulated in the river flowing through a valley, blurs the borderline between past and present, real and artistic. The compression of time and space that so clearly identified the frames of Tarkovsky's *Nostalghia* (merging Russia and Italy) and *Mirror* (merging past and present) cannot be sensed in Mikhalkov.

From this perspective, Konchalovskii may use created settings, but his use of space is honest (as a place for action). Mikhalkov, by contrast, cradles the viewer with the illusion that the authentic space is real and pertains to the present. It is not; it is merely a filmic location.

Notes

1 See Tarkovsky (1999). They worked on *Steamroller and Violin*, *Ivan's Childhood*, *Andrei Rublev*, and a fourth script, *Antarctica*.

2 Rerberg had worked on *Uncle Vania*, *Nest of Gentlefolk* and *Asia's Happiness*.

3 Konchalovskii's Soviet films include *Asia's Happiness* (*Asino schast'e*, also known as *Istoriia Asi Kliachinoi, kotoraia liubila da ne vyshla zamuzh*, 1967, released 1988), *A Romance about Lovers* (*Romans o vliublennykh*, 1974) and the epic *Siberiade* (*Sibiriada*, 1979). The American films include *Maria's Lovers* (1984), *Runaway Train* (1985), *Tango & Cash* (1989), *The Inner Circle* (*Blizhnii krug*, Russia/Italy, 1991) and *The Odyssey* (USA, 1996). After his return to Russia he made a sequel to *Asia's Happiness* entitled *The Little Speckled Hen* (*Kurochka Riaba*, Russia, 1994), and *House for Fools* (*Dom dlia durakov*, 2002).

4 In 1979 the topic of stage adaptations and their relation to the literary original formed the subject of issues 5 and 6 of the journal *Teatr*. Konstantin Rudnitskii's seminal study (Rudnitskii 1981) appeared soon afterwards. Between 1979 and 1981 the weekly *Literaturnaia gazeta* and the journal *Literaturnoe obozrenie* published a large cluster of articles on prose adaptations. Another major debate was generated by Viktor Rozov's article (Rozov 1980) in which he described the heavy use of often bad adaptations as an obstacle for young playwrights in getting their works staged in theatres. There followed a series of articles on this subject in *Literaturnaia gazeta* between October 1980 and February 1981.

5 Oleg Tabakov, b. 1937, graduated from Moscow Arts Theatre School in 1957 and founded with Oleg Efremov the Sovremennik Theatre. Since 1983 he has been at the Moscow Arts Theatre of which he became the artistic director in 2000. He founded his own studio theatre in 1986. He has also played numerous roles in film, including Nikolai Rostov in *War and Peace* (*Voina i mir*, 1967).

6 Yurii Bogatyrev (1947–89) graduated from the Shchukin School in 1971, then became an actor at the Sovremennik Theatre (1971–77), and later at the Moscow Arts Theatre. His roles have included Maksakov in *Slave of Love*, Sergei Voinitsev in *Unfinished Piece*, Stoltz in *Oblomov* and Stasik in *Kinfolk*.

7 Mikhalkov largely draws on 'Lady with a Lapdog', but complements his adaptation with scenes, themes and characters from other Chekhov stories. Romano's family life is drawn from 'The Name-Day' ('*Imeniny*'), where the husband of the story's heroine cares little for her until it is too late; Anna's family life bears parallels to that of Anna in 'Lady with a Lapdog', but her relation with her husband, who sees her as an object of pride, echoes 'Anna round the Neck' ('*Anna na shee*').

9 Adapting the landscape

Oblomov's vision in film

Russell Scott Valentino

In the crystal-image there is this mutual search – blind and halting – of matter and spirit: beyond the movement-image, 'in which we are still pious.'

Gilles Deleuze, *Cinema 2: The Time Image*

In his essay, 'What Novels Can Do That Films Can't (and Vice Versa)', Seymour Chatman argues that, as description entails a stoppage of story-time, 'films do not and cannot describe'. Filmic story time is, so to speak, always running, and the brief suspensions in which the author of a literary work might freeze a moment in order to supply descriptive detail are made impossible, or at least highly awkward, by the medium itself:

> Whereas in novels, movements and hence events are at best constructions imaged by the reader out of words, that is, abstract symbols which are different from them in kind, the movements on the screen are so iconic, so like the real life movements they imitate, that the illusion of time passage simply cannot be divorced from them. Once that illusory story-time is established in a film, even dead moments, moments when nothing moves, will be felt to be part of the temporal whole, just as the taxi meter continues to run as we sit fidgeting in a traffic jam.
>
> (Chatman 1992: 409 10)

Chatman's assertion on one level harkens back to the Aristotelian claims of such classical film theorists as Sigfried Kracauer and André Bazin regarding the fundamentally realist nature of cinema.[1] On another, however, sidestepping any implied evaluative claims, it provides an accessible point of departure for coming to terms with the adaptation of descriptive passages from artistic prose to film. Chatman explores several alternative adaptive methods – methods that he claims take advantage of the potential specific to the medium – used by film makers to render literary description and the assertions inherent in it. He draws his examples mostly from the camera techniques employed in Jean Renoir's 1936 adaptation of Maupassant's *Une Partie de campagne*.[2] In this chapter, by contrast, I would like to examine a different kind of adaptation, one in which the literary description and the implicit temporal suspension that accompanies it are highlighted to such an extent that these, rather than any substitutive movement-oriented constituents, assume a centrally *static* role. They do this, moreover, to such an extent as to overwhelm the film's story time, splitting a moment into two contrasting halves, 'one of which', in Deleuze's words, 'is launched towards the future while the other falls into the past' (Deleuze 1989: 81). The resulting double vision is, on one hand, a moment of crystalline purity and reflection, an aesthetic perfection captured and held up for pleasurable scrutiny. On the other, it is nothing more than a stagnant and lifeless 'image'. In both sides of the vision, the literary descriptive moment is given depth and significance by the movement of film that surrounds and contextualizes it.

The scene in question, which concludes Nikita Mikhalkov's 1979 feature, *Oblomov*, uses what is essentially a closing establishing shot (I am aware of the oxymoron) for a distinct purpose: to render a description, convey a series of *assertions* made by the 1859 novel's narrator, and translate those assertions into a pictorial representation. But rather than disproving Chatman's thesis, the scene relies on the observation with which he begins: 'filmic time is implacable. Thus the prolonged suspension of movement at the film's end is both conspicuous and meaningful'.

At issue is more than a simple 'painterly' approach to depiction. Mikhalkov's lugubrious scenic development foregrounds both the novel's emphasis on the dreamy nostalgia of its hero and the ambiguous triumph of an aestheticized life that amounts to a form of metaphysical stasis. The main protagonist's memory of childhood merges with his own child's anticipation of what is to come, yielding a 'crystal-image' that confuses mental and physical time (Rodowick 1997: 79–118). Where, however, Deleuze attributes to the crystal-image a clear restorative function, as suggested for instance in my epigraph, by which we may somehow recapture a lost faith in the world, the frozen moment we shall explore here has far more dubious implications.

The scene is prepared as Shtolz and Ol'ga, now some six or seven years married, sit in separate rooms of their summer house, speaking without facing each other, Shtolz at his desk, Ol'ga at her embroidery table. The windows and doors are open, the sun is shining, children play in the yard. Alekseev, Oblomov's long-time friend, hovers faithfully amidst the children until Ol'ga asks him to fetch her some medicine, which Shtolz appears to eye with disapproval. The superficially idyllic atmosphere is betrayed by an underlying tension in their conversation. A suspicion of dashed hopes and unresolved allegiances lingers in the air. Oblomov has been dead for some years.

Against the backdrop of this taut falseness, Oblomov's child, who is playing with the others in the yard, upon hearing that his mother has arrived at the train station and is on her way for a visit, suddenly rushes headlong into the fields, calling, 'Mama's come! Mama!'. The boy's appearance, voice, and words recall the opening scene in which child-Oblomov tiptoed around his parents' house, waiting for his mother to awaken after her return from a journey the night before. The exclamation 'Mama's come!' from the film's beginning is repeated verbatim numerous times at its end, thereby providing a frame for the film's 'real-time' body, which the backward-looking first scene and the forward-looking last effectively highlight. The child, running towards his unseen mother and calling out to her, disappears into the green, rolling hills, which in turn furnishes a host of suggestive thematic implications.

Mikhalkov's landscapes are among the most unabashedly lush in contemporary film. Indeed, at least one critic has compared their grandeur with the works of Terence Malick, John Ford and David Lean (Simon 1993: 1). On the other hand, dormant village life is also a recurring theme in Mikhalkov's films, one that undoubtedly has its roots in the filmmaker's own childhood relationship with the *dacha* (Gurevich 1999). The landscape that lingers on screen in the last minutes of *Oblomov* is simultaneously consistent with both these tendencies. The village lies just behind as the boy hurries into the tall green grass. The boy himself may be seen either as Oblomov's son rushing to meet his mother in the future, or as a recapitulation of Oblomov-the-child escaping from his nanny into the endless embrace of the earth – in the past. The landscape opens its arms, enfolding the boy in an ever deeper embrace, until he disappears completely. Yet the scene is not threatening. On the contrary, it is characterized by a soothing and unassuming warmth.

The locale thus rendered by Mikhalkov is described in the following terms by Goncharov's narrator:

> The sky there seems to hug the earth, not in order to fling its thunderbolts at it, but to embrace it more tightly and lovingly … . The sun there shines brightly and warmly for about six months of the year and withdraws gradually, as though reluctantly, as though turning back to take another look at the place it loves and to give it a warm, clear day in the autumn, amid the rain and slush. The mountains there seem to be only small-scale models of the terrifying mountains far away that frighten the imagination. … The river runs gaily, sporting and playing; sometimes it spreads into a wide pond, and sometimes it rushes along in a swift stream, or grows quiet, as though lost in meditation, and creeps slowly along the pebbles, breaking up into lively streams on all sides, whose rippling lulls you pleasantly to sleep. … Everything there promises a calm, long life, till the hair turns white with age and death comes unawares, like sleep.
>
> (Goncharov 1993: 296)

Lest the persistent personifications suggest a romantic idealization, Goncharov's narrator takes care to emphasize that poets would likely be unsatisfied by the locale. The moon there shines with equal good nature at poets and non-poets alike. No nightingales serenade the poetic soul, and indeed, the region's inhabitants are much more likely to keep a caged quail in their yard. Moreover, the dreamer would never succeed in seeing an evening

> in the Swiss or Scottish style, when the whole of nature – the woods, the river, the cottage walls, and the sandy hills – is suffused with the red glow of the sunset, against which is set off a cavalcade of gentlemen, riding on a twisting, sandy road after having escorted a lady on a trip to some gloomy ruin.
>
> (Goncharov 1993: 296)

Instead of romance, comfort is the dominant mode, a quiet, sleepy comfort that infuses everything from the low hills and sky to the unpretentious villages and snug, familiar living spaces. The gentleness of the view, its nurturing caress, is associated with the mother figure through the little boy's disembodied voice in Mikhalkov's rendition (the scene does not occur in the novel), which calls, 'Mama!' while gradually disappearing into the green. But just as Oblomov's character is filled with ambiguities, so the closing association of the earth with the mother, which is actually prepared much earlier, suggests an uneasy acceptance of the landscape of Oblomov's dream, a drowsy, lethargic safety that triumphs in effect over the vitality Oblomov keenly observes in the natural world.[3] It also, I shall claim, asserts the triumph of an aestheticized world over an actual one, a dream-reality, or victory of the virtual over an acceptance of the real world as such.

At first glance, Ol'ga's and Shtolz's plan to lure Oblomov into real life appears to represent an alternative to a life lived in dream, and this, in fact, is a long-standing interpretation of the novel. But closer consideration suggests the opposite is the case. The supposed 'reality' in which Ol'ga and Shtolz live their lives turns out to be yet another idealized dream-world, one that they themselves have manufactured. In effect, Shtolz and Ol'ga attempt to draw Oblomov into their own aestheticized vision of the real, one that fails them both miserably in the end. In what I shall describe below as a supremely modern vision, one dream of reality, one fantasy of the world's 'ontological consistency' (Žižek 1989: 68), competes with another as Oblomov's dream is set against the artificial pretence of Ol'ga and Shtolz.

The musical introduction of Ol'ga, her off-camera performance of the 'Casta Diva' cavatina from Bellini's *Norma*, conveys a realm within which she develops throughout the film.[4] While suggestive of beauty and lyricism, it also represents an assumed, Western, non-Russian orientation to life. In the context of Russia's troubled relationship to Western Europe, to the questions of development and spirituality vis-à-vis the West that plagued both nineteenth-century writers like Dostoevsky, Turgenev, and Goncharov, and have continued to plague twentieth-century Russian and Soviet filmmakers like Tarkovskii, Sokurov, and, I would claim, Mikhalkov, one effect of this initial linkage of Ol'ga to West European romantic opera is to draw her authenticity (her 'Russianness') into question. It suggests an image conceived in aesthetic categories rather than the 'soul', 'Mother', or 'earth' that Mikhalkov's ending invokes.

While such a reading of Ol'ga may at first appear overly harsh, especially when one considers that she is a potential savior to the work's lethargic hero, several key scenes support it. Ol'ga encourages Oblomov in his studies for purely superficial effect. He is not changed in any fundamental way (as if the change she and Shtolz desire would necessarily be a good thing). Nor is she particularly interested in what he has to say about the subjects he is studying as part of his projected transformation.

Notebook in hand, Oblomov announces that he has completed his assignment and begins to read: 'The Renaissance is divided into three periods, the trecento, the quattrocento, and the cinquecento'. Ol'ga does not listen. She is more interested in contemplating the picturesque view, which, she exclaims impulsively, is spoiled by a bush in its centre. A painter, she maintains, would not have put a bush in the centre of a painting like this. At the same moment that she is expounding on the spoiled aesthetics of the view, he lapses into an adoring consideration of her profile, a three-quarter view from behind, which uncannily —and consistently, considering the text Oblomov has just been reading – echoes Florentine Renaissance depictions of women. The sequence thus appeals to aesthetics, to beauty's ability to guide, strengthen, even transform the life of man, which is prepared by the introduction of Renaissance associations: in short, *virtutem forma decorat*.[5]

Ol'ga's effect on Oblomov, the attempt to prop him up and draw him into the realm of predominantly Western aesthetic categories by which to organize his experience, is concentrated in this little gem of symbolization and especially in his response: after she has gone, he eyes the bush, taking its measure as if questioning what he himself is worth, then removes his jacket, rolls up his sleeves, and, amidst a series of grunts and groans, proceeds to tear it down. Ol'ga transforms him into a man of virtue, a hero inspired by a beautiful ideal. Thus, in a reenactment of one of the most charged tropes of West European culture, he *looks up to her window* waiting for her to rise the next morning. Perhaps more importantly for this discussion, he is now prepared to transform the world and his own place in it to suit her aesthetic demands upon it.

The artificial aestheticizing impulse is played out in the issue of whether the area of their fateful encounters in this part of the work is a garden, a *sad* – a Russian word connoting a relatively small, naturally planted space, or a *park* – an obviously imported word connoting something more like a French garden. The distinction is emphasized in the speech of the servant Zakhar, who, being a simple Russian, cannot remember the Russianized foreign word even to convey to his master the essential information that the Il'inskiis are awaiting him there. It is Ol'ga who is most closely associated with seeing the space and the activities that occur within it as park-like.

While Oblomov looks on from behind a tree, Ol'ga's male guests engage in a variety of simulated activities. One plays a fake trumpet on his hand. Two others pretend to box, while a third scores their points. The women look on with excited encouragement, judging their performances. The pipe organ music drowns out their words and laughter, though not before it becomes clear that they are all speaking French, not Russian, while the music itself recalls the previous, empty (from the hero's point of view at least) socializing through which Shtolz guided his sleepy friend in St Petersburg.

In this scene, the semantic hesitation over exactly what kind of a space this should be designated – as *sad* or as *park* – is resolved through the party's definitively *park*-like activities. Moreover, the space's definition by means of the behavior of Ol'ga's friends is analogous to the transformation of the landscape by means of Oblomov's removal of the troublesome bush, at Ol'ga's suggestion. This is not a subtle distinction. Making the space into a *park*, with its foreign derivation and conventional atmosphere, determines to a great extent the meaning and scope of the activities that take place within it. In a *park* one *plays games*.[6]

Another, equally important demonstration of what I am calling the aestheticizing impulse may be found in the coach-riding scene towards the end of the film, when Oblomov, Shtolz and Ol'ga are struck by the fact that it has been only four months since Shtolz's departure for Western Europe. Now, riding in a coach in nineteenth-century Russian society is an activity marked by a host of cultural associations, from the destiny of the country and the essence of rural life, to drunken coachmen and stealing a bride. It is not, however, associated with opera. Indeed, if any songs go with coach riding they are coachmen's songs, not Italian arias.[7] The elderly baron's ill-fated departure illustrates the point. Outraged at the thought of the old lecher's proposal to Ol'ga, Oblomov pursues him on foot screaming at the top of his voice. But his self-righteous demands to stop are inaudible above the raucous singing of the baron's driver. When, in the later coach-riding scene, the trio break into song to celebrate their happiness, it is Ol'ga's song they choose – Casta Diva – and when Shtolz tries to sing it as a coachman would, in the *Russian* manner, it is she who takes the situation in hand and demonstrates how to do it properly, according to the conventions of the genre.

That Ol'ga nearly succeeds in effecting the fateful change in Oblomov becomes clear in the letter-writing scene, in which Oblomov decides he must renounce his love for her own good, and he 'must do it alone' ('*Ia odin dolzhen!*'). The clichéd posturing, which is prepared by the ridiculously pretentious and artificially dramatic conversation between Oblomov and Alekseev, is little more than a pretext for creating a romantic obstacle to their happiness, for drawing out the tension in their lives, making Oblomov feel alive and Ol'ga cry so that he can watch her suffer, suffer with her, feel the agony of their separation, and so on. She, however, is frightened by her near success and tells him he has written the letter precisely in order to create her suffering and see how she will react. At that moment, he exclaims, 'What a thought!' and realizes that she is right. He immediately sees his action for the inauthentic, imitative posturing that it was, and he is cured. But she is not. He lapses into his former, genuine, soft kindness and sincerity, entertaining thoughts of marriage and inviting Alekseev to come and live with them if he should happen to move with his wife to the ancestral home. His delightful overnight slumber in the gazebo brings on a final flashback of Oblomovka, a morning awakening to the caresses of his mother and her invocation to prayer, which parallels his return to himself.

When Oblomov is cured, he turns to the earth. When he thinks of marriage, he imagines his mother, his ancestral home, the warm dream of familial life that has consoled him in the past and now consoles him in the present and in his dream of the future. It is true this is just a dream, but what he has just been cured of was a dream too, and a foreign dream at that.

Ol'ga's awakening to the falsity of the role she has played comes much later, namely, in her final appearance of the film. She is ill. Alekseev fetches her medicine. Shtolz observes from a distance, eyeing the vial, and talks to her over his shoulder. She listens but responds unwillingly. She wants to break off relations with a woman he calls 'her friend'. She no longer sings. Most tellingly, her tormented expression at the news that the mother of little Andrei, Oblomov's orphaned son, is on her way to visit, along with the boy's obvious joy, makes her transition complete. Her previous pretence to operatic song, the pretence of a faded friendship, the pretences of an obviously unfulfilling marriage – all these pale before the pious, authentic love of the boy for his mother. It is not a question of Ol'ga's having merely made the wrong choice in selecting Shtolz over Oblomov. That would simply romanticize her and provide too facile a response to the gamut of problems that Goncharov's novel, and Mikhalkov's adaptation of it, set forth.

These problems have to do with the onset of modernity in mid-nineteenth-century Russia, with the rise of a money economy, the perceived instrumentalization of things and people, the loss of faith, heart, authenticity, truth and love, which many assumed were the natural complements of modern conditions. Let us consider how the scope and demeanor of such changes are circumscribed by Mikhalkov's adaptation.

Two essential constituents must be considered in this regard: the watercolour depictions of St Petersburg and of Shtolz's home that begin contrasting scenes – Oblomov on his couch and Shtolz's leave-taking from his father respectively – and the accompanying voice-over narration read directly from the book, with the occasional rustle of a turning page and the clearing of a throat. The fact that the narration re-emerges most conspicuously when the film becomes a series of watercolor stills once again illustrates Chatman's insight about the implacability of cinematic time. The temporal suspension of each is complementary to the other, and both prepare the eventual suspension, without narration, of the final scene.

In the first case, we see the pictures and then hear the words; in the second, the words and pictures occur simultaneously. But in both, the sequence moves from narrated pictures to 'movement-image' action, from literature to film, in effect recapitulating the activity of the adaptation itself. True as this may be, there is more to the pictures than a mere iconic representation of the literary source.

Following the warm, intimate opening dream sequence of Oblomov as a child on his parents' estate, cared for by everyone, anticipating the awakening of his mother, each cold imperial structure in the opening sequence of watercolours of snowy St Petersburg seems to float in context-less isolation. While every structure is a recognizable monument to that great 'abstract and intentional city', none is recognizable in its actual surroundings.[8] Indeed, as depicted, the buildings have no surroundings but snow drifts and bare trees. It is as if the defenceless child of the dream, in passing into the modern, West European spaces of the capital, has entered a barren, inhuman wasteland of stone and frozen concrete, where he has been rendered, as the first scene depicts him, sluggish, sleepy, inept, and apathetic.[9] Add 'indebted' and 'increasingly isolated', and one gets a picture of the landed aristocrat divorced, deterritorialized, shall we say, from what made him what he was, i.e., from the land and its tax-paying inhabitants. Indeed, the absentee landlord of mid-nineteenth-century Russia was a problem of national well-being and national identity at one and the same time. For the aristocracy of the day, the question of how the country should proceed was intimately linked to how this social type would solve his problems.[10]

The decontextualized landscape paintings suggest two levels of alienation: first, the alienation of St Petersburg from authentic Russian culture as a whole,[11] which is implicitly contrasted to the countryside scenes and, especially, the bath-house scene, in which Shtolz and Oblomov discuss the meaning of life; and second, the alienation of the individual in modern society. The theme of modernity as a series of socio-economic material and conceptual transformations is broached only in passing in the film: under the loud pipe-organ music that suggests empty bustle, Shtolz tries to explain to Oblomov the workings of the stock market, a new institution in 1859 Russia, when Goncharov's novel appeared (Hoch 1991). 'You sell at 5/8', he says, 'and buy at 3/4. 'Three-quarters of what?' asks Oblomov. 'What? Haven't you understood anything yet?' says Shtolz. Oblomov's is a very good question, for the 'whole thing' out of which Shtolz is making fractions exists only as an abstraction, a consensual fantasy among the traders in the market. The fantasy upon which Shtolz builds his fortune, and by extension his entire busy-ness life, is implicitly compared, through this brief but telling exchange, to the fantasy of Oblomov's existence, his desire for complete belonging.[12]

There is, moreover, a compelling equivalency implied here to the fantasy by which Shtolz and Ol'ga attempt to give Oblomov's existence new meaning. Shtolz's plan, which only becomes apparent in the end, is to provide Oblomov with a fantasy – the possibility of marriage to Ol'ga – by which to channel his energy into a positive result. Shtolz, the business man, sees his friend Oblomov as a kind of investment, a failing enterprise as it were, which he attempts to prop up through artifice long enough for some 'real' value to be generated. Ol'ga's much vaunted lack of pretence is precisely the means that are called for in order to take in such an authentic soul as Oblomov. But the future promise to pay, on which the value of such modern phenomena as stocks and bonds might be extended indefinitely, must inevitably come due in the life of a man. When it does in this case, the morally questionable results of 'trading in human souls', demonstrate a long-standing Russian anxiety in the face of modern Western notions of social and political selfhood.

Such notions are contrasted to the theme of belonging, which runs throughout the film, and which is most strongly expressed in the bath-house scene.[13] It is here that Oblomov describes to Shtoltz his thought about the 500-year-old tree outside his window, the leaves of which have a sense of purpose and togetherness. He reiterates the notion to Ol'ga later. I suspect that this again expresses what is only hinted at in the opening sequence: *Oblomov* is not just a historicization of the waning of the aristocracy. It is also a lament on the disappearance of the pre-modern, old Russian, communal, familial, estate values that characterized life at Oblomovka. These include the very friendship that Shtolz in effect destroys by attempting to apply manipulative, objectified, modern methods to it. Such an interpretation, it should be emphasized, was unthinkable by Soviet critics in 1979: Oblomov was, for the Soviet system, an example of the worst form of aristocratic decay. The disease of Oblomovism or 'Oblomovitis' was an epithet to be hurled at the decrepitude of both aristocratic and bourgeois society, which Soviet society had, in Khrushchev's famous formulation, overcome and surpassed.[14] Showing the positive qualities of his hero, and denigrating Shtolz's essentially instrumentalist attitude towards life at the same time, could have easily been a dangerous occupation for a filmmaker without Mikhalkov's connections.[15]

In the end, Casta Diva is both aesthetically alluring and morally pernicious, for it is part of the secular, imported Western culture of nineteenth-century aristocrats that led to the slow erosion of their influence and importance in Russian spiritual life. The use of the Russian church music at the very end might hold up this line of thought, as the little boy is 'released' into the nurturing Russian countryside to the sound of Rakhmaninov's 'Now lettest thou thy servant depart, O Lord', with its undulating pulse, like life itself, under the single tenor voice. It might were it the last sound we hear, but it is not. Just as the choir begins its descent into the depths that Rakhmaninov supposedly desired to resound at his own funeral, the annoying electronic musical theme that has accompanied the dream sequences comes alive once again, appearing to overpower the chorus, and the single disembodied voice of the boy is heard wafting upward from the fields below: 'Mama'! This complex of gestures amounts to a slowing and then a final suspension of the temporal flow, the result of which is the stasis, the stagnation, of a picture that is passed unchanged from frame to frame in violation, in the sense proposed by Chatman, of the medium. It is a forced reversal of the opening sequence and of the technique by which the novel was adapted. It is thus simultaneously a return by one step in the process of artificially aestheticizing life and an implicit recognition of the rigidity and inauthenticity of the aesthetic image itself. In other words, the film conspicuously 'removes all the bushes' and does what it 'cannot do', thereby baring its own inadequacy in the face of the real.

Notes

1 I have in mind the many attempts by these authors to evaluate specific films on the basis of some conception of 'aesthetic validity', that is, the degree to which a film adheres to an a priori definition of the virtue of the medium (for example, as essentially 'photographic' or 'realistic'). Such attempts have fallen into disrepute in film studies, most likely because of their clear teleological, and hence my term, 'Aristotelian', foundation.

2 For a brief overview of problems in film adaptation in general, see Andrew (1984: 96–106). The transition from issues of evaluation in film theory to more recent concerns with ideology, spectatorship, subjectivity, and so on, is treated carefully in Cassetti (1999).

3 The adult Oblomov dreams of his mother as he lies in the grass, hearing the sounds of pulsating nature all around, the rustling of the leaves, and, says the narrator, 'two tears form at the edge of his closed eyes' (Goncharov 1993: 302).

4 Besides the direct references to the cavatina, as sung by Ol'ga, the musical theme re-echoes in Goncharov's characterization of the mode of life at Oblomovka: 'The way to live had been settled once and for all and taught to them by their parents, who had accepted the teaching ready-made from the grandparents and those from the great-grandparents, with the injunction of keeping it whole and undefiled *like Vesta's fire*' (Goncharov 1993: 315, emphasis added).

5 The phrase is found on the back of Da Vinci's portrait of Ginevra Benci; it may be best translated as 'Beauty adorns virtue'.

6 In this connection, the fact that Ol'ga runs into the forest, away from the *park*, before declaring her love to Oblomov may indicate the authenticity of her feelings or, at the very least, an impulse to be outside the conventional world she normally inhabits when she makes the declaration.

7 I am indebted to Oleg Timofeyev of the University of Iowa for this observation.

8 Dostoevskii designated St Petersburg in *Notes from Underground*: 'the most abstract and intentional city in the whole world' (Dostoevsky 1972: 17).

9 This is essentially a secular riff on the tendency to see St Petersburg as inspired by the demonic in nineteenth-century Russian literature. For a thorough treatment, see Connolly 2001. Goncharov's attitude was, as usual, somewhat ambivalent. See, for instance, Valentino (1999: 78–80).

10 Compare, for instance, the depiction of Konstantin Levin in *Anna Karenina*, where, even some fifteen years after the emancipation of the serfs, Tolstoi was still wrestling with and proposing solutions.

11 See for instance, Aileen Kelly's fine overview of this strain in St Petersburg mythology in Kelly (1997).

12 On the rise of imaginary or fantasy-based forms of property in Europe, see for instance Pocock (1975: 464 and *passim*).

13 Mikhalkov's *bania* scenes – another well-known instance occurs in *Burnt by the Sun (Utmomlennye solntsem,* 1993*)* – suggest an essentialist's approach to the Russian soul.

14 The term appears in Goncharov's novel but became a rallying cry for Russian left-radical critics upon the appearance of Nikolai Dobroliubov's polemical essay, 'What is Oblomovism?' ('*Chto takoe oblomovshchina?*') in the May 1859 number of *The Contemporary* (*Sovremmenik*).

15 Western audiences are unlikely to know that Mikhalkov's father was an important communist party member, an officially sanctioned poet, author of, among other works, the lyrics to the Soviet National Anthem. The relatively high status of the Mikhalkovs in Soviet society, their distance from the concerns of everyday people, severely compromised the reception of Nikita Mikhalkov's documentary film, *Ol'ga*, in the eyes of many Russian viewers, particularly Soviet émigrés.

10 'Imperially, my dear Watson'

Sherlock Holmes and the decline of the Soviet Empire

Catharine Theimer Nepomnyashchy

> The means of expression *in being different* would express different things – not the same things in different ways… . We talk as if adaptation were a matter of translation, like passing from one language to another, when in fact it is a matter of passing from one *form* to another, a matter of transposition, of reconstruction.
>
> Jean Mitry[1]

By the beginning of the twenty-first century, we have a tendency to take cinematic adaptations of literary works as a matter of course, because they are so ubiquitous a feature of the movie and television industry. Yet any astute scholar of film adaptation recognizes that the transposition of a literary work into film involves a complex semiotic process. Most important, the technical modifications demanded by the differences between the two media – in the simplest terms, the need to convey in pictures what was originally related in words – require different forms of 'reading'. Equally interesting, in this context, is the fact that the original and the adaptation entail, at least potentially, different interpretive communities, to use Stanley Fish's phrase. In other words, each medium carries with it its own 'baggage': its own conventions, intertexts and cultural status. I would submit that the situation becomes even more complicated when the adaptation is also a 'translation' – that is, when a literary work produced in one national culture is adapted into cinematic form in another linguistically and politically (taken in the broadest sense of the word) alien environment. In this chapter, I would like to take up the challenge to scholars of film adaptation thrown down by James Naremore, who, deploring scholars' preoccupation with 'fidelity', has called for 'a broader definition of adaptation and a sociology that takes into account the commercial apparatus, the audience and the academic culture industry';[2] Naremore has maintained, more specifically, that 'we need more writing about adaptation of 'low' or pop-cultural texts, and we need to think about how certain texts are adapted cross culturally' (Naremore 2000: 10, 12). I would like to explore these issues as they manifest themselves in the Soviet adaptation of the so eminently British adventures of Sherlock Holmes. More particularly, I hope to show that the

Soviet transposition and translation of Sir Arthur Conan Doyle's works, which themselves retain the imprint of the socio-political context in which their author wrote, also indelibly bear the marks of their time: the decline of the Soviet empire.

As I suggested from the outset, every adaptation of a well-known literary work carries baggage, but few projects drag with them such a heavy burden as do the adventures of Sherlock Holmes. Over the course of time, over 160 actors have played the character in plays, feature films, made-for-television versions, and on radio, and 'S[herlock] H[olmes] has been filmed more times than any other fictional character, ranking second is Dracula' (Anonymous 2004). To complicate matters, there was a pre-cinematic visual and theatrical culture at work in the construction of Sherlock Holmes in the popular imagination. Thus, among those features of the character of Holmes that have become 'canonic' some of his trademark traits are not mentioned in the original stories at all, among them the deerstalker hat, the magnifying glass, the distinctive pipe, and the phrase 'Elementary, my dear Watson'. The by now iconic hat and magnifying glass appear to have been the inventions of Sidney Padget, in his illustrations for the first editions of the stories published in *The Strand Magazine*.[3] By the same token, the phrase 'Elementary, my dear Watson' was evidently used by the first actor to portray Holmes, William Gillette, and was made famous by the film actor probably most closely identified with Holmes even today, Basil Rathbone. Gillette appears also to have introduced the calabash pipe as a Holmes accessory, reputedly because it better suited his face than the more modest variants suggested by the original stories.[4] Arguably, then, the 'adapted', largely visual as opposed to verbal Holmes has long since displaced his literary prototype in the mind's eye.

As far as the mark left by the times on the original Holmes stories is concerned, moreover, there is a growing literature on the Sherlock Holmes tales as representations of British imperial ambitions and fears and on Conan Doyle himself as an apologist for empire.[5] Edward Said, in *Culture and Imperialism*, relegates Conan Doyle's works to the 'genre of adventure-imperialism', classing the creator of Sherlock Holmes among those writers of his age for whom 'empire is everywhere a crucial setting' (Said: 1994: 155, 163).[6] Among the more interesting analyses of Holmes' imperial resonance are Laura Otis's postulation of Holmes as an 'imperial immune system', an antigen against the dangerous infection of the foreign colonial which erupts in crime in the metropolis (Otis 1998), Leslie Haynsworth's contention that the counterpoint between Holmes and Watson embodies the tension between the demands of empire abroad and the stability of domestic life at home (Haynsworth 2001), and Sheila Sullivan's argument that the Holmes adventures represent an attempt to redefine British imperial pre-eminence in light of rising challenges in the late nineteenth and early twentieth centuries from Germany and the United States (Sullivan 1998).[7] To reiterate here for the sake of clarity, my primary question is not so much the question of the 'faithfulness' of the Soviet adaptation to the original Holmes stories, but rather what happens to the adventures of Holmes and Watson when they are transplanted onto Soviet soil. More specifically, what happens to the implication in empire of the original Holmes texts when they are recreated in a new time, place and ideological context? Do the Soviet adaptations in any way perform analogous cultural work in their new homeland?

Before exploring the deeper theoretical and exegetical issues raised by the Soviet multi-series adaptation of Conan Doyle's texts to film, let me outline the basic parameters of the project. Between 1979 and 1986, eleven episodes of made-for-television adaptations of some of Sir Arthur Conan Doyle's more famous works were produced for Soviet television. They were directed by Igor' F. Maslennikov, and they featured Vasilii Livanov in the role of Holmes and Vitalii Solomin in the role of Watson. The episodes were grouped into five segments, most of which creatively combined different Holmes stories. The first two episodes aired in 1979, entitled 'Acquaintance' and 'Bloody Inscription', put together the first of Conan Doyle's Holmes tales, the novel *A Study in Scarlet*, with one of the best-known stories, 'The Speckled Band'. This adaptation thereby created a fluid cinematic narrative of how the detective and his chronicler took up residence together at 221B Baker Street and used one of Holmes' more celebrated cases as Watson's initiation. Three episodes were aired in 1980 –'The Master Blackmailer', 'Deadly Flight', and 'Hunt for the Tiger', based respectively on the stories 'The Adventure of Charles Augustus Milverton', 'The Final Problem' and 'The Adventure of the Empty House'. This second series combined one of the later Holmes stories with the tale of the detective's purported demise plummeting into the Reichenbach Falls locked in a death grip with his archnemesis Dr Moriarty and his return by popular demand. In 1981, *The Hound of the Baskervilles* was produced in two episodes, and in 1983, two episodes presented under the title 'The Treasures of Agra' united the novel *The Sign of the Four* with one of Conan Doyle's most celebrated stories, 'A scandal in Bohemia', which features the only hint of romance in Holmes' career: the detective's fascination with the adventuress Irene Adler. Finally, in 1986, the final two episodes, under the title *The Twentieth Century Begins*, were aired, the first adapted from the stories 'The Engineer's Thumb' and 'The Adventure of the Second Stain' and the second – from the stories, 'His Last Bow' and 'The Adventure of the Bruce-Partington Plans'. The creation and airing of the series, one of the most popular television events of the Soviet period, spanned the twilight period of what I pointedly term here the Soviet Empire, a period roughly coterminous with the period from the invasion of Afghanistan to the beginning of glasnost.

So the first set of questions that beg our attention concern the meaning of the choice of the adventures of Sherlock Holmes for adaptation in the first place and the more immediate cultural events that would have conditioned the Soviet audience's expectations and reception of the project. Certainly we should recognize the making of the series as part of the resurgence of detective fiction – especially the works of such 'classic' mystery writers as Conan Doyle and Agatha Christie – during the post-Stalin period after decades of being ostracized from official Soviet culture. Also, the late 1960s saw the emergence of the genre of the television mini-series in the USSR, and the earliest and most popular of these productions were adaptations of crime and spy fiction, most notably the first Soviet TV mini-series, the 1966 *The Meeting Place Cannot be Changed* (*Mesto vstrechi izmenit' nel'zia*), and what remains probably the most popular instance of the genre, the 1973 espionage thriller, *Seventeen Moments in Spring* (*Semnadts' mgnovenii vesny*). We should also note in this regard the airing in the USSR in 1971 of the BBC multi-episode adaptation for television of John Galsworthy's *The Forsythe Saga*, which was so popular with the Soviet viewing audience that it emptied the streets of Moscow during showings. This historic event both demonstrated and whetted an appetite for British period drama on the part of the Soviet public. Comments made by Igor' Maslennikov, which highlight the shaping force of generational experience, suggest how these trends converged in the making of *Sherlock Holmes and Doctor Watson*. Maslennikov had the following to say about political engagement in the years following the Khrushchev thaw: 'At first I did want to make political films. Iurii Chernichenko and I wrote a screenplay, 'Virgin Soil', righteous and stern. But we were told: 'What's the matter with you? You want to make a film about victims when Brezhnev himself was first secretary?' From that time on I promised myself not to make films on current events' (quoted in Bakushinskaia 2001). In a similar vein, when asked by one interviewer whether his wartime childhood had made him want to make movies about war, Maslennikov responded, 'No, on the contrary, I wanted people to recover (*chtoby liudi otdokhnuli*) from the war' (quoted in Skliarova 2001). The Sherlock Holmes project then coincided with the spirit of the time, with the urge to evade the rigours and political disenchantments and pitfalls of the age, or in Maslennikov's words, '"Holmes" was pure chance. I have no interest in detective literature. I had never seriously read Conan Doyle. It was just a very good screenplay. Iulii Dunskii and Valerii Frid brought it – funny and, most important, it had that which lived and lives in me: playing at being British (*igra v anglichanstvo*). It's boyishness for adults' (quoted in Rtishcheva 2000).

Here we should recognize that the relative cultural space or status occupied by this sort of adaptation in the Soviet Union as opposed to the West was not necessarily the same, and in this respect the question of readership or viewership becomes key. In this context, it would not be amiss to recall that while the driving force of the building and maintenance of empire as well as of the creation and consumption of culture in nineteenth-century Britain was the market, the place of the market in those spheres was arguably taken by ideology in the Soviet Union. While this necessary oversimplification glosses over complexities and nuances, it nonetheless has merit within the context of the subject at hand. The original Holmes stories may be seen as particularly notorious instances of the junction between market, literature and empire. Conan Doyle, a savvy observer of consumer demand, conceived the stories as a blatant bid to make money by his pen. He was so spectacularly successful and so resentful that Holmes' celebrity distracted from what he considered his more serious literary labours that he famously killed off his own sleuth. The popular clamour was so vociferous and the financial remuneration so lucrative, however, that Conan Doyle was finally induced to resurrect his hero.[8] To the extent that the popularity of the Holmes stories among the middle-class readership of the day has been convincingly traced, at least in part, to their ability to help readers negotiate the anxieties created at home by the maintenance of empire abroad, we can discern a fairly direct connection between the market at home and the exploitation of foreign resources.[9] In contrast, in the Soviet Union both the production of culture, disengaged from any direct accountability for making a profit, and the expansion of empire, were driven, or were perceived as being driven by very different considerations; ostensibly the empire grew to spread the same project of building communism Soviet domestic culture was to serve.

In attempting, then, to understand whether the Soviet viewer of *The Adventures of Sherlock Holmes and Doctor Watson* took anything more from the experience than pure enjoyment and respite from the unremitting lip service to political seriousness of late Soviet life – whether, that is, the series resonates with the mechanisms and tensions of the maintenance of the Soviet multi-national state – we might better look for relevant comparison not to the original readers of the Holmes stories in nineteenth-century Britain, but to the American public television audience in the late twentieth century. As we know from that experience, the adaptation of literary classics for public television negotiates a liminal cultural space, designed to appeal to an audience with cultural 'pretensions'.[10] While there would seem to have been something of the same sort of snobbery in play in Soviet culture, we must acknowledge that the Soviet cultural system, quite apart from immediate political considerations, was constituted out of markedly different power relations which were inextricably linked with the Soviet imperial cultural hierarchy. Two points would seem to be most important to make in this connection. The first is the generally acknowledged priority of literature over film in Soviet culture, or, perhaps more accurately, the literariness of Soviet film, which not only had profound effects on the technical realization of cinematic narrative in Soviet film works, but also, arguably, facilitated the blurring of the boundaries between serious and frivolous cultural artifacts. In other words, the relevant cultural divide in the USSR was less between 'high' and 'low' culture than between unacceptable, excluded cultural products, dissident or otherwise, and those works given the official imprimatur of publication or production. By the same token, the relative lack of discrimination between the personnel, resources and technical parameters of feature film and made-for-television cinematography in the Soviet Union also served to reshuffle the cultural structure to which we are accustomed in the West. Both of these factors were integrally implicated in the nature of the Soviet system and must be taken into account in the analysis that follows of how we are to understand the semiotic significance of the Soviet rendering of Sherlock Holmes.

One of the most striking aspects of the Soviet adaptation, which speaks to the points just made, is its self-consciousness in locating itself in an ongoing tradition, which is reflected most obviously, first of all, in strategies that draw attention to the fact that the Soviet Holmes is very much the iconic Holmes of the ongoing visual and cinematic tradition and, second, in cinematic quotations. To give just one of the many possible examples of the former, there is a moment toward the beginning of the second series when Holmes poses with his trademark pipe against the window of the Baker Street flat and holds the pose long enough to highlight the traditional Holmes profile. As far as cinematic citation is concerned, toward the beginning of the first series, after Watson has just moved in with Holmes and still does not know the nature of his flat mate's profession, Holmes beckons the new lodger into his room, shows him an array of photographs and asks if he is acquainted with any of the people in them. Watson somewhat squeamishly responds in the negative, while Holmes maintains that he knows them well. The particularly shady characters exhibited, however, appear all to be shots from vintage films, including Lon Cheney Sr in his famous make-up for his role in the silent film of *Phantom of the Opera*.[11] This sort of cinematic 'in joke' signals the film's appeal, above and beyond its accessibility to a more general educated audience, to the more rarefied reaches of the creative intelligentsia who might have had the opportunity to see more obscure foreign films and therefore might appreciate the joke. That is, the Holmes films, with their easy familiarity with the foreign cinematic tradition and fondly ironic stance towards their predecessor texts, would seem to be geared to an audience as much of those who produced culture in the Soviet Union as of those who consumed it. Through the same device, moreover, the film draws attention to its artistry as well as to its foreign ancestry: Holmes is as much a fiction as the villains he collects.

Similar instances in which the series acknowledges the temporal and cultural difference inherent in its appropriation of the Holmes tradition include Watson's overblown reaction to the disclosure that Holmes is a detective. In the original scene from *A Study in Scarlet* in which Holmes reveals to a bemused Watson, unable to make sense of the curious array of talents Holmes displays, what his profession is, the revelation entails a relatively lengthy explanation, which begins: 'Well, I have a trade of my own. I suppose I am the only one in the world. I'm a consulting detective, if you can understand what that is' (Conan Doyle 1930: 24). The film version, on the other hand, openly acknowledges the fact that it is separated from the original by the legacy of the Conan Doyle stories themselves, by the tradition spawned by the character of Sherlock Holmes. Thus, when Holmes finally discloses his profession to Watson – after a far more prolonged and elaborate period of speculation that rises to suspicion on the part of Watson (to a consideration of which we will return below) – Watson immediately launches into an immoderate, repetitive, and sheepish refrain on the theme of how of course it was so obvious he should have figured it out for himself, that is, the once obscure, virtually unprecedented profession of private detective becomes a matter of course precisely because of Holmes' many successors in the intervening years. In the wrap-up scene of 'The Speckled Band', moreover, the adaptation neatly negotiates a flaw in the original story while at the same time creating a 'textual' resonance absent in the prototype. When Holmes explains to Watson how he deciphered the mystery of 'The Speckled Band', which depends on the premise that reptiles have the faculty of hearing, Watson breaks in and asks Holmes if he has not read a recent journal article laying out the argument that snakes are deaf. Holmes immediately occupies a backup position provided by the original story. This manoeuvre functions to establish an affectionate, but ironic distance from the original, by acknowledging the obsolescence of Conan Doyle's scientific knowledge, thereby underscoring the pastness of the prototype text in a manner that, as we shall see, resonates most especially with the concluding series of the project. The generally classy stylization that marks the choreography of movement and witty banter throughout the series, rising to its summit in the concluding episodes as well, has a similar effect.

André Bazin, in his seminal discussion, 'Adaptation, or the Cinema as Digest', raises the issue of the equation of highbrow culture with difficulty: 'The clichéd bias according to which culture is inseparable from intellectual effort springs from a bourgeois, intellectualist reflex. It is the equivalent in a rationalistic society of the initiatory rites in primitive civilizations. Esoterism is obviously one of the grand cultural traditions' (quote in Naremore 2000: 22). While Bazin evokes (and disparages) this distinction specifically to call it into question as an alibi for privileging literature over film in the study of adaptation, his observation serves us well here when we apply it in the opposite direction. In other words, the Soviet adaptation of Conan Doyle's classic popular fictions styled itself a highbrow artefact precisely because it not only triggers elitist cultural knowledge (as in the case of the film citations noted above), but also because of the sophistication of its crafting which, I would argue, demands from the viewer a relationship to the text more commonly associated with the reading of literature or at least of art film.[12] This is particularly notable in the high level of narrative cohesiveness that binds together the series made of multiple Holmes stories. In sum, unlike the sort of 'classy' adaptations of literary works produced for the BBC and US public television, which seek to appeal to a more educated, higher-brow audience by trading on the cultural capital of the source text while at the same time rendering the text more accessible, the Soviet adaptation of the adventures of Sherlock Holmes exhibits aspirations to high culture status in the devices of its own narrative construction which call both for effort and esoteric knowledge on the part of the viewer. While unquestionably enjoyable for and accessible to an uninitiated audience as well (albeit one most likely well read in advance in the Conan Doyle texts), the series of films depends on witty devices to claim an elite cultural space, reminding us of the privileging of high culture, especially the classics of nineteenth-century Realism, which was a hallmark of the Soviet cultural establishment and, in fact, one of the reflexes for establishing imperial legitimacy by asserting the Soviet Union's claim to be heir to the cultural achievements of the past.

Here, I believe, we reach the heart of the issue we must broach before taking a closer look at the series itself. Precisely because of the political context in which *The Adventures of Sherlock Holmes and Doctor Watson* was created – a context that rested on the absorption into politics of all aspects of Soviet life – the series' very disengagement from contemporary issues must be taken as a significant factor in the way the series was read by its audience. I would argue, in this context, that despite a basic strategy of the film to defuse analogy, the titillation lay precisely in the 'imperial nostalgia' in which the adaptation of the original is drenched, the underscoring of its distance from the present in time and space, so that an audience adept at reading between the lines must have found part of the *jouissance* afforded by the cinematic text to lie in a multiplicity of potential relationships to be postulated between the antiquated, bourgeois values of the text and the realities of the Soviet present. As other critics have commented, most notably Maurice Friedburg in his seminal *Russian Classics in Soviet Jackets*, the problem of how to defuse the value systems of pre-revolutionary texts inherently at odds with the ideological premises of the Soviet system was a major and complexly negotiated challenge faced by Soviet culture (Friedburg 1962). *The Adventures of Sherlock Holmes and Doctor Watson* aestheticizes this challenge by 'museumizing' the original tales. In other words, the very painstaking recreation of the stories as period pieces, punctuated by the persistent integration of the exhibition of sculptures and other period art works into the stage sets, has the same effect as does removing a potentially subversive monument to a hero of a deposed culture from a public space into a museum; it would seem to aim at taking that work of art out of dialogue with the present. Ironically, as we shall see, when the trope of the museum is realized in the final instalment of the series, *The Twentieth Century Begins*, it has the effect of laying bare the device, of reclaiming nostalgia as a form of ironic commentary on the loss of innocence that haunts the present.

Given the series' self-reflexivity and self-consciousness, it is not surprising that motifs of gaze, voyeurism and surveillance are recapitulated and resonate throughout the eleven episodes, culminating, as we shall see, in the concluding sequence of *The Twentieth Century Begins*. In this context, the series, I would argue, walks a fine line between cinematic play and references to the police state. Moreover, not only does Watson find himself at one point a murder suspect (which is not the case in the original story), but suspicion and spying frame the series. Thus, in the first episode before he learns Holmes' true profession, Watson, who claims never to poke his nose in other people's business, imagines, in a scene in a park, that he is under surveillance by Holmes' cronies and himself spies on Holmes and comes to the conclusion that his flatmate is the central criminal mastermind of London. By the same token, in the last episode, based on a story in which Watson does not even appear, Watson again spies on Holmes, and decides that he is working as a German spy. When both Holmes and the Baker Street landlady Mrs Hudson, who has been helping him in disguise, reveal themselves as patriots working in the interests of Britain, Mrs Hudson announces to Watson: 'Sherlock Holmes has rendered amazing service to Great Britain, and I am happy to bask in the glow of his glory'. Whilst we shall return to a consideration of the concluding episodes of *Sherlock Holmes and Doctor Watson* shortly, let us note here that towards the end of the series, Holmes becomes less private detective and more government agent, working to stave off the threat to empire posed by the looming twentieth century. I would go so far as to contend that Holmes, especially in relation to Watson, becomes a mirror and model for intelligentsia viewers, negotiating the perilous tensions between friendship, trust, patriotism, justice, and integrity, on the one hand, and the invasiveness of the demands of the state, on the other.

As we move to an examination of certain key moments in the series that illustrate how it addresses itself to its viewers, we should note from the outset that there are any number of ways in which the films signal to their audience a rather sophisticated awareness of their status as a translation. The opening credits of *The Hound of the Baskervilles* – which form a clever and elaborate counterpoint to the episodes as do all the framing sequences in the serial – provide a particularly pointed example. A document appears on the screen at the beginning which is meant to represent the manuscript of the Baskerville legend in English, but a grid is placed over the letters, which are decoded into Russian.

To explore further what gets lost – and gained – in translation, let us look first at a simple trace of the pressure of the times on the text – and a reminder of the still very active interference of Soviet censorship in 1979. To make my point, let me first cite the opening paragraphs of *A Study in Scarlet*, which is also beginning of the Holmes corpus:

> In the year 1878 I took my degree of Doctor of Medicine of the University of London, and proceeded to Netley to go through the course prescribed for surgeons in the Army. Having completed my studies there, I was duly attached to the Fifth Northumberland Fusiliers as assistant surgeon. The regiment was stationed in India at the time, and before I could join it, the second Afghan war had broken out. On landing at Bombay, I learned that my corps had advanced through the passes, and was already deep in the enemy's country. I followed,

however, with many other officers who were in the same situation as myself, and succeeded in reaching Candahar in safety, where I found my regiment, and at once entered upon my new duties.

The campaign brought honours and promotion to many, but for me it had nothing but misfortune and disaster. I was removed from my brigade and attached to the Berkshires, with whom I served at the fatal battle of Maiwand. There I was struck on the shoulder by a Jezail bullet, which shattered the bone and grazed the subclavian artery. I should have fallen into the hands of the murderous Ghazis had it not been for the devotion and courage shown by Murray, my orderly, who threw me across a pack-horse, and succeeded in bringing me safely to the British lines.

Worn with pain, and weak from the prolonged hardships which I had undergone, I was removed, with a great train of wounded sufferers, to the base hospital at Peshawar. Here I rallied, and had already improved so far as to be able to walk about the wards, and even to bask a little upon the veranda, when I was struck down by enteric fever, that curse of our Indian possessions. For months my life was despaired of, and when at last I came to myself and became convalescent, I was so weak and emaciated that a medical board determined that not a day should be lost in sending me back to England. I was dispatched, accordingly, in the troopship *Orontes*, and landed a month later on Portsmouth jetty, with my health irretrievably ruined, but with permission from a paternal government to spend the next nine months in attempting to improve it.

(Conan Doyle 1930: 15)

Aside from highlighting the centrality of Watson's role as narrator of the stories, a key problem for any film adaptation, this beginning vividly illustrates what Joseph A. Kestner terms 'the persistent querying of the Empire in the Sherlock Holmes canon' (Kestner 1997: 7). I have included this passage in full, because it demonstrates precisely how his experiences defending British colonial interests leaves Watson physically broken, literally infecting him with 'the curse of our Indian possessions'. In the Soviet version, on the other hand, Afghanistan, which the Soviet Union invaded in December 1979, becomes simply 'the East' (*vostok*) or, later, 'the Eastern colonies' (*vostochnye kolonii*). This minor and apparently predictable alteration nonetheless indicates that the censors saw not only the possibility of a Soviet audience drawing an analogy between one imperial project and the other, but the danger of that analogy. Moreover, especially since this suppression was apparently common knowledge in certain circles at the time,[13] the very word 'colonies', substituted for the geographical name, potentially highlights the imperial analogy the censor sought to defuse. In the original it is precisely in Afghanistan that Watson contracts the disease that brings him at the beginning of *A Study in Scarlet* destitute, wasted, and all but friendless to London and to 221B Baker Street and Holmes. In the

Soviet version, despite passing references to a wound received abroad, Watson appears hale and hearty and far from friendless from the beginning, which marks the change in his role throughout to more of an equal to Holmes than a foil. In fact, quite a number of Holmes' lines are actually given to Watson in the series, which is, after all, entitled *The Adventures of Sherlock Holmes and Doctor Watson*, thus giving Holmes' sidekick equal billing up front. In fact, the leitmotif of male pairs or brothers is established in the first scene and runs throughout, displacing the aloof, misanthropic detective of the original from centre stage. One episode in particular helps to demonstrate how this affects the relationship between Holmes and Watson. Shortly after sending Watson into a funk by deducing the sad facts of the doctor's brother's decline and demise (as he does in the original as well), Holmes, looking out the window of the flat, challenges Watson to deduce what he can about a gentleman passing by. Watson gives it a good shot, but Holmes then adds a startling number of personal details. When Watson professes himself flabbergasted by Holmes' powers, the detective bursts into laughter, claps Watson on the back, and announces that the passing man is his brother (*rodnoi brat*), Mycroft Holmes, who will also come to play a much greater role in the series than he does in the original texts.

As in the original stories, crime most often originates in the series from contact with the foreign, whether East or West. Thus, Jefferson Hope, the murderer in the first two episodes based on *A Study in Scarlet*, is an American who has lost his beloved to the tyrannical and polygamous Mormons. Here, though, I want to draw attention to the portrayal of another 'American', a portrayal that departs markedly from the original text, as a comparison of the description of Sir Henry Baskerville from Conan Doyle's story and the filmic adaptation demonstrate:

> Our breakfast-table was cleared early, and Holmes waited in his dressing-gown for the promised interview. Our clients were punctual to their appointment, for the clock had just struck ten when Dr. Morimer was shown up, followed by the young baronet. The latter was a small, alert, dark-eyed man about thirty years of age, very sturdily built, with thick black eyebrows and a strong, pugnacious face. He wore a ruddy-tinted tweed suit, and had the weather-beaten appearance of one who has spent most of his time in the open air, and yet there was something in his steady eye and the quiet assurance of his bearing which indicated the gentleman.
>
> 'This is Sir Henry Baskerville', said Dr. Mortimer.
>
> (Conan Doyle 1930: 15)

By contrast, Nikita Mikhalkov, who plays Sir Henry in the Soviet production, is an exuberant, opinionated American who first appears in a large and imposing fur coat. (The fur, by the way, which he gives away to the butler Barrymore when he decides to dress like an Englishman, a transformation that does not occur in the original, becomes the mark by which the convict Seldon's body is initially misidentified as Sir Henry's.) Mikhalkov's Sir Henry, first in his fur and later in his chaps, reminds one of nothing more than a cross between Mr West and his cowboy sidekick Jeddy in Lev Kuleshov's classic silent film *The Adventures of Mr. West in the Land of the Bolsheviks*. Perhaps most interesting in this context is the fact that the ludicrousness of Sir Henry Baskerville's failure as an American to mimic an Englishman successfully, which is periodically underscored, only serves to throw into relief how well Russians in this series are acting 'Englishmen', just perhaps a distant echo of Dostoevsky's Pushkin speech in which the essence of Russianness, and a Russian imperial manifesto of sorts, lies in the Russian ability, as manifested in Pushkin's characters, to 'become' the foreign other and therefore function as the great reconciler of nations. Certainly, here, Russians appear remarkably more adept at mimicking, even absorbing and thereby appropriating, the foreign than is the equally remarkably inept American. Yet this 'talent' inevitably carries with it an anxiety about the instability and permeability of national identity, an anxiety that (as the recurring motifs of disguise, masking and unmasking, betrayal, eavesdropping suggest) may be symptomatic of homo sovieticus of the late Brezhnev period.

The last segment of the series, *The Twentieth Century Begins*, which aired in 1986, is edgier, darker, and quirkier than the others. After all, the primary mystery in the first episode of this segment, aired at the outset of glasnost, concerns the threat of the making public (*oglashenie*) of a state secret, specifically an immoderate letter written by a ruler which could lead to war if revealed. Moreover, as indicated above, throughout the stories combined here, Holmes acts in the interests of king and country. It is the threatening twentieth century and a nostalgia for a simpler age which preceded it that pervades these episodes from the beginning, as the written text which scrolls down the screen after the beginning of the opening sequence in the eleventh and final episode makes clear. Punctuated, as the final episodes are periodically, with pictures of goose-stepping troops and twentieth-century transport clearly meant to epitomize the inroads of technology on a dying way of life, the sequence ends: 'The time of dear old England drowned in Lethe and together with it the Adventures of Sherlock Holmes'. Mycroft Holmes appears periodically at his desk, surrounded by technical gimmickry and even in a gas mask, apparently prepared for an imminent outbreak of chemical warfare. As already noted, Mycroft Holmes plays a much larger role in the Soviet series than he does in the original, on occasion, like Watson, being given some of Holmes' lines. By the end, he becomes an incarnation of the state bureaucracy and its technical power rendered threatening by his own machine-like, but also vain, demeanour. The villains in the final episode are all Germans, while Holmes, following the original, poses as an Irish-American, a colonial subject once removed who justifiably works with the Germans to subvert the empire that oppresses his homeland. Of course, as we have seen, just at the moment when Watson, listening in on a conversation between the disguised Holmes and the German spy, is convinced that Holmes has sold out, the denouement reveals Holmes to be on the side of right as always, despite his lack of interest in politics in the early stories.

At this point, toward the end of the final episode, we see the number combination of the German spy's safe automatically tumble to that most significant date, August 1914, identified by Solzhenitsyn and others as the beginning of the end of the Russian empire. Looking back to what Akhmatova called the beginning of the twentieth century from the hindsight of the beginning of the end of the Soviet empire seven decades later, this final segment is fraught with anxieties about the uncertainty of identity and allegiance in the twentieth century and about the dangers and promise (it will bring the movies, after all) of technology. Watson, Holmes, and Mrs Hudson (the landlady of the Baker Street apartment, who also plays a much larger role here) become ordinary people left behind and powerless to stop the relentless advance of history. The film ends with the director, Maslennikov, himself appearing in a series of frames, screening on an antiquated projector a sequence of a man and woman dancing on a pier over the water. In the end we are brought back to play, but through the prism of a brooding nostalgia for the empire, and the chivalry that was its best defence.

In this regard, the most striking feature of *The Twentieth Century Begins*, as I suggested earlier, is that the trope of the museum becomes the orienting feature of Holmes's portrayal here. As early as the second serial, when Holmes appears to have died along with Moriarty, Mrs Hudson, in a departure from the original text of 'The Final Solution', proposes to preserve Holmes' rooms untouched and create a museum in his memory. In the final episodes, Holmes returns from retirement in the country to the Baker Street apartment which is in the process of being turned into a museum, furniture shrouded in sheets and adorned with a bust of Holmes himself, which is pointedly moved from place to place and posed, confronting Holmes with himself frozen in time and lifeless. He appears as the last outpost of a simpler imperial age and a more innocent and naive belief in the powers of reason and science about to be swept away by the horrors of a century ruled by mass movements, war, and the unleashing of previously unimaginable technological horrors. Holmes, in fact, is brought back from the museum, and contemporary life suffers by comparison.

So what do *The Adventures of Sherlock Holmes* have to say about the Soviet empire and why was the series so popular? Perhaps because, like the original Conan Doyle stories, the Soviet TV series accepts the mantle of empire, while, perhaps, more so than its predecessor, subverting it. Perhaps, in the end, that is why Watson the chronicler more and more displaces Holmes the deducer and defender as the series progresses.[14] It may be too late to contain the evil forces unleashed by history, but the story still remains to be told – in literature and in film.

Notes

1 Cited in Griffith 1997: 25.
2 As most recent commentators on film adaptation have pointed out, the issue of fidelity to the original work, which inevitably privileges the literary work over the film it inspires, remains the primary principle by which not only the popular audience, but even scholars and theorists judge adaptations.
3 In a 2001 interview Igor' Maslennikov confirmed that he had consulted the Sydney Padget illustrations in making *The Adventures of Sherlock Holmes and Doctor Watson* (Skliarova 2001).
4 See for example, Nisbeth 2004.
5 See for example, Symons 1979: 69.
6 It is useful to cite here Said's working definition of imperialism: 'As I shall be using the term, "imperialism" means the practice, the theory, and the attitudes of a dominating metropolitan center ruling a distant territory; "colonialism", which is almost always a consequence of imperialism, is the implanting of settlements on distant territory. ... Neither imperialism nor colonialism is a simple act of accumulation and acquisition. Both are supported and perhaps even impelled by impressive ideological formations that include notions that certain territories and people *require* and beseech domination' (Said 1994: 9, his emphasis). Said is careful to distinguish Western European imperial projects from Russia's on the basis of the fact that Russia expanded into adjacent territories, and, of course, he is concerned with the nineteenth century.
7 For other interesting discussions of Sherlock Holmes and empire, see Arata 1981, Thompson 1993 and Porter 1981.
8 Ironically, in interviews, including those cited in this chapter, Maslennikov, speaking from the vantage of the post-Soviet Russian market economy in cultural production, has repeatedly compared himself to Conan Doyle in this respect, lamenting the fact that he is so identified as the creator of the Soviet Sherlock Holmes that what he believes to be his more serious work is slighted.
9 Said, for instance, maintains: 'And in Europe itself at the end of the nineteenth century, scarcely a corner of life was untouched by the facts of empire, the economies were hungry for overseas markets, raw materials, cheap labor, and hugely profitable land, and defense and foreign policy establishments were more and more committed to the maintenance of vast tracts of distant territory and large numbers of subjugated peoples' (Said 1994: 8).
10 See, for example, Stasio 2003 for a discussion of the recent PBS decision to air a new remake of *The Hound of the Baskervilles* in the 'Masterpiece Theater' series, rather than in the 'Mystery!' series, thereby conferring on it the status of a literary masterpiece.
11 This quotation also serves to draw attention to Holmes as himself a master of disguise.
12 Maslennikov's repeated allegation that the superiority of his adaptation of the Sherlock Holmes stories lies precisely in the fact that Watson rather than Holmes is his focus is telling this context. Thus, Maslennikov has maintained, 'You know why our film is recognized as the best? Because in the others there is no Watson – there is no actor who 'played' Holmes in order to illuminate him. Inasmuch as all Conan Doyle's stories are written by the person of Watson, he finds himself in the shadows, out of the picture, his character is inscrutable' (quoted in Skliarova 2001). In other words, in Maslennikov's version the writer is given pride of place over the detective.
13 I would like to thank Vitaly Chernetsky for pointing this out to me.
14 On Watson's role as chronicler eclipsing Holmes in the original stories, see Haynsworth 2001, Conroy 1992, and Kestner 1997.

Part IV

From text to screen, Soviet to post-Soviet

Re-interpreting the myth

11 'I love you, dear captive'

Gender and narrative in versions of *The Prisoner of the Caucasus*

Joe Andrew

For at least the last two centuries, Russia's troubled relationships with its 'deep south' have provided the material for a variety of cultural expressions. As Julian Graffy has noted: 'The Caucasus region has long fascinated Russians as the nearest manifestation of the unfathomable Orient, and nineteenth-century Russian literature abounds with encounters between young Russians (often army officers) and this Muslim part of their empire' (Graffy 1998: 34). Pushkin's verse tale of 1822 *The Prisoner of the Caucasus* may be seen as the primary inaugurating version of this story (although there are some antecedents); certainly it should be seen as a watershed, and is a work which produced a plethora of imitations in high and low culture (Layton 1994; Goscilo 2003). Pushkin's work was the basis for Lev Tolstoi's identically titled story of 1872. This story in turn was reworked by Sergei Bodrov in his 1996 film, also called *The Prisoner of the Caucasus* (though Tolstoi's name does not appear in the credits). My primary purpose is to offer a reading of these versions, principally from the aspect of gender and narrative. Generally, I will focus on the two later versions, one an 'interpretation' (Goscilo 2002) of the other, although occasional mention will also be made of Pushkin where appropriate. I begin with the image of men in the works, and relations between men.

The men

In Pushkin's work, and continuing through both the Tolstoi and the Bodrov, the world depicted in these Caucasus tales is primarily that of men, and one that is based in different ways on male bonding. Echoing Pushkin's foundational work, comradeship plays an important part in Tolstoi's tale. The primary hero, Zhilin, and his fellow captive Kostylin, are conventionally opposed types, fit versus fat, brave as against cowardly, and so on. Both at the beginning and later, however, their destinies are conjoined. It is their shared bravado in deciding to leave the safety of the wagon train which leads to disaster. More significantly, it is when they first try to escape that the issue of male bonding as the priority comes to the fore. Although the cowardly and portly Kostylin is reluctant to attempt the escape, Zhilin persuades him to do so, but soon regrets it. As the increasingly fractious and maimed Kostylin holds him back, Zhilin ruefully reflects, 'The devil made me drag this great lump with me. I would have been long gone on my own' (Tolstoi 1963: 243).[1] Kostylin almost seems to read his mind, and urges Zhilin to press on alone, to which Zhilin responds: 'No, I won't go on, it's not right to leave your comrade' (ibid.). Indeed, he now carries Kostylin for as long as he can, and they are captured. The primacy of male fellowship is reconfirmed at the conclusion. Zhilin's second bid for freedom succeeds, and he is surrounded by a joyous group of 'comrades'. Zhilin tells them of how he had been taken when on his way home to get married: 'No, it's clear now, that's not my destiny' (ibid.: 248) he opines, and decides to remain in the Caucasus, as a man among men. The right order is thus re-established. Male bonding will also be an important motif in Bodrov's film, especially in the comic-heroic sequence of semi-naked wrestling by the mountain stream, as well as in the relationship between Zhilin and Sasha, to which I will return as a separate issue.

While comradeship may well be the desired norm in these three accounts, each version also discloses the dark underbelly of male–male relationships. In all three the primarily male environment is deeply militarized, to the extent that one might say that to be a (true) man is to be a warrior. Bodrov's film alone questions this equation. Tolstoi's story begins and ends on notes of military action. In both the nineteenth-century tellings of the story, the warrior's horse is valorized. Thus, Zhilin addresses his steed as '(dear) little mother' ('*matushka*'), and much painful and graphic detail is devoted to its death during Zhilin's capture. Women, however, are largely absent from both these versions. The unnamed Circassian woman and Dina will play key roles in the captives' stories, but, otherwise, there is almost no mention of women in Tolstoi and Pushkin, even though the bulk of each story is set in the midst of the *aul* (Caucasian mountain village) of the local tribes-people.

Each of the two earlier versions is really only concerned with men, and, above all, with male violence. In all three tellings, the basic plot situation involves men seeking to prove their own manhood by attacking, imprisoning and, if necessary, killing other men. In Tolstoi, for example, Zhilin inspires the admiration of his captor, Abdul-Murat, by standing up to their demands, while the film wrestling scene is again significant in this regard. In all three there is considerable gruesome, and sometimes gratuitous, violence. Here we should remember the threatened and actual violence against Zhilin during and after his capture in Tolstoi, or the interpolated story of how Hassan's tongue was cut out in a Siberian prison in Bodrov.

The endlessly repeated cycle of male violence, of male blood vengeance, is introduced in Tolstoi in the form of another interpolated narrative, before becoming a central theme in Bodrov's film. For Tolstoi, vengeance is something the tribes-people engage in and that marks them as 'savages', while in Bodrov the Russian army is at least as culpable in this regard.

Tolstoi's Zhilin is told the story of the unnamed 'old man' who had once been the leading warrior of his people. He had eight sons, seven of whom had been killed by the Russians, while the eighth had gone over to the Russians. In an echo of Gogol's *Taras Bulba*, the father had hunted down and killed his own son.

Others have already noted the centrality of vengeance in Bodrov's version.[2] Graffy notes that the locale depicted in the film 'is a place of immemorial codes – about dress, about marriage, about deference to elders and, above all, about vengeance for wrongs suffered' (Graffy 1998: 35). Violent revenge takes many forms here. Dina tells Zhilin two stories: firstly, in a close reworking of Tolstoi, about the old man whose two sons had been killed by the Russians, while the third is now working for the Russians; and secondly, of how Hassan had lost his tongue after being imprisoned for murdering his wife who had run off with a (presumably Russian) geologist. The old man's execution of his treacherous third son is brought into the on-screen diegesis, and precipitates the crisis that nearly costs Zhilin his life. But now the Russians are at least as blood-thirsty. Shortly after Dina's two stories, Sasha tells Zhilin, with no little zest, how he hopes to return to kill Abdul, Hassan and Dina. When Zhilin demurs, Sasha replies 'Well, you have to, Vania. This is a war' ('*A nado, Vania. Eto voina*'). Towards the end of the film Major Maslov attempts to reassure Zhilin's mother, who assumes her son will now be killed, by telling her that 'We'll avenge our sons'. The final sequence of the film proper has Russian gunships flying over the freed Zhilin, perhaps to attack the *aul* where he has been held.[3] This striking visual homage to *Apocalypse Now!* reveals one of the key features differentiating literature from cinema, with the spatiality of the latter contrasting with the temporality of the former. (Interestingly, Bodrov tends to be at his most expansive cinematically in sequences which are absent in the textual predecessor. Another such moment is the graveyard climax, to which I shall return. For the moment, let it be noted that the decision to invent episodes absent from Tolstoi seems to have liberated Bodrov's cinematic imagination.)

More broadly, the Russian army in the film version is depicted in an almost entirely negative light. From the very first frames Bodrov skillfully interweaves political satire with an at least implicit gender-based critique of the army's methods. For example, the opening sequence suggests the ritualized humiliation of the conscripts, who are subjected to routine medical inspections, including an eye-test while completely naked! The almost complete absence of dialogue in this episode again marks the film off from its literary precursor – and, again, this sequence is (self-evidently) absent from the Tolstoi text.

The other captive in the Caucasus, Sasha, is a fascinating study. Certainly, through him Bodrov seeks to question the integrity of the post-Soviet army, as Gillespie and Zhuravkina have suggested (Gillespie and Zhuravkina 1996: 57). At the same time, the film clearly seeks to interrogate masculinity *as such* through his persona. For most of the film he is the embodiment of sardonic machismo, from the opening shot of him riding on the front bumper of an APC, through his reckless bravado during the ambush, his bloodthirsty desire for revenge, to his callous murder of the local shepherd during the doomed escape bid. At the same time, Bodrov seeks to explore the undercurrents of this flamboyant machismo. At almost exactly the mid-point of the film, the two captives celebrate Sasha's birthday by getting drunk. Later, as the two men sit chained together but back to back, and with stirring patriotic martial music on the soundtrack, Sasha breaks down into uncontrollable sobs, and almost reaches for Zhilin's hand. As before, the absence of dialogue in this, another invented scene, enhances the dramatic impact of the film version. In the end, however, he reverts to type, and pays a heavy price. Significantly, his execution (again absent from Tolstoi) is one of the most graphically violent of the film: he is forced to watch his own throat being cut, with an almost ceremonial sword. He must die, unlike his cowardly prototype Kostylin, because his brand of machismo makes him a man of death. As Gillespie and Zhuravkina note: 'In the figure of Sasha, we see that those who wage war destroy not only others, but themselves' (Gillespie and Zhuravkina 1996: 58). (Interestingly, he makes two posthumous appearances in the film, and seems much more at peace now he is dead.)

Bodrov also radically reworks the relationship between Zhilin and his fellow captive by comparison with Tolstoi's story. In Tolstoi, Kostylin is really only a structural figure, there to act as an illustrative foil for the real hero. In the film, Sasha is the more 'senior' figure, both as the older man, and as the professional soldier. The relationship between the two provides an interesting gloss on the theme of male bonding. For much of the film Sasha is the embodiment of the army in his relationship to the conscript, doing his best to humiliate and terrify the younger man, often as sadistically as possible. This is especially apparent when he tells him that the army is too poor to ransom them both, and that Zhilin will have his throat cut. Later he relents, and 'reassures' Zhilin that he may well be ransomed but 'you can kiss your balls goodbye!' Gradually, however, he softens somewhat towards the young conscript, especially, as already noted, in the birthday sequence. In the end, however, his aggressive masculinity will lead to his own death.

In all three versions of the story, the captive in the Caucasus is freed, although through different agencies. In thematic terms, there are different rationales as to why the author allows the particular hero to live. In the film version this issue becomes especially acute, as it is the only one in which one captive lives, while another dies. We have seen why Sasha must die, but why does Zhilin live? The answer lies at least in part in his life-enhancing qualities, a kind of femininity, if you will, which enables him both to establish good relations with his captors, particularly Dina, and means that he does not follow the death-dealing path of masculinity. In this sense, as in others, Bodrov has radically re-conceptualized Tolstoi's character. From the very beginning he is evidently not part of the male world of killing. In the ambush sequence, he does not even have a gun in his hands, but stands with his hands over his ears. In the film we only once see him with a weapon, when he cradles the gun for which Sasha had murdered the shepherd. But Zhilin almost seems to be unsure what the gun is for, and inadvertently fires its single bullet, thereby leading to their recapture.

The most significant departure from both the nineteenth-century versions, however, can be seen in the episodes which culminate in Zhilin going free. The discourse here hinges again on (male) vengeance. After he has been recaptured, Zhilin, as in the Tolstoi story, is put into a stinking pit. Dina comes to him in the film and tells him that he will die tomorrow, in revenge for the death of her brother, who was to be exchanged for Zhilin, but who has been shot in the chaos after the old man had shot his own son. Zhilin asks her to help him escape. At first she says she cannot, but then brings him the key. He is released from his shackles, and she helps him out of the pit. In Tolstoi, Zhilin leaves Dina to the tender mercies of her presumably vengeful father and brother. Bodrov's Zhilin, however, declines to escape because, he realizes, 'They won't forgive you'. Dina's father, Abdul-Murat, arrives and, despite Dina pleading for Zhilin's life, Abdul tells her: 'Russians have killed your brother; now we must kill Russians'. This simple message of stark retribution encapsulates so much of the film's take on male identity. There is no political or religious motive in Abdul's words: it is simple blood vengeance. This is what men have done in this region for centuries.[4] In a series of powerful images Bodrov suggests that death is everywhere, as Abdul takes Zhilin through a graveyard where the tombstones almost dwarf the humans, with Dina following behind. It should be noted that this episode is an excellent example of what Goscilo has called 'the vertical axis of intensification' (as opposed to literature's 'horizontal axis of plot accumulation'), in that this iconography of death, absent from Tolstoi, is conveyed purely visually (Goscilo 2002). Equally, there is no dialogue in these sequences, lending even greater authority to the pictorial image. At the last minute, however, Abdul does not take his revenge, but seems to have learned the futility of the endless sequence of killing. Here the captive of the Caucasus does not *escape*, but is *released*, a crucial shift in emphasis. The final moments of the film suggest that male violence can be overcome. We hear Zhilin's voice over a series of black and white stills, concluding with a shot of Dina. He speaks of his return to Russia and hopes to see in his dreams the people he had encountered in the Caucasus and 'whom he had loved'. For all the ambiguity of the final action shot of the film, the threatening gunships, the film as a whole ends with words of love, spoken by a man. The pictorial and verbal here stand in a montage relationship, each as counterpoint to the other. In this relationship, each has equal validity: one does not cancel the other. There is another way for men to behave: to be a man does not necessarily equate to killing other men.

Narrative

All three versions of *The Prisoner of the Caucasus* essentially tell the same basic story of how a Russian is captured by people of the Caucasus, is imprisoned, and eventually leaves. This core plot has ancient antecedents, and Pushkin, Tolstoi and Bodrov weave variations on an archaic structure. This is indeed significant. Iurii Lotman has suggested the following typology for plot: 'The elementary sequence of events in myth can be reduced to a chain: entry into closed space – emergence from it'. This '*chain*' may be reinterpreted as *'death – sexual relations – rebirth'* (Lotman 1979: 168, 173). And it is precisely this 'death leading to rebirth/resurrection' plot that all three captives embark upon, and, in one sense or another, encounter the immobile heroine (Lotman ibid.; de Lauretis 1984: 103–57). Furthermore, the 'closed space' they each enter will have significant gender implications, 'inasmuch as closed space can be interpreted as "a cave", "the grave", "a house", "woman" (and, correspondingly, be allotted the features of darkness, warmth, dampness)' (Lotman 1979: 168). Let us consider the stories in these terms.

In each work the plot is initiated by precisely the motif of 'entry into closed space'. Again, Bodrov seeks both to develop Tolstoi's version, and to render it in a very visual way, in the sense that we see Zhilin being brought into the village on no less than four occasions, after the aborted exchange, after the mine-clearing incident, and then his attempted escape, as well as when he is first captured. In nearly all of these sequences, moreover, Dina watches him being brought into the space of the village. The cinematic medium here draws attention to its own *dominanta* of spatiality, as opposed to the temporality of literature (Goscilo 2002; McFarlane 1996: 27–8), in that Dina stands in the frame of a doorway as Zhilin enters the frame of the screen. This repeated topos verges, in fact, on a visual pun. Looked at differently, Dina could be said to stand in the place of the viewer, which reinforces the sympathy Bodrov seeks to create around her person.

In all three versions it is emphasized that the space is, in a sense, doubly enclosed, in that not only are they brought into the village, but this settlement is surrounded by majestic, but forbidding, mountains which will make escape difficult. As in so many other regards, the medium of film allows the spectator to *see* the significance of this element, with the mountains becoming much more than a mere backdrop. As Gillespie and Zhuravkina note: 'The Caucasian mountains provide not only a majestic backdrop, but are filmed in such a way that they assume the status of dramatis personae' (Gillespie and Zhuravkina 1996: 58). In all three versions the *aul* and its people are presented as intrinsically alien, although there are significant variations in their treatment. For Tolstoi, the 'Tartars' are presented as virtual savages, even if Dina, and, to a lesser extent, her father, Abdul-Murat, are sympathetically drawn. When Zhilin is captured, it is by 'two stinking Tartars' (ibid.: 228). Later the account given of their incomprehensible speech, of their eating habits and their attitude to Zhilin all emphasize their primitive manners, from a 'civilized', European perspective. The self/other (*svoi/chuzhoi*) opposition is handled very differently in Bodrov's film. To be sure, the *aul* where Zhilin and Sasha are held is shown as a primitive, almost medieval place, with its stony streets and use of mules for threshing, but the values of the local people reveal them to be, if not 'noble savages', then at least the equal of the Russians. In this context, it should be noted that it is Abdul who breaks the cycle of the *lex talionis*.

Each text suggests that we should see imprisonment as a kind of death. In Tolstoi, Zhilin's capture is linked to death, that of his mare, while, when he arrives in the village, he is shackled, shoved into a barn and locked up. Bodrov echoes both his antecedents. Zhilin and Sasha are rendered unconscious in the ambush and arrive in the village, tied over two horses, seemingly lifeless. They too are thrust into a tomb-like barn, and soon shackled together. Both Tolstoi and Bodrov intensify the motif cluster of entry into closed space/death/the grave as if to reinforce its significance, and their awareness of it. As punishment for their attempted escape, as well as to prevent further escapes, both Zhilins are placed in a deep and 'damp' pit. That this represents the grave is especially obvious in the film when Zhilin is filmed from above, asleep, looking for all the world like a man lying in his tomb. (It is while lying in this 'grave' that he has his first visit from Sasha, who is, of course, really dead.)

In Lotman's terms, for the typological hero to be reborn from his narrative death, he must engage in 'sexual relations' at least in structural, narratological terms. In Tolstoi, Dina is only thirteen, but is contextualized in her own culture as almost of marriageable age. Zhilin and she become friends, and when he is thrown in the pit Zhilin clearly attempts to 'seduce' her into helping him escape, by making more dolls and other animals for her. This relationship is encoded as 'sexual relations',[5] and it is through this relationship that Zhilin is enabled to escape.

Bodrov's treatment of the relationship between Zhilin and Dina is immensely more significant than in Tolstoi's original, although here too their friendship should be termed 'sexual relations' only in the narratological sense. Even so, on many occasions the film seeks to lend their relationship a sexual aureole. A link between them is established very early on. When Zhilin first regains consciousness he looks through the stable door and sees Dina looking at him (Dina again standing in for the viewer). He winks, and she runs off. At first she shares the general hostility towards the Russians, declaring that 'they have pigs' blood' in them, a deep insult on the lips of a Muslim. Very soon, however, the young woman, still really a girl, is drawn to the very unmacho Russian soldier. As in Tolstoi, he fixes Abdul's watch, and she observes his skilled handiwork with a half-tender, half-guilty smile. In Tolstoi Zhilin makes her a doll. Here it is the rather less patronizing, emblematic bird puppet (Gillespie and Zhuravkina 1996: 58). It is on this occasion that they first talk, and their conversation is about when she will be married. Dina and marriage, possibly to Zhilin, is a topic that frequently reoccurs. Dina is teased by some younger children because she allegedly 'fancies' one of the Russians. As soon as Zhilin and Sasha return from mine-clearing Dina brings him some milk and food. She has just put on some of her grandmother's very flamboyant jewellery, which Zhilin admires, so she explains what it all is. This elicits from him the words: 'You're very beautiful' ('*Ty ochen' krasivaia*'). Once he has been recaptured Dina visits him, and again they talk of her possible marriage. Zhilin tells her he would marry her if he could. The two Zhilins regain their freedom, and, typologically, this is because they have been reborn by virtue of their relationship with the local woman, although the closure of the structure varies. Tolstoi's Dina assists Zhilin's escape, and is abandoned to her fate. Bodrov's Dina helps Zhilin escape, but he declines to run, because of what might happen to her. Throughout the film there has been much more substance to their relationship than in either earlier version, and this accounts, perhaps, for his selfless gesture. This response on his part, in turns, paves the way for Abdul's change of heart: he too is reborn. Love may not conquer all, but love does lead to some kind of peace. And if the relationship between the hero and the heroine means that she transcends the structural functionality of Tolstoi, then Bodrov's treatment of women, as well of gender more broadly, is immensely more interesting than in Pushkin or Tolstoi. It is with the depiction of women that I conclude.

Images and roles of women

Women are conspicuous in the Pushkin version by their absence. His world is one in which men fight men, and take women as 'black-eyed captives'. Not once in the whole tale is there a real image of a real woman. Indeed, the only female character in the work of any significance is the Circassian woman, and she is largely a conventional figure, a literary type. The heroine is in some senses, at least, defined by her positionality: she is part of the 'closed space' the prisoner enters.

Tolstoi's *Prisoner* is different in many ways. The central female character, now given a name (Dina), is much more developed, and women generally play a more significant role. The story is, indeed, immediately different in that it introduces a maternal presence, and, if only symbolically and structurally, this is an important addition to the Pushkinian template. The whole plot may be said to have been initiated by Zhilin's mother, in that her letter to him, in which she asks him to visit her before she dies and also to meet the fiancée she has found for him, is the cause of his leaving the safety of the fort in which he is serving.

Zhilin's mother is, however, a marginal figure. Rather more central to the narrative is Tolstoi's equivalent to the Circassian woman, Dina. In many regards, she is an altogether more credible figure than her predecessor, although, ultimately, she will remain just as functional and instrumental. In nineteenth-century fiction, the convention was that the reader had to know what the woman looked like. Dina's portrayal is *purely* descriptive, and lacks the sexualization or even fetishization which was so common, but even so, the very first words about are revealing: 'A girl ran in – rather slim and thin, about thirteen and facially similar to the black Tatar. She was clearly his daughter. She also had black, clear eyes and her face was beautiful' (Tolstoi 1963: 230). Eikhenbaum has written of this work: 'There is no psychological decoration, no digressions, no descriptive details' (Eikhenbaum 1974: 72), yet, for all the stylistic minimalism of this story, Tolstoi still seems to feel it necessary in the first reference to the only significant female character in his story to emphasize her physical frailty, to define her in terms of the dominant male of the environment, and to inform the reader that she is attractive! Her frailty is also emphasized on her last appearance. She tries to help Zhilin knock off his shackles, 'But her little arms were like little sticks – they had no strength at all' (Tolstoi 1963: 246). Her emotionalism is emphasized here as elsewhere. Frustrated by her own weakness she bursts into tears, and this is also her reaction when Zhilin bids farewell: 'Dina burst into tears, covered her face with her hands' (ibid.: 247). At this point she also exhibits another trait commonplace in nineteenth-century depiction of irrational young women: that is, their frenetic, animal-like activity. Here, in tears, 'she ran off up the hill, jumping like a little goat' (ibid.: 247). Indeed, when we had first met her, she gave Zhilin some water, and when he handed it back to her, 'she jumped back, like a wild goat' (ibid.: 231).

Thus, although Dina is generally a rather more realistic figure, her character is barely developed, and is hardly less stereotypical than that of her predecessor. Equally, her role in the story is almost entirely functional, and she has no existence separate from Zhilin, except, as we have already seen, in relation to her father. Like the Circassian woman, and although she is really only a child, Dina is here presented as a nurturing, almost maternal presence. Her first action is to bring Zhilin some water, at her father's behest. Soon, she brings him bread, and later milk, as well as meat and other food. As part of his charm offensive Zhilin models dolls for her, and she is seen 'rocking it like a baby, cooing to it' (ibid.: 235). In the work as a whole, however, women play very little role, and this applies to Dina as well. At the end her presence is crucial, but, again in consonance with the pattern identified by de Lauretis, she acts merely as the Donor, as the instrument which enables Zhilin to escape. She helps him out of the pit, and sends him on his way, his pockets stuffed with food. The question as to what will be done to her by way of retribution for this act of treachery is not even addressed.

In some aspects, Bodrov's film closely follows Tolstoi's story, although, as Gillespie and Zhuravkina have noted, the film 'has introduced significant changes to the subject-matter'. For them, perhaps the most significant alteration is the sympathy and understanding shown for the local people, 'for Tolstoi makes no effort to portray the Tartars from within, to understand their grievance or show any sympathy for their culture' (Gillespie and

Zhuravkina 1996: 56–7). Graffy also notes that Bodrov 'shows a startling even-handedness in his depiction of the victims on *both* sides' (Graffy 1998: 34–5, his emphasis). Indeed so, but what strikes me as an even more fundamental alteration is the greatly expanded role of women, as well as the immensely more significant part they play in the film. We see this in the depiction and role of Dina, the part played by Zhilin's mother, and by the overall, visually realized presence of women in the film. This is, of course, especially remarkable given that this is primarily a film about armed conflict, traditionally a genre in which women's role is usually marginal at best. Thus, apart from Dina, we see several other women in the *aul* where Zhilin and Sasha are held. Early on there is the old woman in the barn; later there are a couple of scenes of threshing corn which involve women exclusively, while we also see women baking bread. To be sure, these are traditional functions for women, but at least they are seen to be physically present, and to play an active part in the local society and culture.

In Tolstoi Zhilin's mother plays no part in the actual story, even if her letter triggers the entire action. In the film version she is an important and active presence. The first sequence involving her is indicative. In a series of shots which deliberately echo Soviet iconography, she is seen reading a letter from her son, written before his capture. At a desk in front of adoring primary-school children she emerges as the quintessential maternal figure of Soviet propaganda posters: warm, caring and loving. Her role and significance as a real mother, as opposed to a symbolically maternal presence, are soon reiterated. Abdul instructs his two prisoners to write to their mothers to intervene to save them. In an inversion of the situation in Tolstoi's tale, Sasha writes to a false addressee, the long dead cook of the orphanage he has been brought up in. His motherless status partially explains his emotional cruelty. In reverse, Zhilin's humanity stems from the devotion of his mother. As he writes to her, he is sure 'she will come like a shot', and later recounts the story of the well which demonstrates her great love for him. Before this we have already seen her receiving Zhilin's second letter which tells her that he has been captured. Bodrov echoes the earlier scene in the classroom, but with significant differences. Now we see her alone in her room which is bedecked with children's drawings, including one of a fort, and she almost collapses from the emotional pain, the very image of the Mater Dolorosa. This physical realization of her suffering, with its echoes of traditional Christian, as well as Soviet iconography, is an essential ingredient of the much greater role the film gives Zhilin's mother.

This woman is not limited to mere emotionalism, but begins to take an active, potentially critical part in the story. We next see her trying to persuade Major Maslov to actually do something to free her son – and belabours him when he claims that there's nothing to be done! Undeterred, she arranges a meeting with Abdul herself: she seeks to break the vicious circle of male vengeance. When they meet, she speaks first, trying to find common ground by telling Abdul that she is a teacher, as his son had been.

For now, this gesture of human commonality is rebuffed, but perhaps the seeds of his later relenting are here sown.

If Zhilin's mother is essentially a completely new factor by comparison even with Tolstoi, then Dina is a development out of Tolstoi's work, to such an extent, it should be said, that her significance is immensely enhanced. That this will be part of Bodrov's project is seen very early on. As the two prisoners are carried into an apparently deserted *aul*, the film cuts to Dina who stands watching them arrive. This shot announces that she will be a key player. Moreover, as already noted, she stands for the viewer, so that, to a certain extent, the film is tracked from her point of view. This sequence also initiates a remarkable use of framing shots for her. Throughout the film, but especially in the first half, Dina is almost always seen framed in a doorway. More often than not, as in this opening sequence, she is actually standing in the doorway, or, as when she tells the two interpolated stories, she is sitting by the entrance to a building. The opening shot is recreated more or less exactly when Zhilin and Sasha return after the mine-clearing episode: again we see Dina standing framed in exactly the same doorway as at the beginning. Equally, when they are taken off for this expedition, she watches them go, standing in the doorway to her bedroom. Now, this may be merely for picturesque effect, but, it seems to me, it also has a symbolic role. Dina will, as we know, attempt to liberate Zhilin. In this sense, the iconography presages her future role: she stands on the threshold of his freedom and will act as the door to his liberty, as well as representing the entrance to a new way of being. The acutely visual representation of this symbolic role further underscores the centrality of the pictorial iconography in the film by way of contrast with the underlying tale from Tolstoi.

In narrative terms, Dina plays a much bigger role than any female character in the previous two versions. Again, the opening shot of her hints at this. This suggestion is immediately reinforced. The two Russians are taken into the barn which will be their prison, and Dina runs on ahead to spread a sheepskin on the floor for them. As in Tolstoi, she is sent by her father to fetch them water and, in another echo of both earlier versions, she will later bring them bread and milk. While her father discusses with the elders what should be done with the prisoners, Dina is in the background, helping to make the distinctive local bread. More generally, she is frequently seen apart from Zhilin; that is, she is shown to have a separate existence, and is not merely a plot function. We see her threshing wheat, talking to other villagers, and there is an affecting scene with her father in which he tells her how much he loves her, anticipating his later act of humanity. Another critical scene is when we see her in a circle of much older women as they formally lament the dead. She is very much part of the local community and its culture. Again, the dramatic, intensely *visual* realization of this scene reveals and underscores Dina's enhanced significance. Dina is also, crucially, an active mediator of this culture. It is highly significant that it is she who tells Zhilin the stories of the old man and his sons, and of Hassan's tongue.

That this role of story-telling is allocated to a woman, and a very young woman at that, marks a radical break with tradition.

In his deployment of Zhilin's mother and, even more so, of Dina, Sergei Bodrov would clearly seem to have been attempting not merely to retell Tolstoi's tale in a contemporary, topical setting (the Chechen wars), but to give it a radical new twist, by contrasting the greatly enhanced role of the feminine with the exposé of male violence. We see the significance of Dina and Zhilin especially towards the end of the film where the masculine way leads increasingly to death, while the feminine potentially leads to life and liberty. In the climactic sequences, vengeful male violence reaches its apogee, as Sasha kills twice during his bid for freedom, and is then brutally executed; the old man shoots his own son for his treachery, and in the ensuing confusion Abdul-Murat's son is shot, an event which seems certain to lead to the reciprocal death of Zhilin. At the same time, Zhilin's mother is an important witness, looking on with horror at the shooting, and watching the moving scene of Abdul receiving the body of his beloved son. (As a female witness to these acts of male violence and its consequences, she too stands for the viewer, so that, the viewer is constructed as female, and as opposed to male violence.) Meanwhile, Dina attempts to set Zhilin free, and then follows behind as her father seems bent on more violent revenge. The final live shot of Dina has her sitting on a tomb, her black head-dress whipped around in the wind, looking, for all her association with Islamic culture, just like the Mater Dolorosa of Christian tradition, iconography influenced, perhaps, by Pasolini's Virgin Mary in *The Gospel According to St Matthew*. (Again, the witness/viewer is female.)

It should also be noted none of these sequences appear in the Tolstoi tale. Moreover, there is almost no dialogue, so that the narrative at this point is advanced almost entirely by the rapid switch from one episode to another, and by the striking iconography in the graveyard sequences. In other words, and this is generally true throughout the film, the 'invented' scenes are also those which are rendered in most purely cinematic terms. Goscilo has commented à propos Murnau's version of *Dracula*: 'Murnau's version exemplifies cinema's ability to interpret (in Zorkaia's definition of *interpretatsiia*) a literary text through a director's bold, imaginative reading and render it in visual terms' (Goscilo 2002). *Mutatis mutandis* this applies exactly to Bodrov's 'interpretation' of Tolstoi.

Ultimately, in its final minutes, the film leaves the two ways in the balance. Zhilin is freed; then we see the menacing gunships, and then we hear Zhilin's voiceover, talking of his mother, and of his love for Dina and the others he had encountered. Bodrov is not so naive as to suggest that a young woman of the Caucasus and a widowed mother will end centuries of male violence, but his film certainly does intimate that there is another way. Moreover, the viewer is invited to identify with the female point of view. In any event, by comparison with Pushkin and Tolstoi, as well as other versions of the Caucasian tale, the role of women has been enormously enhanced.

Notes

1 It should be noted that his name derives from the Russian for crutch '*kostyl'*'.

2 In this regard, the genesis and circumstances of the film version merit attention. As Gillespie and Zhuravkina have noted, 'we are in no doubt that the action takes place during the Chechen war' (Gillespie and Zhuravkina 1996: 57). (In fact, the idea of updating Tolstoi's story came from the scriptwriter, Boris Giller: Bodrov himself has suggested that the could have taken place in Bosnia or Afghanistan – or even Mexico!) In turn, his treatment of the war, and especially his sympathetic portrait of the local fighters, provoked controversy on the film's release in Russia. More broadly, this film can be seen as part of a trend over the last twenty years in which Russian cinema has reflected the real-life encounters between Russia and the Muslim world, encounters which have generally been very difficult for both sides (Graffy 1998: 34).

3 Gillespie notes that the Russians seek only revenge, by sending in helicopter gunships to pound Abdul-Murat's village into the dust (Gillespie forthcoming). In my view the ending is by no means as certain as this.

4 Bodrov has argued that, while others have seen his film to be about the Chechen war, for him wider issues are at stake: 'We spoke not so much about war as about human lives and tragic, bloody events. People say that we have made an anti-Russian film. But I think when we are dealing with war, both sides are right and wrong' (quoted in Gillespie and Zhuravkina 1996: 59).

5 Indeed, we should see it in these terms. It is surely not unimportant that all three authors here considered depict a relationship with a female member of the local community. Their tales would have been quite different if the 'Donor' had been a young man, for example. This is not to suggest that such a relationship could not be construed as 'sexual', although this is highly unlikely in the context of nineteenth-century official literary culture. That such a 'same-sex' relationship could indeed be constructed as 'sexual relations' is now evident in the light of Makanin's own, rather different reworking of the Caucasian tale. For an illuminating discussion of all this, see Goscilo (2003).

12 Post-Soviet film adaptations of the Russian classics

Tradition and innovation

Anat Vernitski

Film adaptations are a form of dialogue rather than translation. If translation is a way to engage with an author, creatively yet humbly acknowledging the author's primacy, adapting a literary work to film is a dialogue between equals. Tarkovskii once said that 'literature … ceases to be literature when the film is already made' (quoted in Mikhailovich 1994: 4). Such a transformation does not necessarily assume a loss of the literary qualities of the source text as is often feared when a film adaptation is made. Film based on literature is a work of art in its own right, yet at the same time it is enriched by its dialogue with the literary work. In such a dialogue, what Bakhtin termed as 'the Word of the Other' (*chuzhoe slovo*) is evident in the film, which often – especially in the case of Russian and Soviet film adaptations – assumes a familiarity with the literary source. The spectator experiences the Word of the Other (the author of the literary source) as a continual presence throughout the film, whether the filmmaker supports the author's discourse or, rather, subverts it. The opposite process also happens when the spectator who has watched the film adaptation then reads or re-reads the literary source. In this case, the filmmaker's interpretation almost hijacks the author's original discourse. Due to the visual and aural concreteness of the film, the reader's imagination is forever trapped within the representation of the characters and locations as they are presented in the film.

This relationship between the literary source and its cinematic adaptation has particular qualities in every literary-cinematic dialogue. In post-Soviet film adaptations of Russian nineteenth-century literature, intersections between literary source and film adaptation mark post-Soviet artistic and cultural sensibilities. Bakhtin states that in certain literary genres, such as folk tales and Classical Greek adventure novels, intersections are a significant device. By the term 'intersection' he means occasions at which a character returns to a place already visited when the character was young, mature or in old age (Bakhtin 1981:120). By analogy, we may say that when post-Soviet cinema adapts Russian nineteenth-century literary texts, which were already in the past adapted by Soviet cinema, such intersections occur. The same metaphorical place – the literary text – is revisited in a new period in the life of Russian society. This revisiting is bound to reflect the changing social and cultural conditions, as well as afford a comment on the interrelations between the three key periods in modern Russian cultural history: the nineteenth-century, the Soviet period and the post-Soviet period.

The present chapter concentrates on several examples of post-Soviet Russian film adaptations of seminal texts of Russian nineteenth-century literature: Pushkin's 'The Captain's Daughter' ('*Kapitanskaia dochka*'), Leskov's 'Lady Macbeth of the Mtsensk District' ('*Ledi Makbet Mtsenskogo uezda*'), and Dostoevskii's *The Idiot* (*Idiot*). In treating these films, I aim to present the richness and multiplicity of approaches to adapting the classics in a period when Soviet ideological restrictions on art had been lifted. I also wish to explore whether there are common concerns characteristic to post-Soviet Russian art illustrated by its relationship with the Russian classics. I suggest conjunctures relating to the specific way post-Soviet culture expresses itself through cinematic dialogue with the canon of Russian literature, a canon that serves as a metonymy of the Russian past.

In his book *Novel to Fiction*, Brian McFarlane claims that the question of the fidelity of a screen adaptation to its literary origins is the most commonly discussed, yet the least interesting question (McFarlane 1996: 8–11). What is more important is whether a film adaptation becomes a work of art in its own right. Following McFarlane, I shall concentrate on the way a film adaptation constructs its dialogue with the literary origin. Fidelity is more vaguely defined than the originality of the dialogue, since plot, characterization, themes or ideological context can all be considered of paramount importance when establishing whether a film adaptation is true to its original. As there is no consensus among critics regarding these components, it is not surprising that the status of a film adaptation as loyal to its origin or not is also debatable. If a film adaptation is not expected to conform, but rather to react to the literary source, all of these components may be examined. Moreover, such an investigation frees the film adaptation from total servitude to the literary work it adapts and thus allows for a more open discussion of the genre.

The film *Russian Revolt* (*Russkii bunt*), directed by Aleksandr Proshkin in 1999, is an adaptation and amalgamation of two Pushkin texts concerned with the Pugachev rebellion: 'The Captain's Daughter' and 'The History of Pugachev' ('*Istoriia Pugacheva*'). The film was clearly made to coincide with the 200th anniversary of Pushkin, an event that was much commented upon in Russian press, media and scholarly publications during that year. The film is a historical drama, taking great pains to reconstruct eighteenth-century Russia, the period discussed in Pushkin's texts. It does not allow, therefore, for a representation of the inevitable tension between Pushkin's time and the time he depicts. This tension is felt by the reader of 'The Captain's Daughter' because of Pushkin's use of archaisms mingled with his nineteenth-century language in the novella; in the film the visual images and the archaisms match each other, providing a seamless texture, in which the nineteenth-century layer is less noticeable. Moreover, for the filmmakers and the spectators of the film, Pushkin's time is also a thing of the past. The tension between past and present in Pushkin's novella is therefore eliminated in the film adaptation.

The issue of eliminating differences is even more noticeable due to the fact that the film is based on two different texts written in different genres, 'The Captain's Daughter' being a fictional novella, and 'The History of Pugachev' a historical treatise. In a review of the film, the critic Viktoria Belopol'skaia notes that a problematic aspect of the combination of the two texts in the film *Russian Revolt* is that while 'The Captain's Daughter' is written from the point of view of the protagonist, the young officer Grinev, there are events described in 'The History of Pugachev' which he is not witness to (Belopol'skaia 2000: online). When the film uses scenes from both texts, the point of view of Grinev, which serves at the beginning of the film as a focus of consciousness as it is 'The Captain's Daughter', is confused by the representation of events such as the imprisonment of Pugachev, which Grinev could not have seen. Therefore, the film lacks a consistent sense of time and location. Proshkin's wish to retain the literary features of both the novella and the historical treaty results in a collapse of meanings.

Yet, this amalgamation clearly serves another purpose required by post-Soviet concerns. In a rethinking of Soviet ideology, one of the concepts most refuted in Russian culture nowadays is that of the idealization of revolution. If the Pugachev rebellion was depicted in Soviet cinema as a heroic uprising of the people against oppressive tsarist authorities, this post-Soviet film disputes the Soviet notion in its very title, which hints at Pushkin's famous maxim: 'A Russian rebellion is senseless and merciless' ('*Russkii bunt – bessmyslennyi i pezposhchadnyi*').[1] We may say, therefore, that while the Pushkin text is subverted, what emerges is a specifically post-Soviet text. Although the time and place of the literary source is kept intact in the film adaptations, the amalgamation constitutes a statement against the Soviet treatment of the topic itself. The need to use not only 'The Captain's Daughter', as previous adaptations did, but also 'The History of Pugachev', arises from the fact that the historical treatise includes many more details about the violence and horror of the rebellion. The elimination of the tension between Pushkin's time of writing and his subject mentioned above also effects a concretization of the anti-revolutionary message of the film in the here and now of post-Soviet Russia. The post-Soviet position expressed in the film, therefore, constitutes a shift of emphasis, expressing the specific ideology of its anti-Soviet reaction.

Yet post-Soviet dialogue with the literary canon is not only constructed on the ideological level, but is also expressed in film's metatextual relations with literature itself, as well as in cultural revisions of literary-based concepts. Such a metatextual approach is evident in the film adaptation *Katia Izmailova* (released in Russia as *Evenings Around Moscow* (*Podmoskovnye vechera*)). The critic Anninskii wrote regarding the 1989 film adaptation of Leskov's 'Lady Macbeth': 'Leskov gives filmmakers opportunities, he bequeaths them questions. The answers are anyway ours; you cannot hide behind the classics' (Anninskii 1990: 69). And indeed most film adaptations of this novella, characterized by its potentially problematic themes of sex and violence, were made in times of social change and unrest in Russia, whether that of the NEP or the post-Soviet period.[2]

The last film adaptation of this novella to date is Valerii Todorovskii's *Katia Izmailova*, made in 1994. Todorovskii's title is, significantly, the short informal form of the heroine's name which hints at the filmmaker's intention to move the action of the film to the contemporary scene. In Leskov's novella she is always Katerina, the lady of the estate, so that the new form of her name constitutes a new interpretation of her character. The film does not just transform the story into a new medium, to use McFarlane's term, but is an adaptation in which 'novelistic elements ... find quite different equivalence in the film medium' (MacFarlane 1996:13).

In his review of the 1989 film *Lady Macbeth*, the critic Anninskii provides the context for the reception of this film in Russia. He explains that Leskov's conservative (or anti-radical) political views made him suspicious to Soviet publishers, so that not all of Leskov's writings were published widely in the Soviet Union. The texts chosen to be published were those which could show the writer as a witness of the people's suffering under the Old Regime. Yet Leskov was always part of the classical literary heritage in Soviet times, and *Lady Macbeth* was never banned. Anninskii explains that Soviet criticism, as could be expected, interpreted Leskov's tale in a class-oriented social context with Katerina portrayed as a victim of the oppressive bourgeoisie. On the other hand, popular perceptions of Katerina took a different approach and she was viewed as a victim of her own great passions. Thus, as Anninskii notes, the official appreciation joined the popular one in portraying a picture of Katerina as a victim, a sinner who should, nonetheless, be pitied. A post-Soviet adaptation of *Lady Macbeth* which departs from such Soviet views of the protagonist is bound to express its stance in relation to these moral and psychological positions.

In his article about contemporary film adaptations of the Russian classics, David Gillespie points to the most prominent departure of Todorovskii's film from Leskov's story, namely the fact that Todorovskii transports the plot into the present. As Gillespie puts it, the heroine of the film 'is no Lady Macbeth, doomed by the strength of her own passion and ambition, but rather a modern, self-aware woman with intellectual and cultural aspirations' (Gillespie 1999: 120). In *Katia Izmailova* the plot is radically re-shaped. Katia is the typist of the famous writer Irina Dmitrievna, her mother-in-law. Katia begins an affair with Sergei, a carpenter who works in the family dacha. When the mother-in-law discovers the affair and challenges Katia, the latter causes her death by depriving her of her medicines. Later she confesses the love affair to her husband, whom her lover then kills in a fight. Katia and Sergei continue, not by planning their future riches as they do in Leskov's tale, but by re-writing the ending of Irina Dmitrievna's last novel. A detective investigating Katia's husband's disappearance and modelled on Dostoevskii's Porfirii Petrovich is introduced into the story. When Sergei starts an affair with a former girlfriend, Katia picks her up in her car and drives them both to their deaths from a bridge over a deep river.

Leskov's story is set among merchants and workers, and it reflects disillusionment with the moral values of post-emancipated Russian society. *Katia Izmailova* is set among the intelligentsia, which brings Leskov's disillusionment up to date. The intelligentsia's moral role was indeed emphasized in certain nineteenth-century political theories, yet most of them also insisted on the common people as the source of privileged values which the intelligentsia should adopt (hence the famous 'going to the people' movement). In late Soviet and post-Soviet culture it is the intelligentsia, rather than 'the people' (*narod*), who are considered the bearers of moral principles. Thus, when in *Katia Izmailova* the action unfolds in the surroundings of the intelligentsia, the uneasiness felt by the audience is more acute. Like Leskov's text, the film is set in the countryside. However, Leskov's novella concerns provincial folk, while in the film the urban characters leave their usual habitat and move to their dacha in the provinces for the summer. They do not belong to the countryside (except Sergei, the lover, who lives in the village); rather they invade it. The defamiliarized setting of Leskov's novella becomes the all-too-familiar setting of modern urban culture.

The scene of the move to the dacha, moving from urban to rural as if to 'defile' it, is significant. In this scene, Katia, her husband and her mother-in-law travel by car and cross a bridge to their dacha. As they are found exactly in the middle of the bridge above the river, the mother-in-law cries out to Katia, who is driving, to be more careful. The camera angle changes from the passengers' eye-level to a long shot at the very moment when they cross the river. By the end of the film, we see the crossing of the same bridge in the fatal scene of Katia's suicidal murder of her rival. The crossing of the river in both cases is a transition to a different dimension, a radical and irretrievable change. According to Bakhtin, the traversal of a bridge is an example of the crossing of a threshold, which always marks a significant moment in a narrative. It is 'the chronotope of crisis and break in life … in this chronotope time is essential, instantaneous; it is as if it has no duration and falls out of the normal course of biographical time' (Bakhtin 1981: 248). In this film the threshold scenes are on both occasions emphasized through a repetition of their visual markers, in which location is the same but time changes. Thus the chronotope in each case is both linked with, and juxtaposed to, the other, creating an internal dialogue between them. The threshold scenes, as Bakhtin puts it, transcend biographical time and acquire a structural significance when they mark first the beginning of crisis, then its tragic resolution.

The opening of the film emphasizes its central theme, not sex and murder as the plot of Leskov's tale may suggest, but writing. This is a modern film not only in the fact that it changes the plot to a modern-day story, but also in its self-reflexivity. We hear typing before we hear any other sound. The first *words* of the film are a quotation, as Irina Dmitrievna dictates her new novel to Katia. Yet the first *image* we see revealed behind the page is Katia's, whose face appears behind the page as she types. This image represents Katia's later attempts to usurp Irina's Word and replace it with a happy end to Irina's novel.

The scene of Sergei's seduction of Katia is conducted against the background of writing and typing. The word becomes the location of intimacy as well as identity. Yet as in the previous scene, the text is not Katia's. At the beginning of the seduction scene, Sergei asks Katia what she is writing, and she answers 'I'm not writing, I'm typing'. This distinction inevitably links the seduction scene to Katia's position regarding Irina Dmitrievna's text.

After Irina's death, Sergei and Katia change the ending of Irina Dmitrievna's last novel. Instead of the novel's original tragic ending, they choose a happy conclusion. It is significant that even in this scene Katia does not create, but rather types Sergei's words. In this respect, the relationship between them corresponds to that of the characters of Leskov's tale. Katerina, the bored merchant's wife, has some books at home but she is not interested in reading. The scene of her seduction by Sergei happens when he visits her to ask for books, explaining that he enjoys reading. In Todorovskii's film Sergei tells Irina Dmitrievna, the writer, that he has read her novels from cover to cover. Katia, on the other hand, when asked her opinion of Irina Dmitrievna's new novel, admits to not reading it as she was concentrating on the typing. But later it will be Katia who brings the 'corrected' manuscript to the publishers, claiming its supremacy over the original one in the name of love and happiness. As in Leskov's tale, the man possesses the Word, yet the woman is in charge of the action.[3]

Katia's status in the film is further degraded when Sergei starts an affair with his ex-girlfriend. This is represented again by a scene of subliminal typing: the girl gives him a back massage, imitating a children's verse about typing. Thus the humiliation of Katia, who witnesses the scene, is complete when her rival takes over her functions and indirectly mocks her work as a typist just as the late mother-in-law used to. The metatextual shift of attention from murder to writing reflects Todorovskii's revised emphasis. Instead of Leskov's provincial setting, which is equated in his novella with raw emotions and violence, Todorovskii's modern urbanism is highlighted by the metatextual context.

The rewriting of Irina's novel serves as a metatextual commentary on the making of Todorovskii's film. As Katia in the film appropriates the novel of a well-known established writer, Irina Dmitrievna, so Todorovskii appropriates Leskov's text in creating an independent artistic statement. As Gillespie notes, the literary game continues in the introduction of the police inspector Romanov, a figure based on Dostoevskii's Porfirii Petrovich (Gillespie 1999). In his interrogation of Katia, he tells her of his past experiences in investigating criminal cases. In fact, all of these 'cases' are the plots of Russian canonical nineteenth-century texts: Tolstoi's *Anna Karenina*, Dostoevskii's *Crime and Punishment* (*Prestuplenie i nakazanie*) and Ostrovskii's 'The Thunderstorm' ('*Groza*').

The scene of the move to the dacha heightens the metatextual nature of the film, but also links metatextualism back to the motifs of passion and violence in Leskov's text through the choice of the literary works mentioned (all which contain motifs of passion and violence) and by their presentations as cases solved by the police inspector. It is also, in a sense, Todorovskii's metatextual statement. The literary figures, whom Katia does not recognize (as we remember, she does not like reading), are easily recognizable by the audience. In the world of the film, the fictional characters of the Russian classics become modern real-life figures for Romanov and Katia. In the same way, Leskov's characters, which in the novella 'Lady Macbeth' are removed from the modern audience by time and space, become real to the audience: not archaic and rural, but urban and contemporary. We are no longer able to defend ourselves from Leskov's depiction of violence and horror; we have to face up to its reflection in our own experiences. Furthermore, the use of the Russian classics by the investigator mirrors the use of Leskov's text by the director of *Katia Izmailova*. Thus, Todorovskii's contemporary urban film becomes a mouthpiece for post-modern sensibilities in post-Soviet Russia.

A different approach to the dialogue of post-Soviet cinema film adaptations with the double baggage of nineteenth-century and Soviet cultural and ideological spaces is exhibited in the controversial film *Down House* (*Daun Khaus*), based on Dostoevskii's *Idiot*. As Nikita Lary notes in his monograph on Dostoevskii in Soviet film, Dostoevskii was always seen as a threat to Soviet ideology (Lary 1988: 9). Lary qualifies this observation with a statement that Dostoevskii's revolutionary youth was considered useful for the purposes of Soviet ideology, which is one of the reasons he was not banned altogether. It was Dostoevskii the religious thinker who constituted the real danger. Already in the 1920s Nikolai Berdyaev noted that Russian communism had to juxtapose itself to religion, and especially to Russian Orthodoxy as the religion most associated with the Russian people, in order to assert its own 'atheist religion' (Berdyaev 1961). At the same time Aleksei Losev pointed out that Bolshevism assumes a 'dialectics of myth', in which it fights against religion not as a rejection of religious sentiment but as 'another religion' (Losev 1992: 498–9; Esaulov 2000: 49). The contemporary critic Ivan Esaulov explains that in the early 1920s Russian communism positioned itself against Christianity, because Christianity was a feature of public and private consciousness under the Old Regime. Later, communist ideology took a step forward and characterized itself as essentially anti-Christian (Esaulov 2000: 50–1). As this opposition is so central to Soviet ideology, Soviet cinema's relation to Dostoevskii's texts is inevitably problematic. It is not surprising, therefore, that *The Idiot* was hardly adapted for the Soviet screen.[4]

Post-Soviet cinema is now free from the constraints regarding the spiritual dimension of Dostoevskii's works. When in 2001 director Roman Kachanov released *Down House*, his contemporary adaptation of *The Idiot*, he was working in the context of complete eclecticism and an absence of ideological barriers. Yet this film, surprisingly, avoids all treatment of the religious context of Dostoevskii's novel.[5] *Down House*, and especially the history of its production, provides an interesting commentary on post-Soviet interpretations of the classics in the context of religion and spirituality, again bringing together the cultures of nineteenth-century, Soviet and post-Soviet Russia.

Like *Katia Izmailova*, *Down House* transposes the action of its literary source not only temporally (it is set in contemporary times) but also spatially (the action takes place in Moscow). If Pyr'ev's Petersburg setting emphasizes the nature of this 'most fantastical city' by his use of heavy grey-blue fog in the outdoors scenes, Kachanov's *Down House*, filmed in a pseudo video-camera style, eliminates, through the change of scene, the cultural attributes associated with the Petersburg myth. *Down House* (the Russian film is given this English-language title, probably in order to undermine ironically Dostoevskii's status as a Russian national icon) places the characters of *The Idiot* in the modern, commercial Moscow of the New Russians, and thus brings home the materialist context that Pyr'ev, who made a historical drama, banished to the historical past.[6]

The materialist context is highly significant in the novel *The Idiot*. An obsession with money and status, most notably in the attempts to organize Nastasia Filipovna's marriage as a financial arrangement, in Rogozhin's use of money as a sign of his passion for Nastasia Filipovna, and in the changing circumstances of Myshkin when he inherits a large sum of money. Myshkin's attempt to base his relationships with others on love and brotherhood fails to destabilize the materialistic and self-interested nature of the society he finds himself in. One may say that the conflict between spiritual values and materialism is the underlying structure of the novel. Like *Katia Izmailova*, *Down House* brings the central concerns of the literary source home to a contemporary audience that is supposed to see the film as a mirror of itself rather than a historically remote entity. Retaining the materialist context, Kachanov's adaptation is the most radical example among the films discussed in this chapter.

The film is a disjointed work, resembling in its style a video clip. But it does follow the central plot line of Dostoevskii's novel, its disjointed form acting as a comment on the wish of the filmmakers to transpose Dostoevskii into the contemporary cultural scene. In the film, Myshkin, son of a Russian émigré family, meets Rogozhin, a businessman, and Lebedev, on the Zurich–Moscow bus. (In Dostoevskii's time the third-class rail carriage would contain the people who nowadays travel on the less comfortable, but much cheaper, international bus.) Myshkin's self-absorption, so different from his all-embracing involvement with others in the novel, is expressed in the film by the fact that he is a computer programmer who spends many hours in the virtual world, and the fact that he constantly listen to music on his personal stereo. Computers and personal stereos are the most expressive means of denoting the mental solitude available to an individual nowadays. Several of the characters take drugs, yet Myshkin stresses that he does not need the help of chemical substances in order to be transported into the world of the imagination. Nastasia Filipovna's appearances on the screen are characterized by a rapid succession of shots set apart from the rest of the film through a distinctive montage effect, hinting at her contradictory nature. Rogozhin, who had exchanged crosses with Myshkin, shoots him from his pistol. The Epanchins discuss monetary matters in their private gym. Gania is offered three vans full of (rotting) meat in return for his marrying Nastasia Filipovna. The film ends with Rogozhin's inviting Myshkin to a meal made of Nastasia Filipovna's legs. In the words of the scenario writer, Ivan Okhlobystin, Dostoevskii ends his novel with the most shocking image of his period, and Okhlobystin attempted to match this with an image that would be as shocking in our times (Okhlabystin 2002: online).

Indeed, shocking is how most critics saw the film. Both reviews of *Down House* in *Iskusstvo kino* state that the film is made only in order to shock the audience and attract publicity. Igor' Mantsov even sees in it the arrogance of filmmakers who feel they are beyond the realms of art (and critics!) (Mantsov 2001a: 35–7). Elena Kutlovskaia claims that the style of the film recalls the children's television programme '*Eralash*' (Kutlovskaia 2001: 161–6), in which several comic episodes about the same characters are strung together (although in *Down House*, regardless of its parodic nature, the episodes are clearly sequenced according to Dostoevskii's text). The TVTs Russian television channel, in its talk show 'Courtroom in Action' ('*Sud idet*') went as far as to denounce the film as an amoral affront to national and religious values. These harsh accusations spring from the irreverential treatment of the classical writer, but also from the special role of the scenario writer, Okhlobystin, in the contemporary Russian media and it is this that I now want to explore.

The figure of the actor – a visual reflection of the real body, a sign of the person – carries with it the weight of the actor's recognizable, media-generated, figure. It is impossible to ignore the knowledge the audience has about the actor, including his or her previous roles in films. In the case of *Down House*, the figure of Okhlobystin functions particularly strongly, as he is both the scenario writer and the actor playing the role of one of the main characters, Rogozhin. Thus the media-projected image of Okhlobystin bears direct relevance to the perception of the film in the context of post-Soviet culture.

Ivan Okhlobystin, actor and scenario writer, a familiar figure in show-business circles, announced publicly in autumn 2002 that he intended to stop working in cinema and become an Orthodox priest. He was ordained by the time *Down House* was released. The idea of a priest writing the scenario to a film of a classical novel featuring drugs, cannibalism and other controversial issues became much more shocking than the film itself. Various rumours appeared in the Russian press concerning Okhlobystin's ordination: that it was a PR move, that he was ordained without being subject to the appropriate procedures, that his ordination took place in Tashkent because other dioceses would not agree to it. Yet already in 1989 Okhlobystin presented on television the religious programme 'Canon', and some of Okhlobystin's acquaintances testify that his interest in the church is not a fleeting one. Following a short period of serving as a priest in Tashkent, he has taken charge of a parish in Moscow, where he had always lived. Two years after the release of *Down House*, Okhlobystin is writing a book about the Russian Patriarch Alexi II, as well as working on a television adaptation of *The Lives of the Saints*.

Regarding *Down House*, Okhlobystin published in April 2001 an open letter, in which he stated that no longer saw himself as linked to the film, having chosen a different way of life. He explained that as actor and scenario writer he was never able to express the spiritual questions that had always concerned him. This is significant, especially in the case of *Down House*, a film which not only pays, albeit perfunctory, deference to the plot and the psychological complexity of Dostoevskii's novel, but also deals with the spiritual questions that it poses. One may say that in writing the scenario to this film Okhlobystin tried to engage with Dostoevskii's religious dimensions, failed, yet began the journey that finally led him to the Church of Sophia the Divine Wisdom in Moscow. Ending his 'open letter', he writes: 'as he died, Ivan Okhlobystin asked your forgiveness' ('*umiraia, Ivan Okhlobystin prosil u vas proshcheniia*'). He signs himself 'Fr Ioann Okhlobystin' ('*Sviashchennik Ioann Okhlobystin*'), thus stressing the outmoded, religious version of his name, Ioann, which replaces the common, secular version of the name, Ivan (Okhlobystin 2002: online). As in the title of the film *Katia Izmailova*, the change of proper names becomes a vital carrier of meaning. Okhlobystin further explained that 'due to a series of mistaken choices he had made, he became associated with a disgusting legend that never expressed who he really was' (ibid.).

It seems that *Down House* expresses the real concerns of a 'lost generation' in contemporary Russia, one which found itself oscillating between the wild capitalism of the world of the New Russians and the renaissance of religious sentiments together with the ever strengthening role of the Russian Orthodox Church. Dostoevskii's *Idiot*, in its spiritual concerns on one hand and its emphasis on the materialist context in which characters operate on the other, seems the most suitable source for a cinematic adaptation to illustrate this contemporary crisis, in a society which is both capitalist oriented and spiritually articulate. Dostoevskii's *The Idiot* is a seminal text for the relationship between materialism and spirituality; it even may be seen as a rod by which to measure one's allegiances regarding these opposing concepts. The fact that the adaptation of this text by Kachanov and

Okhlobystin is an act of negation of old ideas rather an affirmation of new values is, therefore, highly significant.

In a recent article, Igor' Mantsov states that the Soviet past is a source of trauma accompanied by masochism and perverse enjoyment (Mantsov 2001b: 66). This may be the reason why contemporary Russian filmmakers, who have wearied of the bleak and violent films based on the Soviet period that proliferated in the early years of perestroika, prefer to engage with a past more readily accepted as worthy of emulation. In *Russian Revolt* the historical context is retained, yet through the amalgamation of two Pushkin texts and through the visual concreteness of the cinematic medium, a new, distinctively post-Soviet anti-revolutionary statement is made. *Katia Izmailova* and *Down House* both transpose nineteenth-century canonical texts into a post-Soviet context, yet their use of the contemporary material is different. *Katia Izmailova* converts Leskov's text into a post-Modernist self-referential narrative. *Down House* sarcastically points to the radical changes in attitudes to religion and spirituality after the fall of the Soviet Union. Yet all three films engage creatively with their literary sources in order to create their own artistic statement, acknowledging at the same time the paramount significance that nineteenth-century literature still has for post-Soviet culture today.

Notes

1 Besides a pre-Revolutionary adaptation made in 1914 (directed by G. Libken and S. Veselovskii in Iaroslavl), there were two adaptations of Pushkin's 'Captain's Daughter' made during the Soviet period: one in 1928, directed by Iu. Tarich (Sovkino) and another in 1958, directed by V. Kaplynovskii (Mosfilm). Neither of these films use 'Pugachev's History' as an additional source to the adaptation.

2 The first adaptation of this tale was the silent film *Katerina Izmailova*, subtitled 'Ledi Makbet Mtsenskogo uezda', and directed by Sabinskii in 1926, of which both parts 1 and 4 are lost. An adaptation of Shostakovich's opera 'Lady Macbeth of the Mtsensk District' was made in 1966, with the famous soprano Vishnevskaia in the leading role. This film concerns me less here as it is not a direct adaptation of Leskov's text, but is instead mediated through the operatic text, itself already a visual form of art. The other two adaptations were both made during and after perestroika. In 1989 Roman Balaian directed *Lady Macbeth of the Mtsensk District*, and in 1994 Valerii Todorovskii directed Katia Izmailova.

3 In Leskov's novella it is Katerina who initiates all the murders committed by her and her lover Sergei, a fact that motivates the title comparing her to Lady Macbeth.

4 The first film adaptation of Dostoevskii's *The Idiot* was made in 1910 by Piotr Chardynin, and is one of his first cinematic works. Then, from the Revolution until Stalin's death, no adaptation of this novel was made. Ivan Pyr'ev, the director of famous socialist realist films such as *Tractor Drivers* (*Traktoristy*, 1939) and *A Tale of the Siberian Land* (*Skazanie o zemle sibirskoi*, 1947), had written a scenario for an adaptation of *The Idiot* in two parts already in 1947, yet he had to wait until after the Twentieth Party Congress in order to obtain permission to direct the film. Pyr'ev was a highly influential figure in post-World War II Soviet cinema. He was for several years the director of the biggest studio,

Mosfil'm, and later became the President of the Union of Cinematographers. For part of that period he was even a deputy to the Supreme Soviet of the USSR. It seems that Pyr'ev's strong position in political circles allowed him to venture into the unknown and produce adaptations of such sensitive material as Dostoevskii's novels.

5 This fact is especially surprising since late Soviet cinema had already dealt with issues of spirituality and religion; the strong presence of Dostoevskii's *The Idiot* is sensed in Sergei Solov'ev's heavily religious 1989 film *A Black Rose is a Symbol of Sadness, a Red Rose is a Symbol of Love* (*Chernaia roza – emblema pechali, krasnaia roza – emblema liubvi*).

6 It is not clear what the title *Down House* refers to, and the filmmakers produced no statement in this regard. The word 'Down', it was suggested in reviews of the film, may constitute a short form of the term 'Down's Syndrome', thus denoting a modern term analogous to Dostoevskii's 'idiot' in the sense used in the novel (a person who lacks intelligence as a result of a disability). The word 'house' may refer to the style of dance music that accompanies the film and which the protagonist listens to. The combination 'Down House', in its turn, may denote the habitat of retarded people, expressing the deliberate breaking of social norms and etiquette that is exhibited by almost all the characters in the film.

Bibliography

Aksenov, V. (1981) 'Beseda s pisatelem Vasiliem Aksenovym', *Kontinent* 27: 433–46.

—— (1994) *Sobranie sochinenii*, vol. 1 'Kollegi. Zvezdnyi bilet. Apel'siny iz Marokko. Pora, moi drug, pora. Na polputi k lune', Moscow: Biblioteka zhurnala 'Iunost". Izdatel'skii dom 'Iunost".

—— (1995) 'Tri shineli i nos', *Kinostsenarii* 1: 137–49.

—— (2003) 'V dal'neishem – Dal", in *Oleg Dal'. Vzroslyi molodoi chelovek. Dnevniki. Pis'ma. Vospominaniia*, ed. B. Poiurovskii, Moscow: Olma-Press, pp. 6–9.

Aleksandrov, A.D., Kolmogorov, A.N. and Lavrent'ev, M.A. (eds.) (1963) *Mathematics: Its Content, Methods, and Meaning*, vol. III, Cambridge MA: MIT Press.

Alferov, I. (1946) 'Syn Polka', *Vecherniaia Moskva*, 244 (6915), 17 October: 4.

Alov, A. and Naumov, V. (1989) *Stat'i. Svidetel'stva. Vyskazyvaniia*, Moscow: Iskusstvo.

Altschuller, A. (1999) 'Actors and Acting, 1820–1850', in R. Leach and V. Borovsky (eds) *A History of the Russian Theatre*, Cambridge: Cambridge University Press, pp. 104–23.

Ando, A., Yasuo, U. and Mochizuki, T. (eds) (1994) *A Concordance to Dostoevsky's 'Crime and Punishment'*, vol. 2, Sapporo: Hokkaido University.

Andrew, D. (1984) *Concepts in Film Theory*, Oxford: Oxford University Press.

—— (2000) 'Adaptation', in J. Naremore (ed.) *Film Adaptation*, London: Athlone Press, pp. 28–38.

Andrew, J. (1993) *Narrative and Desire in Russian Literature, 1822–49*, Houndmills: Macmillan.

—— (2002) 'Same time, same place': some reflections on the chronotope and gender in Dostoevsky's "White Nights" ', *New Zealand Slavonic Studies* 36: 25–58.

Anikst, A. A. (1955) 'Byt' ili ne byt' u nas Gamletu?', *Teatr* 3: 62–81.

—— (1971) 'Tragediia prozreniia. Pervye vpechatleniia o fil'me 'Korol' Lir'", *Sovetskii ekran*, 1: 4–5.

—— (1974) *Shekspir: Remeslo dramaturga*, Moscow: Sovetskii pisatel'.

Anninskii, L. (1966) 'Ne v etom delo, tiatia!', *Iskusstvo kino*, 7: 15–20.

—— (1969) 'Smysl krasoty', in *Iskusstvo kino*, 12: 45–52.

—— (1990) 'A esli eto dazhe ne liubov?', *Iskusstvo kino*, 2: 66–71.

Anonymous (1934a) 'Chapaevtsy o Chapaeve', *Pravda*, 20 November.

—— (1934b) ' "Chapaev" v dal'nevostochnoi armii', *Pravda*, 24 December.

—— (1948) 'Molodaia gvardiia', *Pravda*, 284 (11025), 10 October.

—— (2004) 'Basic Sherlock Holmes For You Beginners', online at <http://www.geocities.com/Hollywood/Derby/3418/basicsherlock.htm> (accessed 3 January 2004).

Arata, S. (1981) *Fictions of Loss in the Victorian Fin de Siècle,* Cambridge: Cambridge University Press.

Attwood, L. (ed.) (1993) *Red Women on the Silver Screen: Soviet Women and Cinema from the Beginning to the End of the Communist Era*, London: Pandora.

Aumont J., Bergala, A., Marie, M. and Vernet, M. (1983) *Esthétique du film*, Paris: Nathan.

Averbakh, L. (1931) 'O Furmanove i proletarskoi literature', in A. Bezymenskii *et al.* (eds), *Bor'ba za metod. Sbornik diskussionnykh statei o tvorchestve Dm. Furmanove,* Moscow and Leningrad: Gosudarstvennoe izdatel'stvo khudozhestvennoi literatury.

Babochkin, B. (1968) *Boris Babochkin v teatre i kino*, Moscow: Iskusstvo.

Bakhtin, M. (1981) *The Dialogic Imagination*, M. Holquist (ed.), C. Emerson (trans.), Austin, TX: University of Texas Press.

Bakushinskaia, O. (2001) ' "Igor" Maslennikov: Posle "Zimnei vishni" muzhchiny nazvali menia predatelem', *Komsomol'skaia Pravda*, 26 October.

Barta, P. and Hutchings, S. (2002) 'The train as word-image intertext in the films "Ballad of a Soldier" and "Thief" ', *Intertexts* 6 (2): 127–144.

Barthes, R. (1981) *Camera Lucida*, Richard Howard (trans.), New York: Hill and Wang.

—— (1993) *Mythologies*, A. Lavers (trans.), London: Vintage.

Baudouin, A. and Heller, L. (1991) 'L'image prend la parole: Image, Texte, Littérature dans la période jdanovienne', in W. Berelowitch and L. Gervereau (eds) *Russie-URSS 1914–1991: Changements de Régards*, Nanterre: Documentation Internationale Contemporaine, 140–52.

Bazin, A. (2000) 'Adaptation or the Cinema as Digest', in J. Naremore (ed.), Alain Piette and Bert Cadullo (trans.), *Film Adaptation*, London: Athlone Press, pp. 19–28.

Beaudoin, L.J. (1997) *Resetting the Margins. Russian Romantic Verse Tales and the Idealized Woman*, New York: Peter Lang.

Beliaev, V.S., Macheret, A.V. and Dmitrieva P.F. (eds.) (1973) *Kniga sporit s fil'mom*, Moscow: Iskusstvo.

Belinskii, V. G. (1977) ' "Gamlet", drama Shekspira. Molchanov v roli Gamleta', in his *Sobranie sochinenii v deviati tomakh* (9 vols), Moscow: Khudozhestvennaia literatura (1976–82), II, pp. 7–92.

Belopol'skaia, V. (2000) 'Vkus k ekzotike', Vremia MG, 15 February, online at <http://www.film.ru/process/article.asp?ID=1500> (accessed 15 April 2003).

Benjamin W. (1999) 'The work of art in the age of mechanical reproduction', in J. Evans and S. Hall (eds) *Visual Culture: The Reader*, London: Sage.

Berdyaev, N. (1961) *The Russian Revolution*, Ann Arbor: University of Michigan Press.

Bernstein, L. (1995) *Sonia's Daughters. Prostitutes and Their Regulation in Imperial Russia*, Berkeley, Los Angeles and London: University of California Press.

Beumers, B. (forthcoming) *Mikhalkov: Between Nostalgia and Nationalism*, London: IB Tauris.

Bisztray, G. (1978) *Marxist Models of Literary Realism*, New York: Columbia University Press.

Bleiman, M. (1966) 'Rezhissura—eto professia', *Sovetskii ekran*, 7: 5.

Blok, A.A. (1997a) *Polnoe sobranie sochinenii i pisem v dvadtsati tomakh,* vol. 2. 'Stikhotvoreniia. Kniga vtoraia (1904–1908)', A.V. Lavrov and Z.G. Mints (eds), Moscow: Nauka.

—— (1997b) *Polnoe sobranie sochinenii i pisem v dvadtsati tomakh,* vol. 3, 'Stikhotvoreniia. Kniga tret'ia (1907–1916)', Iu. K. Gerasimov (ed.), Moscow: Nauka.

Bluestone, G. (1957) *Novels into Film: The Metamorphosis of Fiction into Cinema*, Baltimore: Johns Hopkins University Press.

Bodeen, D. (1963) 'The adapting art', *Films in Review* 14/6 (June–July): 349–56.

Bogomolov, Iu. (1994) *Ekrannye iskusstva i literatura: zvukovoe kino*, Moscow: Nauka.

Boym, S. (1994) *Common Places*, Cambridge MA and London: Harvard University Press..

—— (2001) *The Future of Nostalgia*, New York: Basic Books.

Brooks, J. (2000) *Thank You Comrade Stalin: Soviet Public Culture From Revolution to Cold War*, Princeton NJ: Princeton UP.

Buck-Morss, S. (2000) *Dreamworld and Catastrophe: The Passing of Mass Utopia in East and West*, Cambridge MA and London: MIT Press.

Bulgakova, O. (2000) 'Sovetskie fil'my v poiskhakh obshchei modeli', in E. Dobrenko and H. Gunther (eds) *Sotsrealisticheskii kanon*, St Petersburg: Akademicheskii proekt, pp. 146–66.

Cardwell, S. (2002) *Adaptation Revisited: Television and the Classic Novel*, Manchester: Manchester University Press.

Carroll, N. (1996) 'Nonfiction film and postmodernist skepticism', in D. Bordwell and N. Carroll (eds) *Post-Theory: Reconstructing Film Studies*, Madison: University of Wisconsin Press, pp. 283–306.

—— (2001) *Beyond Aesthetics: Philosophical Essays*, Cambridge: Cambridge University Press.

Cassetti, F. (1999) *Theories of Cinema, 1945–1995*, Austin: University of Texas Press.

Caughie, J. (ed.) (1981) *Theories of Authorship: A Reader*, London: Routledge and Kegan Paul.

Caute, D. (2003) *The Dancer Defects: The Struggle for Cultural Supremacy During the Cold War*, Oxford: Oxford University Press.

Chakovskii, A. (1948) 'Nastoiashchii sovetskii chelovek', *Izvestiia*, 23 November.

Chandler, R. (1985) 'Translator's Introduction', in Vasily Grossman, *Life and Fate*, London: Collins Harvill, pp. 7–16.

Chatman, S. (1978) *Story and Discourse: Narrative Structure in Fiction and Film,* Ithaca and London: Cornell UP.

—— (1990) *Coming to Terms: The Rhetoric of Narrative in Fiction and Film*, New Haven CT: Yale University Press.

—— (1992) 'What novels can do that films can't (and vice versa)', in G. Mast, M. Cohen, L. Braudy (eds), *Film Theory and Criticism: Introductory Readings*, New York, Oxford: Oxford University Press.

Chernenko, V. (1962) 'Review of the film *Kollegi*', *Moskovskaia kinonedelia*, 22 August.

Christie, I. (1991) 'Down to Earth: *Aelita* relocated', in R.Taylor and I. Christie (eds) *Inside the Film Factory: New Approaches to Russian and Soviet Cinema*, London: Routledge, pp. 80–103.

Clark, Katerina (1981) *The Soviet Novel: History as Ritual*, Chicago: Chicago UP.
____ (2000) 'Stalinskii mif o "velikoi sem'e", in E. Dobrenko and H. Gunther (eds) *Sotsrealisticheskii kanon*, St Petersburg: Akademicheskii proekt, pp. 784–96.
Clark, K. (2000) *The Soviet Novel: History as Ritual*, 3rd edn, Bloomington and Indianapolis: Indiana University Press.
Conan Doyle, A. (1930) *The Complete Sherlock Holmes*, Vol. 1, Garden City, NY: Doubleday.
Connolly, J. (2001) *The Intimate Stranger: Meetings with the Devil in Nineteenth-Century Russian Literature*, New York: Peter Lang.
Conroy, P. (1992) 'The Importance of Being Watson', in H. Orel (ed.) *Critical Essays on Sir Arthur Conan Doyle*, New York: G.K. Hall, pp. 84–102.
Crofts, S. (1997) 'Ideology and form: Soviet Socialist realism and Chapayev' *Essays in Poetics* II(1): 43–57.
De Lauretis, T. (1984) 'Desire in narrative', in *Alice Doesn', Feminism, Semiotics, Cinema*, London: Macmillan, pp. 103–57.
Deleuze, G. (1989) *Cinema 2: The Time-Image*, H. Tomlinson and R. Galeta (trans.), Minneapolis: University of Minnesota Press.
Dobin, E. (1967) *Gamlet. Fil'm Kozintseva*, Moscow-Leningrad: Iskusstvo.
Dobrenko, E. (1993) *Metafora vlasti: literatura stalinskoi epokhi v istoricheskom osveshchenii*, München: Otto Sagner.
—— (2001) 'The Russia we acquired: Russian classics, the Stalinist cinema, and the past from the revolutionary perspective', *Russian Studies in Literature* 37(4) (Fall): 61–91.
Dobroliubov, N.A. (1962) 'Temnoe tsarstvo', in his *Sobranie sochinenii v deviati tomakh* (9 vols), Moscow-Leningrad: Khudozhestvennaia literatura (1961–64), vol. V, pp. 7–139.
Dolinskii, I. (1945) *Chapaev: Dramaturgiia*, Moscow: Goskinoizdat.
Dostoevski, F. (1960) *Idiot: roman v chetyrekh chastiakh*, Moscow: Khudozhestvennaia literatura.
—— (1972) *Notes from Underground/The Double*, Jessie Coulson (trans.), New York: Penguin Books.
—— (1973a) *Polnoe sobranie sochinenii v tridtsati tomakh*, vol. 5, 'Povesti i rasskazy, 1862–1866', E.I. Pokusaev (ed.), Leningrad: Nauka.
—— (1973b) *Polnoe sobranie sochinenii v tridtsati tomakh*, vol. 6, 'Prestuplenie i nakazanie', V.V. Vinogradov (ed.), Leningrad: Nauka.
Dyer, R. (1979) *Stars*, London: British Film Institute.
Dzigan, E. (1973) 'Poniat' mysl' avtora', in V. S. Beliaev, A.V. Macheret and P. F. Dmitrieva (eds) *Kniga sporit s fil'mom*, Moscow: Iskusstvo, pp. 215–22.
Eagleton, T. (2001) 'Signs, sense and sentiment', *The Times Higher Educational Supplement*, 27 April.
Eikhenbaum, B. (1974) *Lev Tolstoi. Semidesiatie gody*, Leningrad: Khudozhestvennaia literatura.
—— (1982) *The Poetics of Cinema*, Oxford: Holdan.
Eisenstein, S. (1998a) 'The montage of attractions' (1923), in Richard Taylor (ed.) *The Eisenstein Reader*, Richard Taylor and William Powell (trans.), London: British Film Institute, pp. 29–34.
—— (1998b) 'The dramaturgy of film form (the dialectical approach to film form)', in Richard Taylor (ed.) *The Eisenstein Reader*, Richard Taylor and William Powell (trans.), London: British Film Institute, pp. 93–110.

—— (1998c) 'The problem of the soviet historical film', in Richard Taylor (ed.), *The Eisenstein Reader*, Richard Taylor and William Powell (trans.), London: British Film Institute, pp. 145–59.

Ellis, F. (1999) *From Glasnost to the Internet: Russia's New Infosphere*, London: McMillan.

Endlin, M. (1983) *Chapaev v Amerike i dr.*, n.p., Smeshanina.

Esaulov, I. (2000) 'Sotsialism i religioznoe soznanie', in E. Dobrenko and H.Gunther (eds) Sotsrealisticheskii kanon, Sankt-Peterburg: Akademicheskii proekt, pp. 47–58.

Fadeev. A. (1959–61) Sobranie sochineni, 5 vols, E. F. Kipovich, A.G.Dement'ev, E.I.Naumov and L.I.Timofeev (eds), Moscow: Gosudarstvennoe izdatel'stvo khudozhestvennoi literatury.

Faraday, G. (2000) *Revolt of the Filmmakers: The Struggle for Artistic Autonomy and the Fall of the Soviet Film Industry*, University Park: Pennsylvania State University Press.

Fedoseeva-Shukshina, L. and Chernenko, R.D. (1979) *O Shukshine*, Moscow: Iskusstvo.

Ferro, M. (1976) 'The fiction film and historical analysis', in Smith, P. (ed.) *The Historian and Film*, Cambridge: Cambridge University Press, pp. 80–94.

—— (1988 [1977]) *Cinema and History*, Naomi Greene (trans.), Detroit, MI: Wayne State University Press.

Figes, O. (2002) *Natasha's Dance: A Cultural History of Russia*, New York: Metropolitan.

Foley, B. (1986) *Telling the Truth: The Theory and Practice of Documentary Fiction*, Ithaca, NY: Cornell University Press.

Fomin, V. (ed.) (1998) *Kinematograf ottepeli. Dokumenty i svidetel'stva*, Moscow: Nauchno-issledovatel'skii institut kinoiskusstva. Goskino Rossiiskoi Federatsii. Materik.

Fomin, V.I. (1976) *Peresechenie parallel'nykh*, Moscow: Iskusstvo.

Friedburg, M. (1962) *Russian Classics in Soviet Jackets*, New York: Columbia University Press.

Frolov, V. (1963) 'Sasha Zelenin i ego druz'ia', *Iskusstvo kino* 4: 97–99.

Furmanov, D. (1923) *Chapaev*, Moscow: Istpart–Gosizdat.

—— (1960–61) *Sobranie sochinenii*, 4 vols, A.G. Dement'ev A.G.Dement'ev, E.I.Naumov and L.I.Timofeev (eds), Moscow: G.I.Kh.L.

Furnkov, L. (1964) 'Pashka Kolokol'nikov i ego druz'ia', *Sovetskaia Rossiia*, 19 June.

Galadzheva, N.P. (1991) *Oleg Dal'*, Moscow: Soiuz kinematografistov SSSR. Vseoiuznoe tvorchesko-proizvodstvennoe ob"edinenie 'Kinotsentr'.

Gallagher, M. (1963) *The Soviet History of World War II: Myths and Realities*, New York and London: Praeger.

Geller, H. (2000) 'Esteticheskie kategorii i ikh mesto v sotsrealizme zhdanovskoi epokhi', in E. Dobrenko and H. Gunther (eds) *Sotsrealisticheskii kanon*, St Petersburg: Akademicheskii proekt, pp. 435–48.

Giannetti, L. (1975) *Godard and Others: Essays on Film Form*, Rutherford NJ: Fairleigh Dickinson University Press.

Giddings, R. and Sheen, E. (eds) (2000) *The Classic Novel: From Page to Screen*, Manchester: University of Manchester Press.

Gillespie, D. (1999) 'New versions of old classics: recent cinematic interpretations of Russian literature', in B. Beumers (ed.) *Russian on Reels: The Russian Idea in Post-Soviet Cinema*, London: I.B.Tauris, pp. 114–24.

—— (2002) *Russian Cinema*, London: Longmans.

—— (forthcoming) 'Confronting Imperialism: the ambivalence of war in Post-Soviet film', in S. Webber (ed.) *War and Society in Post-Soviet Russia*, Manchester: Manchester University Press.

Gillespie, D. and Zhuravkina, N. (1996) 'Sergei Bodrov's *A Prisoner in the Caucasus*', *Rusistika* No.14, December: 56–8.

Ginzburg, E. (1981) *Within the Whirlwind*, London: Collins and Harvill Press.

Gogol', N.V. (1994) *Sobranie sochinenii v deviati tomakh*, vol. 3, E.S Smirnova, (ed.) 'Povesti', Moscow: Russkaia kniga.

Goncharov, I. (1993) 'Oblomov's Dream', in G. Gibian (ed.) *The Portable Nineteenth-Century Russian Reader*, New York: Viking Penguin, pp. 295–333.

Gor'kii, A.M. (1957) *Pis'ma o literature*, Moscow: Sovetskii pisatel'.

—— (1990 [1934]) 'Doklad Gor'kogo' in *Pervyi vsesoiuznyi s"ezd sovetskikh pisatelei 1934: stenograficheskii otchet*, Moscow: Gosudarstvennoe izdatel'stvo khudozhestvennoi literatury. Reprint, Moscow: Sovetskii pisatel'.

Goscilo, H. (2002) 'Moving Images, Imagination, and Eye-deologies', paper presented at 'Screening the Word' conference, University of Surrey, May 2002.

—— (2003) 'Casting and Recasting the Caucasian Captive', in J. Andrew and R. Reid (eds) *Two Hundred Years of Pushkin: Pushkin's Secret*, Amsterdam and Atlanta: Rodopi, pp. 195–207.

Graffy, J. (1998) 'Soldier, Soldier' *Sight and Sound*, March: 34–5.

Griffith, J. (1997) *Adaptations as Imitations: Films from Novels*, Newark: University of Delaware Press.

Grossman, V. (1958) 'V gorode Berdicheve', in *Povesti. Rasskazy. Ocherki*, Moscow: Voenizdat, pp. 88–103.

Gural'nik, U. (1973) *Fil'm sporit s knigoi*, Moscow: Iskusstvo.

Gurevich, D. (1999) *Masterworks of Soviet Cinema. Images*, 1999. Online at <http://www.imagesjournal.com/issue08/reviews/sovietcinema/> (accessed 21 January 2004).

Hansen, M. (1992) 'Deadly scenarios: narrative perspective and sexual politics in pre-revolutionary Russian film', *Cinefocus* 2(2): 10–19.

Haynsworth, L. (2001) 'Sensational adventures: Sherlock Holmes and his generic past', *English Literature in Transition* 44(4): 459–85.

Heldt, B. (1987) *Terrible Perfection. Women and Russian Literature*, Bloomington and Indianapolis: Indiana University Press.

Heyne, E. (1987) 'Toward a theory of literary nonfiction' *Modern Fiction Studies* 33: 479–90.

Hoch, S. (1991) 'The banking crisis, peasant reform, and economic development in Russia, 1857–1861', *American Historical Review* 96(3) (June): 795–820.

Hutchings, S. (2004) *Russian Literature in the Age of the Camera: The Word as Image*, London: RoutledgeCurzon.

Hutchings, S. and Vernitski, A. (2002) 'Shooting the canon: the role of the *Ekranizatsiia* in Stalinist culture', *BLOK* (Bydgoszcz, Poland) 1: 139–56.

Iutkevich, S. (1971) 'Tsena shpagi. O fil'me Grigoriia Kozintseva "Korol' Lir"', *Iskusstvo kino* 5: 73–88.

Izvolov, N. (2001) *Fenomen kino*, Moscow: EGSI.

Johnson, P, and Labedz, L. (eds) (1965) *Khrushchev and the Arts. The Politics of Soviet Culture, 1962–64*, Cambridge, Massachusetts: MIT Press.

Kassil', L. (1940) 'Timur i ego komanda', *Pravda*, 361, 30 December.

Kelly, A. (1997) 'Where the Dead Smiled,' *The New York Review of Books*, February 20.

Kelly, C. (1998) 'The Retreat from Dogmatism: Populism under Krushchev and Brezhnev', in C. Kelly and D. Shepherd (eds) *Russian Cultural Studies: An Introduction*, Oxford: Oxford UP, pp. 249–74.

Kenez, P. (1992) *Cinema and Soviet Society, 1917–1953*, Cambridge: CUP.

____ (1995) 'Black and white: the war on film', in R. Stites (ed), *Culture and Entertainment in Wartime Russia*, Bloomington and Indianapolis: Indiana UP, pp. 157–76.

Kestner, J.A. (1997) *Sherlock's Men: Masculinity, Conan Doyle, and Cultural History*. Aldershot: Ashgate.

Khrenov, N. (1991) 'Vozdeistvie esteticheskikh gorizontov massovoi publiki na otnosheniia kino i literatury v pervye desiatiletiia XX v.', in A.S. Vartanov, N.M. Zorkaia (eds) *Ekrannye iskusstva i literatura: nemoe kino*, Moscow: Nauka, pp. 220–37.

Khrushchev, N. (1963) 'Vysokaia ideinost' i khudozhestvennoe masterstvo – velikaia sila sovetskoi literatury i iskusstva. Rech' tovarishcha N.S. Khrushcheva na vstreche rukovoditelei partii i pravitel'stva s deiateliami literatury i iskusstva 8 marta 1963 goda', *Novyi mir* 3: 3–33.

Kibirovskii, A. (2002) *Sibirskii tsiriulnik – pravda i vymysel kinoepopei*, Moscow: Eksprint.

Klado, N. (1966) 'Tak v chem delo?', *Iskusstvo kino* 7: 20–25.

Kogan, P. S. (1926) 'Dmitrii Furmanov', *Pechat' i revoliutsiia* 3: 75–82.

Kozhinov, V. (1973) 'Klassika v zhizni naroda i na ekrane' in V.S. Beliaev, A.V. Macheret and P. F. Dmitrieeva (eds) *Kniga sporit s fil'mom*, Moscow: Iskusstvo, pp. 5–21.

Kozintsev, G. M. (1941) ' "Korol' Lir" ', *Teatr* 4: 16–32.

—— (1966) *Nash sovremennik Vil'iam Shekspir*, 2nd edn, revised and supplemented, Moscow-Leningrad: Iskusstvo.

—— (1977) *King Lear: The Space of Tragedy. The Diary of a Film Director,* Mary Mackintosh (trans.), London: Heinemann.

—— (1982–6) *Sobranie sochinenii v piati tomakh*, Leningrad: Iskusstvo.

—— (1994) *'Chernoe, likhoe vremia…': Iz rabochikh tetradei*, Moscow: 'Artist. Rezhisser. Teatr'.

Kozintseva, V. G. and Butovskii, Ia.L. (eds) (1998) *Perepiska G. M. Kozintseva 1922–1973*, Moscow: 'Artist. Rezhisser. Teatr'.

Kriachko, L. (1966) 'Sut' i vidimost", *Oktiabr'* 2: 180–201.

Kriger, E. (1946) 'Syn polka', *Izvestiia*, 246, 18 October.

Kriukova, A. (1998) 'Obrazy i znaki. 'Mne khotelos', chtoby Stalina uvideli kak cheloveka', – govorit Aleksandr Zbruev', *Obshchaia gazeta*, No. 50, 17–23 December.

Kriukova, M. S. (1937) 'Chapai', in V. Popov (ed.), *Skazaniia Marfy Kriukovoi. Skazanie o Lenine, Chapai, Pokolen-boroda i iasnye sokoly*, Moscow: G.I.Kh.L.

Kulinichev, V. (1970) 'Strannye liudi', *Molodoi kommunar* (Voronezh), 18 August.

Kuprianovskii, P. V. (1981) 'Elan' ili Sizov?', *Russkaia literatura* 3: 173–74.

Kutlovskaia, E. (2001) 'Eralash-art', *Iskusstvo kino* 8: 161–66.

Kuznetsov, M. (1965) 'Debiut, obeshchaiushchii mnogoe', in I.N. Vladimirtseva (ed.) *Ekran 1964*, Moscow: Iskusstvo, pp. 136–42.

Lahusen, T. (1997) *How Life Writes the Book: Real Socialism and Socialist Realism in Stalin's Russia*, Ithaca and London: Cornell University Press.

Lary, N. (1986) *Dostoevskii and Soviet Film: Visions of Demonic Realism, Ithaca and London*: Cornell University Press.

Lawton, A. (1992), *Kinoglasnost*, Cambridge: CUP.

Layton, S. (1994) *Russian Literature and Empire. Conquest of the Caucasus from Pushkin to Tolstoi*, Cambridge, New York and Melbourne: Cambridge University Press.

Lefebvre, H. (1991) *The Production of Space*, Oxford: Blackwell.

Lelevich, G. (1923) 'Dm. Furmanov. Chapaev', *Pechat' i revoliutsiia* 6: 189–91.

Leskov, N. (1958) 'Ledi Makbet Mtsenskogo uezda', in V.G. Bazanov (ed.) *Sobranie sochinenie*, Moscow, pp. 96–143.

Levin, E. (1994) 'Ekranizatsiia, istorizm, mifografiia, mifologiia. K tipologii obshchestvennogo soznaniia i khudozhestvennogo mysshleniia', in Iu. Bogomolov (ed.) *Ekrannye iskusstva i literatura: zvukovoe kino*, Moscow: Nauka, pp. 872–894.

Levin, Iu. D. (1988) *Shekspir i russkaia literatura*, Leningrad: Nauka.

Levin, S. K. (1978) 'O dokumental'nosti v sovetskoi proze pervoi poloviny 20–kh godov. Po arkhivnym materialam', in E. G. Bushkanets *et al.* (eds) *Problemy istorii kritiki: poetiki realizma. Mezhvuzovskii sbornik*, Issue 3, Kuibyshev, n.p.

Lévi-Strauss, C. (1962) *The Savage Mind (La Pensée sauvage)*, London: Weidenfield and Nicholson.

Levshina, I. (1970) 'Shukshin protiv ... Shukshina?', *Iskusstvo kino* 2: 40–49.

Leyda, J. (1960) *Kino: A History of the Russian and Soviet Film*, Princeton: Princeton UP.

Losev, Aleksei (1992) *Dialektika mifa*, Moscow: Mysl'.

Lotman, Iu. M. (1979) 'The origin of plot in the light of typology', *Poetics Today* 1(1–2)(Autumn): 161–84.

Lotman, Iu. and Mintz, Z. (1981) 'Literatura i mifologiia', *Trudy po znakovym sistemam* 13, 35–56.

Lukin, Iu. (1962) 'Povest' o vernykh druz'iakh', *Pravda*, 23 September.

Macherey, P. (1976) *A Theory of Literary Production*, London: Routledge and Kegan Paul.

Makarenko, A. (1937) ' "Chapaev" D. Furmanova', *Literaturnyi kritik* 10–11: 102–119.

Mantsov, I. (2001a) 'Kapituliatsiia', *Iskusstvo kino* 7: 35–7.

—— (2001 b) 'Svidetel'', *Iskusstvo kino* 5: 64–7.

Manvell, P. (1971) *Shakespeare and the Film*, London: Dent.

Marsh, R.J. (1986) *Soviet Fiction Since Stalin: Science, Politics and Literature*, London and Sydney: Croom Helm.

McFarlane, B. (1996) *Novel to Film: An Introduction to the Theory of Adaptation*, Oxford: Clarendon Press.

McMillin, A. and McMillin S. (1999) 'Sex, speech and sewing machines: whores' voices and useful occupations in Russian literature', *Slovo* 11: 121–39.

McReynolds, L. (1995) 'Dateline Stalingrad: newspaper correspondents at the front', in R. Stites (ed.) *Culture and Entertainment in Wartime Russia*, Bloomington and Indianapolis: Indiana UP, pp. 28–41.

—— (2003) 'Tsarist Russia's dream factories', in L. McReynolds, *Russia at Play. Leisure Activities at the End of the Tsarist Era*, Ithaca and London: Cornell University Press, pp. 253–91.

Menzel, B. (2000) 'Sovetskaia lirika stalinskoi epokhi', in E. Dobrenko and H. Gunther (eds) *Sotsrealisticheskii kanon*, Saint Petersburg: Akademicheskii proekt, pp. 953–68.

Michalski, M. (2000) 'Olesha, room and the search for a new art form', in C. Kelly and S. Lovell (eds) *Russian Literature, Modernism and the Visual Arts*, Cambridge: CUP, pp. 220–49.

Mikhailov, A.D. (1934) 'Proshloe vstalo pered moimi glazami', *Pravda*, 20 November.

Mikhailovich, V. (1994) 'Evoliutsiia kinoiazyka: novyi etap', in A.S. Vartanov, V.I. Mikhalkovich and E.S. Sabashnikova (eds), *Ekrannye iskusstva i literatura: Sovremennyi etap*, Moscow: Nauka, pp. 2–18.

Mitchell, W.J.T. (1987) *Iconology: Image, Text, Ideology*, Chicago and London: Chicago UP.

—— (1994) *Picture Theory: Essays on Verbal and Visual Representation*, Chicago and London: Chicago UP.

Morley, R. (2003) 'Gender relations in the films of Evgenii Bauer', *Slavonic and East European Review* 81(1): 32–69.

Moss, K. (1993) 'A Russian Munchausen: Aesopian translation', in A. Horton (ed.) *Inside Soviet Film Satire: Laughter With a Lash*, Cambridge: CUP, pp. 20–35.

Mozejko, E. (ed.) (1986) *Vasiliy Pavlovich Aksënov: A Writer in Quest of Himself*, Columbus, Ohio: Slavica.

Nabokov, V. (1974) *Bend Sinister*, London: Penguin.

Naremore, J. (ed.) (2000) *Film Adaptation*, London: Athlone Press.

Nel's, S. (1960) *Shekspir na sovetskoi stsene*, Moscow: Iskusstvo.

Nikol'skaia, T. (1990) 'A. Blok o zhenskom tvorchestve', *Uchenye zapiski Tartuskogo gosudarstvennogo universiteta*, no.881, *Blokovskii sbornik*, no. 10, Tartu: Tartuskii gosudarstvennyi universitet, 32–40.

Nikulin, L. (1934) 'Dlia togo, chtoby zhit'', *Pravda*, 20 November.

Nisbeth, H. (2004) 'What pipes did Sherlock Holmes smoke?', online at<http://sherlock-holmes.hypermart.net/pibes.html)> (accessed 3 January 2004).

Okhlabystin, V. (2002) 'Open letter', online at: <http://ohlobystin.narod.ru> (accessed 30 April 2002).

Ol'gin, V. (1969) 'Fil'm i istoricheskaia deiatel'nost'', *Iskusstvo kino* 12: 38–44.

Orlov, V. (1966) 'Strela v polete', *Literaturnaia gazeta*, 10 March.

Otis, L. (1998) 'The empire bites back: Sherlock Holmes as an imperial immune system', *Studies in Twentieth Century Literature* 22(1) (Winter): 31–60.

Panferov, F. Il'enkov, V., Isbakh, A., Gorbatov, B., Platoshkin, M., Galin, B. and Ilin, I. Pasternak, B. L. (1990) 'Zamechaniia k perevodam iz Shekspira', in his *Ob iskusstve*, Moscow: Iskusstvo, pp. 175–92.

Pertsov, V. (1988) 'Literature and cinema', in Richard Taylor and Ian Christie (eds) *The Film Factory: Russian and Soviet Cinema in Documents 1896–1939*, London: Routledge & Kegan Paul, pp. 164–66.

Piotrovskii, K.P. and Glagoleva, N.A. (eds) (1968) *Sovetskie khudozhestvennye fil'my. Annotirovannyi katalog, tom IV (1958–1963)*, Moscow: Iskusstvo.

Pisarevskii, D. (1981) *Brat'ia Vasil'evy*, Moscow: Iskusstvo.

Plantinga, C. (1997) *Rhetoric and Representation in Non-Fiction Film*, Cambridge: Cambridge University Press.

Pocock, J. (1975) *The Machiavellian Moment: Florentine Political Thought and the Atlantic Republican Tradition*, Princeton: Princeton University Press.

Pogozheva, L. (1964) 'Svoia tema', *Sovetskii ekran* 18: 2–3.

—— (1965) 'Uchastnik spora', *Iskusstvo kino* 3: 70–1.

Popov, V. (1962) 'Review of the film *My Younger Brother*', *L'vovskaia pravda*, 30 October.

Porter, D. (1981) *The Pursuit of Crime: Art and Ideology in Crime Fiction*, New Haven: Yale University Press.

Prokhorov, E.I. (1967) ' "Chapaev" D.A. Furmanova. Istoriia teksta romana', in V. S. Nechaeva and A. G. Dement'ev (eds) *Tekstologiia proizvedenii sovetskoi literatury. Voprosy tekstologii,* Issue 4, Moscow: Nauka.

Prokhorova, E. (2003) 'Can the meeting be changed? Crime and identity discourse in Russian television series of the 1990s', in *Slavic Review* 62(3) (Fall 1993): 512–25.

Pushkin, A. (1949a) 'Istoriia Pugacheva', in M.Tsiavlovskii and S.Petrov (eds) *Sochineniia*, Moscow: OGIZ, pp. 663–705.

—— (1949b) 'Kapitanskaia dochka', in M.Tsiavlovskii and S.Petrov (eds) *Sochineniia*, Moscow: OGIZ, pp. 593–642.

—— (1978a) *Polnoe sobranie sochinenii v desiati tomakh*, vol. 4, 'Poemy, skazki', B.V. Tomashevskii (ed.), Leningrad: Nauka.

—— (1978b) *Polnoe sobranie sochinenii v desiati tomakh*, vol. 5, 'Evgenii Onegin, dramaticheskie proizvedeniia', B.V. Tomashevskii (ed.), Leningrad: Nauka.

—— (1978c) *Polnoe sobranie sochinenii v desiati tomakh*, vol. 6, 'Khudozhestvennaia proza', B.V. Tomashevskii (ed.), Leningrad: Nauka.

Roberts, G. (1999) *Forward Soviet! History and Non-fiction Film in the USSR*, London and New York: I.B. Tauris.

Robin, R. (1992) *Socialist Realism: An Impossible Aesthetic*, trans. C. Porter, Stanford, CA: Stanford University Press.

Rodowick, D. (1997) *Gilles Deleuze's Time Machine (Post-Contemporary Interventions)*, Durham and London: Duke University Press.

Rozov, V. (1980) 'Molodye dramaturgi, instsenirovki i prochee', *Literaturnaia gazeta*, 22 October.

Rtishcheva, N. (2000) 'Igor' Maslennikov: Eto zhe elementarno, Vatson!', *Moskovskii komsomolets*, 30 April.

Rubanova, I. (1963) 'Rebiata nastoiashchie …', *Komsomol'skaia pravda*, 24 January.

Rudnitskii, K. (1981) *Proza na stsene*, Moscow: Znanie.

Rühle, J. (1969) *Literature and Revolution: A Critical Study of the Writer and Communism in the Twentieth Century*, Jean Steinberg (trans. and ed.), London: Pall Mall.

Said, E.W. (1994) *Culture and Imperialism*, New York: Alfred A. Knopf.

Samarin, R. and Nikoliukin, A. (comps.) (1966) *Shakespeare in the Soviet Union*, Avril Pyman (trans.), Moscow: Progress.

Sandler, S. (1989) *Distant Pleasures. Alexander Pushkin and the Writing of Exile*, Stanford: Stanford University Press.

Sartori, Rosalinde (1995) 'On the making of heroes, heroines and saints', in R. Stites (ed.), *Culture and Entertainment in Wartime Russia*, Bloomington and Indianapolis: Indiana UP, pp. 176–93.

Sauerberg, L. O. (1989) 'The novel in transition: documentary realism', *Orbis Litterarum*, 44: 80–92.

—— (1991) *Fact into Fiction: Documentary Realism in the Contemporary Novel*, Houndmills, Basingstoke: Macmillan.

Semenov, A. (1970) ''Strannyie liudi' Shukshina', *Vostochno-Sibirskaia Pravda*, 8 August.

Scholes, R. (1975) *Structural Fabulation: An Essay on Fiction of the Future*, Notre Dame, IN and London: Notre Dame University Press.

—— (2001) *The Crafty Reader*, New Haven, CT and London: Yale University Press.

Sheshukov, S. (1984) *Neistovye revniteli. Iz istorii literaturnoi bor'by 20–kh gg*, 2nd rev edn, Moscow: Khudozhestvennaia literatura.

Shitova, V. (1962) 'Deviat' fil'mov odnogo goda', *Iskusstvo kino* 11: 58–69.

Shklovskii, V. (1988a) 'Where is Dziga Vertov striding?', in R. Taylor and I. Christie (eds) *The Film Factory: Russian and Soviet Cinema in Documents 1896–1939*, London: Routledge & Kegan Paul, pp. 151–52.

—— (1988b) 'The temperature of cinema', in R. Taylor and I. Christie (eds) *The Film Factory: Russian and Soviet Cinema in Documents 1896 – 1939*, London: Routledge & Kegan Paul, pp. 162–64.

Shukshin, V. (1973) 'Edin v trekh litsakh' (interview by S. Vishniakov), *Moskovskii komsomolets*, 11 March: 3.

—— (1981) *Voprosy samomu sebe*, comp. L.N. Fedoseeva-Shukshina, Moscow: Molodaia gvardiia.

Siegel, G. (1970) 'The fallen woman in nineteenth-century Russian literature', *Harvard Slavic Studies* 5: 81–107.

Simon, J. (1993) 'The Russian soul, one Steppe at a time: "The Real Film is Between the Words" ', *Buffalo News*, 11 April.

Skliarova, N. (2001) ' "Igor" Maslennikov: Ot kino, kak ot SPIDa, nel'zia izbavit'sia', *Vecherniaia Moskva*, 14 November.

Smeliansky, A. (1999) *The Russian Theatre after Stalin,* P. Miles (trans.), Cambridge: Cambridge University Press.

Smirnova, V. (1941) 'Stsenarii i fil'm', *Literaturnaia gazeta* 3(5), 19 January.

Sokolov, N. (1999) 'Slav'sia great Russia', *Itogi*, 9 March: 48–9.

Sokolov, Iu (ed.) (1938) *Krasnoarmeiskii fol'klor*, Moscow: Sovetskii pisatel'.

Sokolov, V. (1962) 'Review of the film *My Younger Brother*', *Sovetskaia kul'tura*, 15 November.

Sontag, S. (1991) *Illness as Metaphor*, London: Penguin.

—— (1999) 'The image world', in J.Evans and S. Hall (eds) *Visual Culture: The Reader*, London: Sage Publications, pp. 80–95.

Stam, R. (2000) 'Beyond fidelity: the dialogics of adaptation', in J. Naremore (ed.) *Film Adaptation*, London: Athlone Press.

Stasio, M. (2003) 'Holmes loses the hat, and Watson gets hip', *New York Times Television Guide, 19–25 January*, pp. 4–5.

Sullivan, S. (1998) 'Hands across the water, crime across the sea: gender, imperialist history, and Arthur Conan Doyle's America', *Victorians Institute Journal* 26: 95–120.

Symons, J. (1979) *Portrait of an Artist: Conan Doyle*, London: Whizzard Press.

Tarkovskii, A. (1990) 'Lektsii po kinorezhisere', *Iskusstvo kino* 9: 23.

Tarkovsky, A. (1986) *Sculpting in Time*, Austin: University of Texas Press.

—— (1999) *Collected Screenplays*, Natasha Synessiou (ed. and trans.), London: Faber.

Tass (1948) 'Molodaia gvardiia: novyi khudozhestvennyi fil'm v dvukh chastiakh', *Pravda*, 239, 26 August.

Taylor, R. and Christie I. (eds) (1988) *Inside The Film Factory: Russian and Soviet Cinema in Documents 1896–1939*, London and New York: Routledge.

Thompson, J. (1993) *Fiction, Crime, and Empire: Clues to Modernity and Postmodernism*, Urbana: University of Illinois Press.

Tiurin, I. (1984) *Kinematograf Vasiliia Shukshina,* Moscow: Iskusstvo.

Tolstoi, L.N. (1950) 'O Shekspire i ego drame', in his *Polnoe sobranie sochinenii* (90 vols), Moscow: Khudozhestvennaia literatura, 1928–58, XXXV, 216–72.

—— (1963), 'Kavkazkii plennik', in *Sobranie sochinenii v dvadtsati tomakh*, Moscow: Khudozhestvennaia literatura, 1960–6, vol. 10, 225–48.

Tret'iakov, S. (1924) 'Otkuda i kuda? (Perspektivy futurizma)' *Lef*, 1: 192–203.

Tsiv'ian,Yu. (1989) 'Evgenii Frantsevich Bauer', in P. Cherchi Usai, L. Codelli, C. Montanaro, D. Robinson (eds), *Silent Witnesses. Russian Films, 1908–1919*, London: British Film Institute, pp. 546–50.

—— (1991) 'Early Russian cinema: some observations', in R. Taylor and I. Christie (eds), *Inside the Film Factory. New Approaches to Russian and Soviet Cinema*, London and New York: Routledge, pp. 7–30.

—— (1994) *Early Cinema in Russia and its Cultural Reception*, A. Bodger (trans.), London: Routledge.

—— (1996) 'The tango in Russia', *Experiment/Eksperiment* 2: 306–33.

—— (2002) 'Bauer, Evgenii Frantsevich', in V. Ivanova, V. Myl'nikova, S. Skovorodnikova, Iu. Tsiv'ian, R. Iangirov (eds), *Velikii kinemo. Katalog sokhranivshikhsia igrovykh fil'mov Rossii, 1908–1919*, Moscow: Novoe literaturnoe obozrenie, pp. 498–500.

Turovskaia, M. (1973) 'I moe mnenie ob ekranizatsii', in V.S. Beliaev, A.V. Macheret, P.F. Dmitrieva (eds) *Kniga sporit s fil'mom*, Moscow: Iskusstvo, pp. 222–35.

—— (1995) 'The 1930s and 1940s: cinema in context', in R.Taylor and D. Spring (eds), *Stalinism and Soviet Cinema*, London and New York: Routledge, pp. 34–54.

—— (1997) 'Zhenshchina-ubiitsa v russkom i sovetskom nemom kino', *Iskusstvo kino* 5: 108–13.

Tynianov, Iu. (1977) *Poetika; istoriia literatury; kino*, Moscow: Nauka.

Urnov, D. (1971) 'Dvizhenie vremen', *Iskusstvo kino* 4: 122–36.

V. G. (1923) 'Review of *Chapaev* by D. Furmanov', *Izvestiia*, 15 April.

Valentino, R. (1999) 'Paradigm and Parable in Goncharov's *An Ordinary Story*', *Russian Review* 58 (January): 71–86.

Vartanov, A.S. (1994) *Ekrannye iskusstva i literatura: Sovremennyi etap*, Moscow: Nauka.

Vartanov, A.S. and Zorkaia, N.M. (1991) *Ekrannye iskusstva i literatura: Nemoe kino*, Moscow: Nauka.

Vartanov, A.S., Lipkov, A.I. and Sabashnikova, E.S. (2000) *Ekrannye iskusstva i literatura: televizionnyi etap*, Moscow: Nauka.

Vasil'ev, G. and Vasil'ev S. (1934) 'Kak my rabotali nad 'Chapaevym', *Pravda,* 20 November.

Vernitski, A. (2003) 'Socialist in form, humanist in content: Vera Panova's artistic method in prose and in film', *BLOK* (Bydgoszcz, Poland) 2: 121–41.

Vertov, D. (1984) *Kino-Eye: The Writings of Dziga Vertov*, ed. Annette Michelson, trans. Kevin O'Brien, Berkeley and Los Angeles: University of California Press.

Villasur, B. (2002) 'Classic adaptations, modern reinventions: reading the image in the contemporary literary film', *Screen* 47(1) (Spring): 5–19.

Virilio, P. (1989) *War and Cinema: The Logistics of Perception*, P. Camiller (trans.), New York–London: Verso.

Vishnevskii, V. (1945) *Khudozhestvennye fil'my dorevoliutsionnoi Rossii: filmograficheskoe opisanie*, Moscow: Goskinoizdat.

Vroon, R. (1996) 'Dmitrii Furmanov's *Chapaev* and the Aesthetics of the Avant-Garde', in J. Bowlt and O. Matich (eds) *Laboratory of Dreams: The Russian Avant-Garde and Cultural Experiment*, Stanford, CA: Stanford University Press, pp. 219–34.

Whelehan, I. (1999) 'Adaptations: The Contemporary Dilemma', in D. Cartmell and I. Whelehan (eds) *Adaptations: From Text to Screen, Screen to Text*, London and New York: Routledge, pp. 3–21.

Woll, J. (2000) *Real Images, Soviet Cinema and the Thaw,* London and New York: I.B. Tauris.

Wood, A. (2002) 'Timespaces in spectacular cinema: crossing the great divide of spectacle versus narrative', *Screen* 43(4) (Winter 2002): 370–86.

Youngblood, D.J. (1999) *The Magic Mirror. Moviemaking in Russia, 1908–1918*, Madison and London: University of Wisconsin Press.

Zabolotsky, N. (1994) *The Life of Zabolotsky*, Cardiff: University of Wales Press.

Zalesskii, V. and Kuznetsova, I. (1963) 'Liudi i fil'my', *Nash sovremennik* 4: 179–97.

Zhdanov, A. (1990 [1934]) 'Doklad Zhdanova', in *Pervyi vsesoiuznyi s"ezd sovetskikh pisatelei 1934: stenograficheskii otchet*, Moscow: Gosudarstvennoe izdatel'stvo khudozhestvennoi literatury. Reprint, Moscow: Sovetskii pisatel'.

Žižek, S. (1989) *The Sublime Object of Ideology*, London: Verso.

Zorkaia, N.M. (1976) *Na rubezhe stoletii: U istokov massovogo iskusstva v Rossii 1900–1910 godov*, Moscow: Nauka.

—— (1989) *The Illustrated History of the Soviet Cinema*, New York: Hippocrene Books.

Index

Literary works – authors are shown in brackets following titles. Films – directors and release dates are shown in brackets following titles. *Italicized* page numbers indicate illustrations.

For Product Safety Concerns and Information please contact our EU representative GPSR@taylorandfrancis.com
Taylor & Francis Verlag GmbH, Kaufingerstraße 24, 80331 München, Germany

www.ingramcontent.com/pod-product-compliance
Lightning Source LLC
Chambersburg PA
CBHW071520110726
47908CB00003B/901

* 9 7 8 0 4 1 5 5 4 6 1 2 6 *